The Transformation of Economic Systems in Central Europe

STUDIES IN COMPARATIVE ECONOMIC SYSTEMS

General Editors: Wladimir Andreff, *Professor of Economics at the University Paris 1 Panthéon Sorbonne and Director of ROSES*; Bruno Dallago, *Associate Professor of Economic Policy and Comparative Economic Systems at the University of Trento and President of EACES*; János Kornai, *Allie S. Freed Professor of Economics at Harvard University and Permanent Fellow at Collegium Budapest, Institute for Advanced Studies*; and Hans-Jürgen Wagener, *Professor of Economics and Vice-Rector at the European University Viadrina at Frankfurt/Oder*

Recent developments in different economic systems have presented new challenges to economic theory and policy. Scholars in comparative economic systems have to debate and clarify the nature of the economic system, its place within the economy and the dynamics of its transformation in a comparative perspective.

This new series is designed to contribute to the debate and advance knowledge in the field. It will provide a forum for original comparative research on the economic system and economic performance including important aspects such as economic institutions and their change, economic actors and policy instruments in the transformation process.

The books published in this series will be written by leading international scholars writing in a theoretic or applied way and using either country-specific studies or cross-country comparisons. They will show how economic analysis can contribute to understanding and resolving one of the most important questions facing the world at present and in the future.

Recent titles in the series include:

Struggle and Hope
Essays on Stabilization and Reform in a Post-Socialist Economy
János Kornai

The Transformation of Economic Systems in Central Europe
Herman W. Hoen

The Transformation of Economic Systems in Central Europe

Herman W. Hoen

Royal Netherlands Academy of Arts and Sciences, University of Groningen, The Netherlands

STUDIES IN COMPARATIVE ECONOMIC SYSTEMS

Edward Elgar
Cheltenham, UK • Northampton, MA, USA

Published by
Edward Elgar Publishing Limited
8 Lansdown Place
Cheltenham
Glos GL50 2HU
UK

Edward Elgar Publishing, Inc.
6 Market Street
Northampton
Massachusetts 01060
USA

A catalogue record for this book
is available from the British Library

Library of Congress Cataloguing in Publication Data

Hoen, Herman Willem, 1960–
    The transformation of economic systems in Central Europe / Herman W. Hoen.
        (Studies in comparative economic systems)
    Includes bibliographical references and index.
        1. Europe, Central—Economic policy. 2. Europe, Central—Economic conditions. I. Series.
    HC244.H565 1998
    338.943—dc21   97–47522
                                                CIP

ISBN 1 85898 271 5

Printed and bound in Great Britain by
Biddles Ltd, Guildford and King's Lynn

Contents

List of Tables

Acknowledgements

In a book on processes of transformation in Central Europe, this would have been the place to start with a short story on my childhood in one of the countries in this region. Unfortunately, I am unable to do this, since, during the heyday of the cold war, my playing field was in The Netherlands. Neither parents who escaped the region in 1956 or 1968, nor relatives with roots in the Czech Republic, Hungary, Poland, or Slovakia, can possibly have been an incentive for writing a book on these countries' current transformation from a centrally planned to a market economy. What, then, is the fascination of Central Europe?

Although the region is the centre of gravity in Europe, its history reveals a continuous oscillation between the points on the European compass. The economic historian István Berend, in his recent book on contemporary economic history of the nations in transition, expresses his fears of a revolving rather than a proceeding history, indicating that the political and economic transformation will move the region from the periphery to the periphery (Berend, 1996). I do not completely subscribe to this point of view. The demise of communism was the pivotal event which started an irrevocable path in a westward direction. The path itself may be uncomfortably paved, the scene of many collisions, but is highly interesting to explore. The purpose of this book is to elaborate differences and similarities among the Central European countries in transition striving for political and economic integration with Western Europe. It therefore applies both a historical and a comparative approach and I am more than pleased that this study appears in the 'European Association for Comparative Economic Studies' series.

Writing a book is impossible in solitary confinement. I am, therefore, very grateful to the Royal Netherlands Academy of Arts and Sciences for granting a fellowship after I finished my PhD thesis on Hungary's export performance in the 1970s and 1980s. During this fellowship, I moved from the Department of Economics to the Department of International Relations, both at the University of Groningen. I found this transfer beneficial to this book, since it enabled me to prepare it in an environment consisting of both economists and historians, political scientists, and specialists in international law. I believe an interdisciplinary approach in research focusing on economic transformation in Central Europe to be indispensable. Consequently, I feel indebted to both institutes.

Numerous persons have been helpful during the process of research and writing. I want to express special gratitude to Wladimir Andreff, Wendy Asbeek Brusse, Livia Balász, Maria Baranyai, Henny de Boer, Jaroslav Bohanes, Milán Constantinovits, László Csaba, Bruno Dallago, Michel Doortmont, Hans van Ees, Michael Ellman, Anjo Harryvan, Jan van der Harst, Jan Jacobs, Ívan Gaďourek, Joost Herman, Joop de Kort, Karel Kouba, Sytse Knypstra, Ger Lanjouw, Marie Lavigne, Beppo van Leeuwen, Fieke van der Lecq, Nick van der Lijn, Hajna Istvánffy Lőrincné, Ine Megens, Hetty Meijer, Suzan Nollen, Bart Nooteboom, Hans Renner, Bert van Selm, Wim Slik, Peter Volten, Herman Voogsgeerd, and Hans-Jürgen Wagener. These persons are in no way to be held responsible for any error, omission, or wrong conclusion. For that, the author alone is to blame.

Finally, even though I am daily in a position to thank my wife Hilly Mast for her encouragement in my research, and though my children Iris and Maarten are not even able to read yet, I feel this to be the place to express my gratitude to them. Since I find Central Europe such a fascinating region, the suffering involved in writing this book did not apply to the author, but rather to his family.

Herman W. Hoen,
Groningen, December 1997

Abbreviations

ÁPV Rt	Állami Privatizáció és Vagyon Részvénytársaság (State Privatization and Holding Company Inc.) [*Hungary*]
ÁV Rt	Állami Vállalat Részvénytársaság (State Holding Company Inc.) [*Hungary*]
ÁVU	Állami Vagyon Ügynökség (State Property Agency) [*Hungary*]
CAP	Common Agricultural Policy [*European Union*]
CEFTA	Central European Free Trade Association
CEI	Central European Initiative
CIS	Commonwealth of Independent States
CMEA	Council for Mutual Economic Assistance
CSCE	Conference on Security and Cooperation in Europe
ČSSD	Česká Strana Sociálně Demokratická (Czech Party for Social Democracy)
EBRD	European Bank for Reconstruction and Development
EC	European Communities
ECSC	European Coal and Steel Community
ECU	European Currency Unit
EEA	European Economic Area
EEC	European Economic Community
EFTA	European Free Trade Association
EU	European Union
EURATOM	European Atomic Energy Community
FKgP	Független Kisgazda Földmunkás és Polgári Párt (Independent Smallholders' Party) [*Hungary*]
Fidesz	Fiatal Demokraták Szövetsége (Federation of Young Democrats) [*Hungary*]
FTO	Foreign Trade Organization
GATT	General Agreement on Tariffs and Trade
GDP	Gross Domestic Product
GDR	German Democratic Republic
HZDS	Hnutie Za Demokratické Slovensko (Movement for a Democratic Slovakia)

IMF   International Monetary Fund
ITO   International Trade Organization
KDH   Krest'anskodemokratické Hnutie (Christian Democratic Party)
           [*Slovakia*]

KDNP   Kereszténydemokrata   Néppárt   (Christian   Democratic
           People's Party) [*Hungary*]
KDS   Konzervatívna Demokratická Strana (Conservative
           Democratic Party) [*Czech Republic*]
KDU–ČSL   Křestanská Demokratická Unie – Československá Strana
           Lidová (Christian Democratic Union – Czechoslovak
           People's Party) [*Czech Republic*]
KSČ   Komunistická Strana Československa (Communist Party
           of Czechoslovakia)
MDF   Magyar Demokrata Forum (Hungarian Democratic Forum)
MSzMP   Magyar   Szocialista   Munkás   Párt   (Hungarian   Socialist
           Workers' Party)
MSzP   Magyar Szocialista Párt (Hungarian Socialist Party)
NATO   North Atlantic Treaty Organization
NMP   Net Material Product
ODA   Občanská Demokratická Aliance (Civic Democratic Alliance)
           [*Czech Republic*]
ODS   Občanská Demokratická Strana (Civic Democratic Party)
           [*Czech Republic*]
OECD   Organization for Economic Cooperation and Development
OF   Občanská Forum (Civic Forum) [*Czechoslovakia*]
PHARE   Pologne et Hongrie: Aide pour la Réconstruction des
           Economies (Poland and Hungary: Aid for the Reconstruction
           of Economies) [*European Union*]
PSL   Polskie Stronnictwo Ludowe (Polish Peasants' Party)
PZPR   Polska Zjednoczona Partia Robotnicza (Polish United
           Workers' Party)
SD   Stronnictwo Demokratyczne (Democratic Party) [*Poland*]
SDĹ   Strana Demokratickej Ĺavice (Party of Democratic Left)
           [*Slovakia*]
SITC   Standard International Trade Classification
SLD   Sojusz Lewicy Demokratyczne (Democratic Left Alliance)
           [*Poland*]
SNS   Slovenská Národná Strana (Slovak National Party)
SPC   State Planning Commission
SzDSz   Szabad Demokraták Szövetsége (Alliance of Free Democrats)
           [*Hungary*]

TACIS	Technical Assistance for the Commonwealth of Independent States [*European Union*]
UD	Unia Demokratyczna (Democratic Union) [*Poland*]
ÚGM	Új Gazdasági Mechanizmus (New Economic Mechanism) [*Hungary*]
VHJ	Vyrobni Hospodářské Jednotky (Association of Enterprises) [*Czechoslovakia*]
VPN	Verejnost' Proti Násiliu (Public Against Violence) [*Slovakia*]
WTO	World Trade Organization

1. On the Theory of Economic Transformation

INTRODUCTION

The economic transformation from a centrally planned to a market economy has presented one of the major challenges in contemporary history. In order to fulfil that task, there were neither available experiences to rely upon, nor clear-cut conceptual frameworks available to underpin this shift in economic systems. Moreover, despite great similarities in the communist dictatorships, the political and economic legacy varied enormously among the countries facing the task of creating a market economy. As a result, different strategies were applied, and where policies were similar performances repeatedly diverged, since what was suitable for one country proved inappropriate for another (see World Bank, 1996). That may have made the transformation a frustrating experience for the countries involved, but, at the same time, it constituted an important challenge for social scientists.

This book accepts this challenge of the unknown and focuses on the transformation of economic systems in Central Europe. The countries addressed are the Czech and Slovak Republics, Hungary and Poland. The reasons for restricting the analysis to these countries are many. Suffice it to mention four of them. Firstly, at the start of the transformation, these countries were more or less comparable in terms of their level of economic development. Of course, economic development of Czecho-slovakia in the twilight of the communist era was higher than that of Hungary and Poland. But there are good arguments to cluster these countries when comparing their economic development with other trans-forming economies of the former Soviet bloc (*PlanEcon Report*, various issues). Secondly, these countries are closest to the border of the European Union (EU). The intention to become a full member of the EU was shared right from the start of the transformation and, as will be shown below, this gave impetus to a certain coordination of policies to attain this objective. The EU responded and, by persistently referring to these nations as

'Visegrád' countries, intimated that it would treat them as a geo-political unit (see for example Mizsei, 1993). Thirdly, the reform strategies seem to be more crystallized than elsewhere in Central and Eastern Europe and, therefore, better able to make qualitative assessments regarding the impact of the reforms on economic performance (see European Bank for Reconstruction and Development, 1996(a); World Bank, 1996). Fourthly, the strategies applied in these countries were perceived as different (*ibid.*; Falk and Funke, 1993). Consequently, despite the fact that enormous problems will be encountered, these four arguments to a certain extent better facilitate and enhance meaningful comparisons between countries.[1]

The comparisons made in this book are meant to give a general overview in terms of macroeconomic stabilization and microeconomic restructuring, but it most specifically centres on external economic relations. The economic transformation from a centrally planned to a market economy is pictured within the framework of European economic integration. This implies that external economic relations are pivotal topics in all the chapters. The basic assumption underlying this book is that economic integration and transformation are interdependent. Continuing economic reforms aimed at the creation of a market economy will enhance global economic integration, but, at the same time, attempts to integrate with the world economy and its dominating financial and trade organizations may work as a catalyst to further transformation. Since the Central European countries are so deliberately focused on full participation in the EU, these closest neighbours of the EU have, therefore, drastically shifted trade from East to West and declared reforms in the realm of foreign trade organization that are pivotal in the total transformation process.

Before elaborating the facts of the transformation attempts by the Czech, Hungarian, Polish and Slovak governments, it may be illuminating to explore the extent to which economic theory is able to underpin the transformation. That is the topic of the present chapter. Economists face severe difficulties when suggesting strategies for the transformation from a centrally planned to a market economy in Eastern Europe and therefore the initial optimism about quickly implementing a market economy has proven not to be justified (see Bruno, 1992; Schmieding, 1993). The transformation appears to be a complex process that cannot be accomplished within a couple of years. As mentioned above, apart from different legacies of communism, the dissimilarities in the paths of reform stem from the fact that for this complex process there are no general prescriptive rules, derived either from historical precedents or from economic theory. This introductory chapter focuses on the latter of these two reasons.

Currently, an enormous number of contributions have been published on the issue of transformation, but only a few of these explicitly start from a theoretical viewpoint. Among this restricted group of authors, some tend to be rather pessimistic concerning the extent to which economic theory can provide useful suggestions, as the interdependence between what can be intentionally created and what may accidentally emerge makes the path of reform highly unpredictable (see Wagener, 1993). Others remain static in their analysis by either questioning the merits of the desired economic order (Murrell, 1991), or theoretically underpinning the persistence of the initial economic order (Krug, 1991; Murrell, 1992; Olson, 1992). Hence, theoretical tenets of the transformation from a centrally planned to a market economy still need a lot of research. It is the intention of this chapter to survey the underlying assumptions of different schools of economic thought and to study their implications for transformation policies.

The outline of this chapter on the theory of economic transformation is as follows. The next section surveys the nature of the transformation. This should enable us to formulate conditions that have to be met by economic theories. It boils down to the notion that a change in the economic order implies a complete shift in the set of institutions which focus on decision making with respect to economic activity. Institution building must be at the core of reform economics. The following section deals with neo-classical economics and its implications for a strategy of reform. Neo-classical economists mostly propagate a 'once-and-for-all' jump, but this advice seems to be mainly derived from the desired economic order, rather than from the logic of the transformation. In fact, as neo-classical economics does not explicitly take institutions into account, no general prescriptions are to be expected.

Two alternative theoretical approaches, to wit, Post-Keynesian and Austrian economics, are elaborated in separate sections following the one on neo-classical approaches towards the transformation. Both Post-Keynesians and Austrians are extremely heterodox groups, but they commonly oppose major strands of neo-classical thinking, in particular the concept of Walrasian market equilibrium. Whereas Post-Keynesians view the market system as one essentially in disequilibrium in this respect, the Austrians perceive the market as a process rather than as a reflection of equilibrium. A question being asked is whether these critical views on the core concept of neo-classical economics lead to alternative suggestions for transformation. The closing section summarizes the main findings and sets out the outline of the following chapters.

SPEED AND SEQUENCING OF THE KEY ELEMENTS FOR THE TRANSFORMATION

The exploration of what transformation actually implies should start with trying to understand the concept of economic system. An economic system can be defined as the total of behaviour and institutions that focuses on the satisfaction of needs (see Wagener, 1979, Chapter 1). Constituent elements of the system are the various organizations, profit-making as well as non-profit, the division of property rights, the division of decision-making power, information and motivation structures, and law. An economic system coordinates the activities and interactions of individuals and organizations which take part in it. Hence, the decision-making structure to a large extent determines the nature of an economic order (Eucken, 1990).

With respect to the nature of institutional change, Wagener (1993, p. 6), following the classification originally put forward by the Austrian Carl Menger, distinguishes two paths of development: pragmatic–constructivist and organic–evolutionary change. Pragmatic change is subject to purposeful action, whereas organic change may be the unintended result of a sequential decision-making process, or spontaneous historical development. It is important to note that unintended organic change is not inconsistent with rational behaviour that motivates each step in the chain of decisions. Therefore, it is erroneous to put the rationality criterion as the dividing line between pragmatic and organic change. The distinction has to be made in terms of the ability to return to the initial situation. Pragmatic change implicitly assumes reversibility, whereas organic change does acknowledge path-dependency and hysteresis. This latter view reveals that for the formerly centrally planned economies, the desired economic order cannot be negatively defined. The idea that a market economy would emerge spontaneously as soon as the institutions belonging to a centrally planned economy are removed fails to recognize the phenomenon of irreversibility and the fact that a market economy entails the implementation of new institutions that are pivotal in a market environment. Institution building is at the core of the transformation into a market economy. The task of transformation should, therefore, not be confused with the question of how to dismantle a planned economy.

It goes without saying that the transformation into a market economy entails both kinds of institutional change, pragmatic as well as spontaneous and organic. But the task of the transformation starts with a survey of the possibilities of purposeful attempts to change an administratively co-ordinated economic order, based upon hierarchical relationships and allocated budgets, in which income is not solely dependent upon transactions, to a market-based economic order, characterized by horizontal relations between equal partners of supply and demand, who respond to financial incentives. The agenda for the transformation consists of an enormous list of items which should guide the restructuring of the economy (see Falk and Funke, 1993; Laski *et al.*, 1993). It can be divided into the following four main categories: stabilization, liberalization, privatization, and a number of institutional reforms, in the context of this chapter labelled 'institutionalization' or institution building.

Stabilization

Immediately after the collapse of communism, the Central and Eastern European countries faced the task of stabilizing the economy in order to eliminate an inherited monetary overhang, which severely hindered the advance of economic activity. There exists a broad consensus among theorists and policy makers on the necessity of macroeconomic stabilization as a precondition for successfully starting the process of transformation. However, disagreement on how to achieve macroeconomic stabilization gives rise to many intellectual debates (see Bruno, 1992). Therefore, it is reasonable to include stabilization matters in our discussion of how economic theory can add to the understanding of transformation, especially because stabilization of an economy which stands between central planning and the market does not present a textbook case.

Liberalization

Liberalization of trade, production and prices is closely related to the problem of macroeconomic stabilization, and is often simultaneously raised within the context of the necessity of stabilization (see Berg and Sachs, 1992; Hanel, 1992). It has generally been held that both have to be realized in the early stages of the transformation. Within the context of this study, liberalization is separately listed, since it ensures that prices reflect scarcities in markets and is, therefore, believed to be indispensable for the good functioning of a market. Moreover, liberalization as the basis of the transparency and openness of the market belongs to the core of an economic system co-ordinated by decentralized decision making.

Privatization and Restructuring

The transfer of state ownership to the public received enormous attention after the demise of the centrally planned systems (see Lipton and Sachs, 1990). The major dispute seems to focus on 'how' to privatize, whereas the necessity of large-scale privatization is often taken for granted. But the arguments in favour of privatization are not so straightforward, since state enterprises can operate within an environment which enforces competition (see Sachdeva, 1994; Van Brabant, 1991). However, to the extent that market participants have to be independently acting agents, whose incomes are solely dependent upon market transactions, privatization can be perceived as an important element of the transformation to a market economy. The argument goes that private property is less vulnerable to rent-seeking behaviour. Hence, the ultimate goal of privatization is an improvement in enterprise efficiency.

The efficiency improvement is ultimately dependent upon restructuring of the enterprises involved. Now, the question arises whether restructuring should precede or at least coincide with privatization, as is more likely to occur when state property is sold to the public, or whether it should follow privatization. The latter is more likely to be the case when state property is freely distributed among the public and restructuring is left to the market.

Institutionalization

The category of institutional reforms includes all the measures that are intended to provide a legal framework for the good functioning of markets. These reforms are, of course, closely linked to the establishment of private property rights, but they comprise more. Institutional reforms focus on the legal preservation of established ownership rights, guarantee the freedom of contract, and, most importantly, have to ensure the legal liability of market participants. They should basically support a consistent incentive structure (see Raiser and Nunnenkamp, 1993). Since the collapse of the system of central planning led to an institutional void, in which the law of the jungle threatens to prevail, these reforms deserve high priority on the agenda of the transformation.

Theoretical Dispute

The theoretical debates on current transformation policies are often put into the framework of 'shock therapy' versus 'gradualism'. The dispute concentrates on different opinions with respect to the speed and sequencing of the above-defined categories of economic reforms. The underlying idea is that each of the measures to be taken in the process of transformation involves adjustment costs. The issue is how total welfare costs can be minimized: by implementing all the measures at the same time and at maximum speed, or by sequencing the implementation of the necessary reforms (see Slay, 1994(a)).

The 'shock therapy-versus-gradualism' debate has often been visualized as a J-curve. From a shock therapy approach point of view, it is assumed that after a sharp initial fall in economic activity, recovery will be rather rapid (Berg, 1994; Lipton and Sachs, 1990). Hence, the total costs of transformation will be less than in the case of a gradual transformation policy, for which a more moderate initial decline in economic output is accepted, but as the new system emerges only slowly, recovery is expected to be modest as well. In the most extreme case, the costs of gradual transformation are seen as infinite, since the gap between the desired and the actual economic level will never be closed. The gradualist approach holds that immediate destruction of the old system and rapid conversion to capitalist arrangements is counter-productive (Murrell, 1992). The magnitude of the output decline under the shock therapy regime is seen as too severe and unnecessary, whereas, at the same time, the recovery scenario of a shock approach is contested as well. Crucial in the underpinning of this statement is the 'hoped-for supply' response. This response will only emerge within an appropriate institutional setting, the creation of which necessarily takes time. If the institutional reforms are not crystallized, market forces will not secure the recovery but rather reinforce the economic crisis. It should be stressed, though, that from both points of view, an initial drop in production is believed to be inevitable. There is simply no upward slope right from the beginning. Although the J-curve is not beyond dispute, since output declines may also be due to exogenous shocks (see Brada and King, 1992), both adherents of shock treatment and proponents of gradual transformation mainly contest the steepness of the J-curves and not the transformation crisis as such.

HOW TO DEDUCE 'SHOCK VERSUS GRADUALISM' FROM SCHOOLS OF ECONOMIC THOUGHT

This section analyses the extent to which economic theory is able to underpin the transformation from a centrally planned into a market economy and tries to explore how the proposals for a rapid or a gradual transformation can be deduced from economic theory.[2] The analysis follows the list of the above-mentioned key elements for the transformation and surveys three leading schools of economic thought: neo-classical, Post-Keynesian, and (Neo-)Austrian economics.

Neo-classical School: The Invisible Jump

Neo-classical economics is based upon the assumption of rational behaviour of individuals within the framework of general equilibrium. Under several restrictive assumptions, Walrasian general equilibrium theory ensures Pareto efficiency. Decisions of individual agents are coordinated by market prices, so there is an automatic tendency towards equilibrium of supply and demand on all markets. As the optimum conditions for consumer and producer are specified in the respective demand and supply functions, this equilibrium maximizes all individual utilities.

Standard neo-classical economics does not explicitly take institutions into account. These are assumed to exist, but do not restrict the behaviour of economic agents. The transparency of the market is perfect, while property rights are well defined, completely decentralized, and transferable at any time. In fact, within the neo-classical framework utility-maximizing consumers and profit-maximizing firms are restricted only by budgetary and technical constraints. It implies that transaction costs are assumed to be zero.

In order to take account of non-zero transaction costs, various economists have tried to incorporate institutions within the neo-classical concept. Because of the neo-classical angle of incidence, Eggertsson (1990) refers to these theories as neo-institutional economics, thereby excluding those institutionalists who criticize the rational choice model.[3] Neo-institutional economics basically emphasizes the importance of property rights as these define the extent to which economic agents have the right to use resources, and, subsequently, will bear the consequences of their decisions. Within neo-institutional economics, the system of property rights is broadly defined. It not only comprises a judicial concept, but it also includes social norms. At another level, this broad interpretation allows us to include theories of collective interests and bureaucratization as extended theories of property rights. These public-choice-like approaches focus on rent-seeking and bargaining power of interest groups *vis-à-vis* governments, which represent the legal body that can reshuffle decision-making power over economic resources. In actual fact, receiving a larger share of the pie just implies (re-)allocation of property rights.

What neo-institutionalists further have in common is their emphasis on all kinds of issues related to arranging exchange, instead of on the execution of a gratuitous contract. If production costs are the principal costs within neo-classical economics, transaction costs are at the heart of neo-institutionalism (see North, 1990). In sum, the neo-institutional theory can mainly be considered as an extension of neo-classical economics, that is, new constraints have been implemented. But the idea of rational agents maximizing utility by making choices subject to restrictions has been preserved, and so has the framework of general equilibrium.

Within neo-classical economics, the nature of transformation is a matter of instantaneous adjustment of rational agents without a past. Therefore, pragmatic constructivism prevails among those economists who rely upon this framework. As economic agents behave rationally, economic regularities are universal and non-historic. Hence, the transformation essentially entails the implementation of new rules and the elimination of political resistance, which implies that it should be as fast as possible. Why this appears to be the case will be elucidated below.

The core element of a shock therapy approach towards transformation is rapid elimination of domestic price control by the state. Price liberalization is essential for macroeconomic stabilization as well as for microeconomic restructuring. A general increase in the price level must eliminate monetary overhang, while changing relative prices must improve allocative efficiency. As soon as the aggregate price level is stabilized, relative price adjustments lead to a rational allocation of resources. Producers will economize on the utilization of inputs, while consumers are expected to experience welfare gains, because they will not be forced to substitute initially unwanted for eventually unavailable commodities (Brada, 1993, p. 91). In other words, prices are expected to equilibrate demand and supply. Of crucial importance for the achievement of equilibrium is the rational behaviour of market participants. Independently of any past experience they will optimize utilities.

Thus, although neo-classical economics is static by nature, and therefore has very little to add to the understanding of the transformation into a market economy, the assumption of rationally behaving agents leads to the perception that exogenously implementing the new rules of the game may prove successful. A market economy can be pragmatically constructed by dissolving the institutions of central planning. There is an instantaneous adjustment of agency behaviour, which in fact means that in the pure world of neo-classical economics transformation simply entails a jump from one equilibrium to another. Hence, it corresponds to the removal of unnatural constraints.

But what are the implications for the building of new institutions? The most important task is the implementation of a well-defined system of decentralized property rights. The sooner it can be accomplished, the better it is. It has to be emphasized that on neo-classical grounds speed is the only relevant criterion for the way in which property rights must be transferred from the state to private persons. Here the logic of competitive markets and allocative efficiency applies again. The device for privatization is straightforward from the Coase theorem, which states that under zero transaction costs no matter how the distribution of property rights looks initially, it will always result in the most efficient way. Now the question arises as to what extent the neo-institutional acknowledgement of non-zero transaction costs alters the policy suggestions of immediate decentralization.

As a matter of fact, it hardly modifies any of the policy suggestions for the transformation into a market economy. For instance, from the theory of collective interests, which can be seen as an extended theory of property rights (Eggertsson, 1990), it follows that resistance to reform by special interest groups should be firmly eliminated. So a strong state that looks after maintenance of the agents' new external environment is needed. A system of diffuse property rights, such as emerged from piecemeal reforms in the 1980s, has to be avoided. The failure of these attempts was precisely due to the fact that agents behaved rationally. They could gain specific profits at the expense of the efficiency of the economic system at large. Thus, half-hearted reforms will enlarge the costs of transformation.

Post-Keynesian Economics: The Unpredictable Journey

The assumption of general equilibrium attained by rationally behaving economic agents has been extensively criticized. Two groups of scholars should be mentioned in this respect. The first group relies upon the ideas that often have been labelled as Post-Keynesian and focuses on a market economic system as one essentially in disequilibrium. The other group of economists is affiliated to the (Neo-)Austrian school, which perceives economic systems as being in a constant process of change. Although a common denominator can be found in their emphasis on inadequacy of information, the rationality and disequilibrium concepts to a large extent differ between the Post-Keynesians and the Austrians. Therefore, these groups will be separately dealt with in this chapter. The present section explores Post-Keynesianism.

The classification 'Post-Keynesian economics' can be rather misleading. It assumes common positions, whereas existing differences are enormous. It is even highly questionable whether such a classification makes any sense. But one important common strand makes it at least accepted: all those perceived as Post-Keynesians seem to oppose the neo-classical perception of market equilibrium (Pheby, 1989). In accordance with this general criticism, Post-Keynesians adopt another concept of time. Whereas time in neo-classical economics is a purely logical concept, Post-Keynesians rely upon the concept of historical time (Garretsen, 1992, pp.

68ff). This criticism essentially pinpoints the fact that in neo-classical economics equilibrium exists simply as a final stage. According to Post-Keynesians, this implies that initially the system was not in equilibrium, and it therefore has to be explained which conditions have changed over time. In short, in neo-classical economics, the achievement of equilibrium remains a 'black box'. It is purely static in nature.

The reliance on historical time and the rejection of Walrasian equilibria have important consequences for Post-Keynesian perceptions of the transformation into a market economy in Central and Eastern Europe. The fact that there are historical legacies implies recognition of irreversibility and path-dependency. Constructing a market economy overnight is simply not feasible. The above-mentioned general strands that tend to present cases for gradual sequencing can be further elucidated by considering two items that are assumed to be pivotal in Post-Keynesian economics, namely the theory of interest (Blaug, 1987, Chapter 15; Garretsen, 1992; Leijonhufvud, 1968; Kregel, 1983), and, following from this, the implications of future expectations on investment behaviour and the role of financial institutions (Van Ees and Garretsen, 1993). These two aspects will be briefly dealt with in order to clarify the Post-Keynesian position on transformation.

In neo-classical thinking, monetary and real matters are strictly separated. Keynesians and Post-Keynesians reject this view by taking into consideration that money will not only be used as a means of exchange, but will also serve hoarding purposes. Hence, money is an asset. The demand for hoarding money depends on the interest rate, expectations with respect to changes in the interest rate, and the degree of uncertainty. Thus, contrary to the neo-classical framework in which the interest rate, independently of monetary variables, equilibrates savings and investments, the Keynesian school of economics proposes a monetary interest theory. The interest rate serves as an equilibrator in the money market and fulfils the crucial function of transmitter for the monetary and the real sphere of the economy. Therefore, changes in the stock of money eventually not only lead to a changing price level, as claimed by neo-classicists, but also have an impact on the real side of the economy (see Leijonhufvud, 1968).

The observation that the rate of interest is a monetary phenomenon turned the neo-classical world upside down and had important implications for aggregate investment and employment. Post-Keynesians hold that the interest rate is not determined by marginal productivity of capital, but depends on the speculative motives of money holders. At this point the Keynesian framework comes up with the notion that investing in money for profit-maximizing objectives may imply sub-optimal output and employment levels. So there is a real constraint on investment which is due to competition from money assets (Kregel, 1983, p. 41). The Post-Keynesian emphasis on demand gaps seems incompatible with pragmatically constructing a market economy by applying shock therapy, and, in fact, several authors rested on Keynesian arguments to explain the depth and severity of the transformation crisis (Kregel *et al.*, 1992; Schmieding, 1993).

The Keynesian theory of money, interest and prices, essentially focusing on the transmission of monetary to real economic variables, almost automatically leads to the second point under scrutiny, that is, the role of future expectations and the importance of financial institutions for investments. In Post-Keynesian economics, expectations are interwoven with uncertainty due to information deficiencies. The idea of market disequilibrium within this Post-Keynesian paradigm arises from the existence of imperfect or asymmetric information. It means that if neo-classical conditions of full information do not prevail, relative prices will not be determined by scarcities of the commodities involved, but they will reflect the informational advantages of certain market participants. Thus, in the resulting equilibrium, the welfare conditions are not met. In principle this phenomenon is relevant to all markets, but it seems particularly important to financial markets (Van Ees and Garretsen, 1994). It is important to stress once more, though, that Post-Keynesians reject the notion of market equilibrium, and not equilibrium as such. In other words, an equilibrium may be attained without this implying full employment. To complicate the equilibrium dispute, for instance, Kregel (1983, p. 41) holds that 'The Post-Keynesian position is rather that the market works well enough, but not necessarily on those real variables that may be the goals of government policy.'

Taking the importance of financial markets for the transformation into a market economy in Central and Eastern Europe into consideration, Post-Keynesian starting-points again give rise to opposing a stabilization policy based exclusively on market-conforming instruments. However, contrary to the general Keynesian emphasis on deficient aggregate demand, the argument now focuses on what has been called the *credit crunch*, that is, the lack of short-term bank credits to enterprises (Calvo and Coricelli, 1992). Thus, the argument goes that rapid and general price liberalization, combined with restrictive monetary and fiscal policy, disturbs the necessary development of certain components of liquidity in the short run.

Since financial markets were completely absent in the former centrally planned economies, or at the most functioning at an embryonic stage, investment capital needed for restructuring the economy is to be supplied mainly by banks. Moreover, for the majority of enterprises in Central and Eastern Europe foreign direct investments do not pose a real alternative either. However, the banking sector is seriously constrained in supplying credits. Firstly, they inherited bad portfolios, because under central planning credits resulted from *ex post* adjustment for changes in the real sphere of the economy. Therefore, once a market economy had to replace this passive financial system, the banks started off with the burden of several decades of badly performing loans, and hence were not in a favourable position to generate new investment capital. Besides, restrictive monetary policy, which plays a pivotal part in shock-like stabilization approaches, hindered bringing about a positive climate for investments as well. According to the neo-classical dichotomy of monetary and commodity markets, tight market-based credit ceilings will instead restore equilibrium in commodity markets, if not instantaneously, at least in the short term. Post-Keynesian arguments, however, suggest that stabilization of this kind will turn out to be ill suited to the countries in transition. With respect to the establishment of financial markets, their focus is on informational devices and the necessity of state interference (Stiglitz, 1992). From a Post-Keynesian perspective *laissez-faire* solutions are deemed to lead to non-welfare-maximizing developments, as prices (interest rates) will not reflect the marginal profitability of investments, but will rather be subject to problems of project selection and moral hazard (*ibid.*, pp. 167–9).

The Austrian School: The Creative Destruction of a Planned Economy

Regarding questions of the functioning of different economic orders, the Austrian viewpoint is very well known. The Austrians nourished the famous 'debate on socialism' with their liberal strands, in particular those of Mises and Hayek. Although the debate initially concerned theoretical underpinnings of implementing a socialist economic order, it ultimately focused on the practical feasibility of socialism. Because of problems of complexity and stability, Mises and Hayek responded negatively to this issue (Wagener, 1979, Chapter 2). Contrary to many Post-Keynesian economists, who to a certain extent question the merits of the market mechanism, the Austrians most firmly adhere to the market. But how do the Austrians add to the understanding of the transition from a centrally planned system to a market economy?

Whereas neo-classical analyses start with the assumption of rational behaviour, Austrian thinking relies upon the concept of 'choice behaviour'. According to the first generation of Austrians, notably Menger, choices determine the allocation of resources, and marginal utilities determine prices. So far, nothing seems new. For this reason, the first generation of Austrians are thought to be clear precursors of neo-classical marginalism.

But the picture changes completely when the subjectivist strands of the Austrians are taken into consideration (see O'Driscoll and Rizzo, 1985). Subjectivism has important ramifications for the concept of rationality. If rationality is subjective, there is no such thing as rational choice behaviour, as put forward by neo-classical economics. For the Austrian school, objective rational choice behaviour, that is, economic agents optimizing their utility functions by calculating the model, does not imply real choices, as it means that there is just one that is optimal. The subjectivist approach towards scarcity and fulfilment of needs implies that there exists equilibrium only at the individual level. Therefore, Austrians mostly refrain from statements on national welfare.

Within Austrian thinking, the concept of subjectivism is directly connected to the role of knowledge (Hayek, 1945). According to the Austrians, knowledge is notoriously dispersed and incomplete. Therefore, equilibrium cannot be attained instantaneously, but has to be perceived as the final stage in a long continuing process (see Kirzner, 1979). To put it another way, the market has to be seen as a process rather than as a reflection of competitive Walrasian equilibrium. Only if knowledge were to be perfect, that is, if expectations with respect to behaviour of other economic agents were correct, would it be appropriate to speak of a competitive market equilibrium. However, as stated above, such an equilibrium would in itself thwart the essentials of subjectivism. Thus, whereas neo-classical economists primarily focus on conditions under which there exists a market equilibrium, the Austrian school, just as the Post-Keynesians, tend to be preoccupied with scrutinizing what happens if these conditions are not being fulfilled.[4]

The Austrians also differ from other schools of economic thought by emphasizing the role of the entrepreneur. In this respect, it is common to refer to Schumpeter (1934), according to whom the entrepreneur is the only person who is willing to take risks in an inevitably uncertain environment. Contrary to mechanical routine, which underlies the behaviour of bureaucrats, entrepreneurial action has to be interpreted as innovation. The entrepreneur is a disequilibrating force 'creatively destructing' established ways of doing things. But within the Austrian school, Kirzner in particular opposed this view of entrepreneurial behaviour. This modern Austrian more or less defines the entrepreneur as an arbitrageur, that is, someone responding to disequilibria (Kirzner, 1979, Chapter 3), a notion which is fully compatible with the Austrian concept of the market as a process towards general equilibrium.[5]

Since the Austrians emphasize that decision making is based on purely subjective knowledge, they are not easily to be positioned within the debate on actual transformation in Central and Eastern Europe. With the notable exception of the importance of enforcing a stable monetary environment, the Austrians to a large extent refrain from macroeconomic policy issues, as it does not make sense to construct aggregates on the basis of subjective behaviour. The Austrian approach is microeconomic by nature (see Garretsen, 1992). Hence, with respect to macroeconomic stabilization, there are hardly any lessons to be drawn. But implications for microeconomic restructuring are not straightforward either.

In setting the stage for microeconomic restructuring, one might at first be inclined to suggest a non-interventionist approach, based upon the liberal Austrian philosophy. However, there are strong arguments to see Austrian antecedents in the evolutionary paradigm of economic change, as originally put forward by Nelson and Winter (1982). With respect to problems of transformation, Murrell (1992), strongly opposing a quick and radical change, most profoundly adheres to this approach.

Similar to the biological concept of evolution, the evolutionary theory focuses on selection processes of entry and exit which generate economic development and dismisses the neo-classical preoccupation with allocative efficiency and competition within a framework of general equilibrium. Pivotal for the continuation of development is innovation. Here, Austrian influence starts to glimmer, but it becomes more pronounced when uncertainty and the limits on information processing are taken into consideration. According to the evolutionists, lack of knowledge leads to a craving for routine. In order to extend biological comparisons, the evolutionary theory holds that routine behaviour is in the genes of firms (Nelson and Winter, 1982, pp. 134-6). The emphasis on routines does reflect the notion of historical time, for these operational rules and procedures which guide organizational behaviour are gathered over time. The notion of a rational choice, irrespective of time, is thought to be obsolete. According to the evolutionary theory, economic development is set in motion by a change in the external environment. Past experience embodied in routine action will, of course, imply a continuity in behaviour, but, at the same time, learning-by-doing will perpetuate. Certain routines still seem to be appropriate, while others do not fit any longer. Hence, a selection made by entry and exit will accomplish growth and change. Therefore, within the evolutionary theory, economic development is a continuous adjustment process, which is close to the Austrian concept of organic change.

The implications of the evolutionary theory for the transformation in Central and Eastern Europe are that a shock treatment will be ineffective. This holds true for macroeconomic stabilization policy, as well as for microeconomic restructuring. Both will be elucidated in the remaining part of this section. The evolutionary theory raises the notion that the context in which stabilization policy is applied is extremely important. To be more concrete, market-conforming stabilization within an environment which is neither a market nor a planned economy will have a completely different impact from stabilization in market-dominated systems. Within the evolutionary theory, it is assumed that stabilization should not be solely market-oriented, but should also include direct controls, because these are compatible with routine behaviour within the old system of central planning. What especially counts, in their view, is the legacy of central planning in which enterprises have soft budget constraints. These soft budget constraints led to routines that exhibited a passive monetary system in which credits and debits retrospectively accommodated changes in the real side of the economy. The relative neglect of financial restrictions, for example, will not instantaneously change with the implementation of a tight monetary policy. In fact, an enormous increase in inter-firm credits is predicted, which is no more than behaviourial hysteresis on the part of enterprises. Thus, according to the evolutionist, it is questionable whether market-based stabilization schemes will be effective in societies saddled with the legacy of more than forty years of communism. Besides, the success of stabilization policies crucially depends upon supply responses. If these fail to appear, there is the risk of a 'roll-over' mechanism developing in the crises of transformation. The crucial point from an evolutionary perspective, though, is that rapid supply response is not obvious because of persistence of past behaviour. Consequently, market-conforming stabilization based upon a complete liberalization of prices combined with a tight monetary and fiscal policy may be destabilizing in the context of transformation from a centrally planned into a market economy.

Another item is privatization as part of microeconomic restructuring. It has been dominating the discussion on the transformation into a market economy from the very beginning. For economists and politicians who firmly believe in the merits of shock therapy, privatization is almost as vital as stabilization (Lipton and Sachs, 1990). Some authors, however, moderated this passion for privatization by stressing that it should essentially imply the creation of an economic environment which enforces competition (Van Brabant, 1991). Therefore, the transfer of state property does not require the highest priority. But the logic of rapid privatization has most firmly been contested by the evolutionists (see Murrell, 1991).

In line with the argument on selection by exit and entry, the evolutionary approach is more in favour of the emergence of new private enterprises, which is often referred to as privatization from below. To put it into a Schumpeterian phrase, this would entail the 'creative destruction' of the central planning system. Furthermore, the argument goes that the sale or giving away of state assets will not immediately alter the behaviour of the enterprises involved. Here, of course, persistence of behaviour is the pivotal point. Most surprisingly, and contrary to the view of mainstream economics, however, the evolutionists think privatization will crowd out the entry of new private enterprises. Restructuring and privatizing the state enterprise system is a costly and time-consuming process, and therefore is supposed to compete with resources that can be used for the growth of the new private sector. It has to be noted, though, that in this context of the crowding-out mechanism, privatization is perceived as a step following a costly restructuring of the state enterprise. If restructuring is to follow the transfer of ownership rights, the argument is less convincing, since the maintenance of state enterprises will not free endowments either.

SENSE AND NONSENSE IN THE DEBATE: A TENTATIVE CONCLUSION

The 'shock-versus-gradualism' debate concentrates on different opinions with respect to the speed and sequencing of reforms. Each of the measures to be taken in the process of transformation involves adjustment costs. The issue is how total welfare costs can be minimized: by implementing all the measures at the same time and at maximum speed, or by sequencing the implementation of the necessary reforms. The dispute gave rise to much incomprehension, since the labels 'shock' and 'gradual' make sense only when the type of reform is indicated.

Within this continuing debate, proponents of shock therapy strongly emphasize stabilization and liberalization. Regarding stabilization, they stress the necessity of a restrictive monetary and fiscal policy in order to combat budget deficits and external disequilibria (see Berg and Sachs, 1992; Lipton and Sachs, 1990). The core element of a shock therapy, however, is rapid elimination of domestic price control by the state. As stated above, price liberalization is essential both for macroeconomic stabilization and for microeconomic restructuring. An expected increase in the level of prices has to eliminate the excessive real stock of money. The problem of a monetary overhang can be rather quickly solved in this way. However, price liberalization will also affect relative prices. These will have a positive influence on decisions of producers and consumers. Therefore, once the aggregate price level is stabilized, relative prices lead to an efficient allocation of resources. None the less, stabilization is a necessary but not a sufficient condition for microeconomic restructuring. To a shock therapist, liberalization involves not only the freeing of prices, but also the exposure of domestic enterprises to international competition, that is, the introduction of an internally convertible currency for current account transactions. Shock therapy ultimately rests upon the assumption of general equilibrium. For the achievement of such an equilibrium, the rational behaviour of market participants is of crucial importance. Independently of any past experience, they will optimize utilities by following price information. Within the neo-classical-inspired shock approach, the nature of transformation is a matter of instantaneous adjustment of rational agents without a past (see Hoen, 1995).

Whereas proponents of shock treatment primarily focus on conditions for market equilibrium, adherents of gradualism are preoccupied with scrutinizing what happens if these conditions are not being fulfilled (for example Van Ees and Garretsen, 1994; Murrell, 1992). They strongly suggest that liberalization of prices and foreign trade should be spread over a longer period of time. In the discussion so far, the arguments have particularly focused on the notion that rapid and general price liberalization, in combination with a restrictive monetary and fiscal policy, hinders the important development of certain components of liquidity in the short run (see Kregel *et al.*, 1992; Schmieding, 1993). These solutions are deemed to lead to non-welfare-maximizing developments, since prices (interest rates) do not reflect the marginal profitability of investments, but suffer from project-selecting and moral-hazard problems (see Stiglitz, 1992). Besides, an immediate and definite exposure to international competition may lead to the termination of production which in the longer run could have been profitable. Moreover, they oppose *laissez-faire* solutions because well-functioning markets need special institutions. Some of these institutions have to guarantee that privatization will indeed enforce productive restructuring. In short, advocates of a gradual approach focus on another aspect of the transformation: without proper institutional guidelines with respect to property rights, freedom of contract, liability and competition rules, shock treatment will induce an unnecessary decline in economic activity. They also point to the fictitious aspects of the free market concept. Most specifically, this criticism pinpoints the fact that shock therapists try to implement a kind of capitalism which has ceased to exist long ago. In a more general sense, it focuses on the necessity of state intervention during the period when markets do not yet function properly.

Although the logic of shock treatment or gradualism can to a certain extent be deduced from economic theory, political restrictions determine the ultimate choice. This highly complicates matters and fuels further confusion. Shock treatment is generally perceived to add to the credibility of the transformation strategy in a society which owing to experiences from past communist reforms may be rather sceptical, but at the same time it can be considered a strategy which anticipates a possible reversal once negative consequences are revealed (Roländ, 1994). Therefore, in the perception of shock therapists, successor governments have to be burdened with insuperable costs in case they want to revoke decisions retrospectively (*ex post* political constraints). Authorities would be most susceptible to this kind of 'scorched-earth policy' in a revolutionary atmosphere immediately after the collapse of the communist system. A gradual approach is based on initial political feasibility (*ex ante* political constraints). It focuses on the possibility and the necessity of compromise. Political barriers have to be lifted in advance and, therefore, the policy should reduce expected costs related to a reversal and persuade sceptics to support the reforms for the moment. It seems an obvious strategy in the case where uncertainties about the welfare gains of the transformation dominate the political scene, for instance when past communist reforms resulted in a relatively prosperous inheritance.

To what extent does the derivation of strategies from pure economics differ from the one from which the choice of 'shock' or 'gradualist' approaches is made, that is, based on the nature of political restrictions? As far as the differences are concerned, it has to be pointed out that a transformation policy based on the nature of political restrictions under all possible circumstances assumes system reversibility, even though a gradual approach is intended to reduce costs of return, whereas a shock treatment is meant to maximize them. In this respect, these different angles of incidence further nourish confusion. But there are also similarities, especially related to the ability to implement all the necessary reforms. As stated above, when discussing stabilization and liberalization, rapid implementation seems feasible in principle. But it is not just for political reasons, but also due to technical constraints, that privatization and institution building cannot be prepared in a short period of time, let alone implemented. Therefore, it has to be concluded that governments applying shock treatment will not only be seeking to raise the costs of reversibility, that is the creation of a market as the way of destroying mandatory planning, but for reasons of political survival will also have to consider the feasibility of reforms in the longer run. Thus, the whole 'shock-versus-gradualism' debate may be reduced to a semantic discussion, unless one is willing to distinguish the key elements of the transformation into a market economy.

In the following chapters addressing the transformation strategies in the Czech and Slovak Republics, Hungary and Poland, we shall attempt to avoid the trap of semantic debate by making clear the distinctions in different kinds of economic reforms. Furthermore, path-dependency and hysteresis will be explicitly taken into account. This underlines the importance of communist inheritance – political as well as economic – and assumes that the economic transformation from a centrally planned to a market economy must be regarded as an intricate process in which the political setting permanently determines the degree of freedom for the implementation of economic reforms.

The structure of the book is as follows. The next chapter focuses upon the interdependence of external economic relations and the transformation to a market economy. It elaborates the systemic factors which excluded world market integration, the way in which, to different extents, the countries involved were nevertheless able to deal with important international organizations, and the reform measures which have been taken to overcome this seclusion. As far as the latter aspects are concerned, not only East–West integration will be on the agenda, but also the restoration of mutual trade relations.

The following three chapters deal with transformation policies applied in the Czech and Slovak Republics, Hungary and Poland, respectively. Although the Czech Republic and Slovakia have been independent countries since January 1993, these countries are jointly dealt with in Chapter 3. The reason for this lies in the identical communist inheritance and the shared initial years of transformation policy. Furthermore, since external relations constitute the main thread in the book, special attention will be paid to intermediate trade and payments arrangements established after the split of the Czechoslovak federation. It should be stressed in advance, though, that the fact that both are treated in the same chapter does not imply that the transformation strategies of the Czech Republic and Slovakia are scrutinized simultaneously. Different sections focus upon current issues at stake in the two republics. The basic question addressed in Chapter 4 on Hungary's transformation to a market economy is the extent to which this country was able to take advantage of the reforms which the communist regimes initiated. After the defeat of communist power, the idea was widely held that owing to comprehensive and far-reaching economic reforms in the 1970s and, especially, the 1980s, Hungary was expected to gain a head-start in its transformation to a market economy. Chapter 5 addresses the creation of a market economy in Poland. This economic transformation became a sort of reference model for a shock approach, because of the rigorous stabilization policy, as set in motion in January 1990 with the so-called 'Balcerowicz Plan'. The chapter will scrutinize the advantages and drawbacks of the Polish experience, but, following the line of reasoning set out above, it will also evaluate reform attempts in the field of microeconomic restructuring and institutionalization in order to reconsider the total transformation experience.

After Chapters 3–5 have dealt with the transformation strategies in the four Central European countries, Chapter 6 addresses the external economic performances of these countries in terms of East–West integration. The basic approach of the chapter is to assess the Central European countries' trade performance on the EU market, since, despite sound arguments for restoring mutual trade relations, the share of the EU in the countries' export structure has become the most important. Competitiveness on the EU market is explored by means of a breakdown of export change. The methodological problems are dealt with briefly and an explanation of the calculated results is presented in the framework of a political economy of 'rent-seeking'.

Chapter 7 concludes the book. On the basis of the description in the preceding chapters, it essentially compares and evaluates the Czech, Hungarian, Polish and Slovak transformation from a centrally planned to a market economy. The chapter concludes that the terms 'shock' and 'gradual' are inappropriate and misleading when reconsidering the transformation strategies applied in these countries. Moreover, on the basis of the political economy of 'rent-seeking', it concludes that the legacy of a reformist communist past has not proved to be particularly favourable.

NOTES

1. It might be asserted that these four arguments apply to Slovenia as well. For example, Slovenia is highly developed, is close to the EU border and has the intention of becoming a full member of the EU. Moreover, its reforms are among the most crystallized in Central and Eastern Europe. However, since Slovenia belonged to former Yugoslavia and therefore had a very different legacy, it has been decided not to include the country in this study.

2. This section draws heavily on the author's publication in *Economic Systems* and the *Journal of International and Comparative Economics* (Hoen, 1995; 1997). The publishers of both journals are gratefully acknowledged for their permission to do so.

3. This is an arbitrary matter. In the literature, it is also common to refer to these economists as 'new institutionalists'.

4. To this has to be added, though, that the *tâtonnement* in Walrasian general equilibrium theory is a recognition of an iterative process towards equilibrium. But the process itself has never been a main field of interest in neo-classical economics.

5. According to Blaug (1987, 464–5) this 'Schumpeter–Kirzner controversy' should not be over-emphasized. To a large extent, it can be ascribed to the historical context in which both Austrians published.

2. Transformation and Integration: Mutually Dependent

INTRODUCTION

The preceding chapter addressed the theoretical underpinnings of the transformation from a centrally planned to a market economy and identified macroeconomic stabilization, liberalization, privatization and institution building as the primary elements of the process. However, this should not be understood as a purely internal affair for the respective countries. Immediately after the fall of communism, it was clear that economic transformation and integration with the world economy jointly dominated the way forward. Politically speaking, the two were impossible to separate. Therefore, the present chapter aims to focus on the relationship between transformation and integration.

The post-communist leaders in Central and Eastern Europe had two important reasons to give economic integration with the West a very high priority on the political agenda of transformation. After all, the desire for East–West integration is firmly rooted in current economic theory. The line of reasoning is fairly straightforward. Economic integration interpreted as increasing participation in the international economic division of labour will generate welfare gains, since it enables specialization according to a country's comparative advantages. This was the kind of integration of which – for systemic reasons – the centrally planned economies were so long deprived (see Holzman, 1966; Pryor, 1963). For Central and Eastern Europe, integration with the West became more or less equivalent to seeking contact with and, eventually, entry into, the EU. Although possible claims laid to the structural funds of the EU will certainly have been a significant incentive, positive welfare effects through trade creation are decisive within this line of thought.

Economic integration with the West and transformation from a centrally planned to a market economy are mutually dependent. On the one hand, continuing economic reforms will expedite the process of integration. This holds true in particular for reforms in the realm of foreign trade organization. The organization of foreign trade under central planning made it difficult, if not impossible, to adhere fully to the market rules set by important international monetary and financial organizations and international trade forums, such as the International Monetary Fund (IMF), the World Bank, the General Agreement on Tariffs and Trade (GATT), the World Trade Organization (WTO), and also the Organization for Economic Cooperation and Development (OECD). On the other hand, integration with the West can be perceived as a big stick, which can be used to implement necessary but painful economic reforms. The rules of the game state, for example, that protection of the domestic production can be effectuated only by market-conforming measures. Therefore, quantitative restrictions will have to be replaced by a suitable tariff system, whereas the exchange rate is supposed to have an important allocative function. Henceforth, integration enforces politicians in Central and Eastern Europe to continue the reforms regarding the transformation from central planning to the market. The stick is most profound with IMF loans, not only because of the conditionality of the drawing rights, but also owing to the 'seal of approval'. Integration diminishes the degree of policy freedom, but by referring to the iron will of the international organization, it becomes easier to defend reform proposals in the parliaments of Central and Eastern Europe.

The aim of economic integration with the West raises the question of how the foreign trade organization under central planning impeded the possibilities for world market integration and the extent to which necessary measures have been taken to overcome these impediments. This chapter's outline is as follows. The next section explores the nature of foreign trade under central planning. It will not only be shown that, for systemic reasons, the centrally planned economies were isolated from world markets, but the incompatibility of centrally planned foreign trade and the principles of global economic organizations will also be shown. After having studied these systemic impediments to integration into the world economic order, we scrutinize regional integration during the communist era as an alternative to East–West integration. The remainder of the chapter will focus on East–West and on regional integration after the collapse of central planning. It will be seen that East–West integration will not only speed up economic transformation towards a market economy, but will impel the respective countries to mutual economic cooperation, whether they like it or not.

CENTRALLY PLANNED ECONOMIES AND THE WORLD ECONOMIC ORDER

Centrally Planned Economies and Foreign Trade

The organization of foreign trade under central planning is referred to as a state monopoly. Strictly speaking, this implied that only state-owned enterprises were authorized to conduct foreign trade.[1] In practice, however, the state monopoly on foreign trade implied a lot more. It developed into a specific set of institutions and methods for the conduct of foreign trade (see Gardner, 1983; Matejka, 1986). Within this constellation, the Ministry of Foreign Trade and special Foreign Trade Organizations (FTOs) were the pivotal institutions. FTOs were strictly organized according to sectoral principles and – within a well-defined sector – had exclusive rights to import and export. The separation of production and external economic relations was not just the fruit of ingrained ideological motives, but rather matched with and fitted into the methods of central planning.

As extensively described in the literature about Soviet planning, material balances were used as a substitute for the price mechanism (see Spulber, 1957; Kushnirsky, 1982; Bornstein, 1994). Material balances equate available supply of resources, that is production, import and initial stocks, with the demand for these resources, that is domestic expenditures of consumer and government, deliveries of intermediate output, export and final stocks. In tuning domestic demand and supply, the State Planning Commission (SPC) as the supreme planning authority was unable to solve the model simultaneously, but had to rely upon information to be delivered by subordinate bodies. The supreme planning authority lacked the necessary information regarding the technical coefficients indicating the inputs for the production of a certain commodity, and, by contrast, the alternative uses of available resources. Therefore, the balance had to be achieved through iterative adjustments negotiated with the Sectoral Production Ministries and the Ministry of Foreign Trade.

The planning of foreign trade was part of the total planning process and the two were dovetailed. In the procedure for drawing up the foreign trade plan, imports were given highest priority. Foreign trade was intended to facilitate the realization of the national economic plan designed by the SPC. Only those commodities which could not be produced domestically, or not at an adequate standard, were imported, while exports simply served to finance necessary imports. The consequences of this method, also referred to as the 'import first' method (Pryor, 1963, p. 55ff), were that foreign trade served as a buffer. Since enterprises had to fulfil production targets, it was evident that the information they supplied the SPC stimulated too large a demand (see Kornai, 1980) and, therefore, in the final analysis, foreign trade had to balance demand and supply. Furthermore, exports were seen as a loss. Whereas in market economies exports are often perceived as the engine of growth, they have only a residual status within the system of central planning.

It is evident that this organization of foreign trade breached the principles of specialization according to a country's comparative advantages. The complete separation of foreign trade and domestic production made it impossible to reap the welfare gains of participation in the international division of labour. Instead of a comparison of relative costs – domestic and foreign – absolute import needs for the realization of domestic production targets were the basis of foreign trade activity. 'Comparative advantages' more or less haphazardly appeared on the supply side of the material balance, thereby solving the problem of excess domestic demand. The nature of those commodities which were at the disposal of the export sector differed from time to time and was dependent upon what was more or less available at the final stages of planning.[2]

Incompatible Principles of Centrally Planned Economies and Bretton Woods Institutions[3]

Besides the irreconcilable mechanisms of the foreign trade behaviour of market economies and centrally planned systems, there were, of course, also systemic impediments to planned economies in joining international financial and trade organizations. None the less, even during the period of central planning, several Eastern European countries were members of Bretton Woods institutions, participated in the GATT, or both. Before discussing the extent to which the Czech and Slovak Republics, Hungary and Poland will benefit from these international organizations in their efforts to create a fully-fledged market economy, we shall examine how some of these countries were able to join them at a time when their economy was subject to central planning.

The Soviet Union, Poland and Czechoslovakia were among the founder-nations of the Bretton Woods institutions. The Soviet Union, however, did not join the IMF and the World Bank, while Czechoslovakia's and Poland's membership had already ended within a decade after the creation of the organizations. In the 1970s and 1980s, Eastern European interest in the IMF and the World Bank revived. Romania became a member in 1972 and Hungary and Poland followed in 1982 and 1986, respectively. Romania's rather early application for membership was related to the country's pursuit of relative independence within Eastern

Europe. Hungary's entry in 1982 was part of the process of economic reform and the concomitant desire for further integration into the world economic order. Moreover, the possibility of using new credit facilities was important in view of the country's worsening external debt situation. In the case of Poland, the expected contribution of the organizations to solving the external debt problem was the prime motive for application in 1981. Poland's membership of the IMF and the World Bank was blocked by the United States for a number of years because of political events and the declaration of martial law in December 1981. The renewed entry of Eastern European countries into the Bretton Woods institutions, however, did not automatically imply that the economic policies of the centrally planned economies were better attuned to IMF and World Bank philosophy. To a large extent, these countries kept relying on direct administrative import restriction in their external adjustment process.

Since the Soviet Union participated in the Bretton Woods conference, the tension between an international monetary and financial system based on a market-oriented philosophy and the nature of centrally planned economies was already at stake already during the formative years of the IMF and the World Bank. The problems were most explicit regarding the role to be played by the IMF.[4] Apart from problems related to the position of the Soviet Union within the Bretton Woods institutions and the requirements of members to supply statistical information on gold, foreign-exchange reserves, the balance of payments, national income and price developments, a primary dispute appeared to be the role of the exchange rate. One of the basic ideas concerning the new international monetary system was that exchange rates were a matter of international concern. The IMF would supervise members' exchange rate polices in such a way that changes in parities exceeding a certain threshold would require its consent.[5]

For a market economy, this concern for the distortive effects of exchange rate manipulation is indeed justified. In centrally planned economies, however, the role of exchange rates is totally different. As discussed above, the state is directly involved in international trade through its monopoly on foreign trade. The size and structure of trade flows is determined by the central plan. Consequently, the role of prices and exchange rates in deciding these is very limited. Exchange rates merely fulfil the function of translating foreign currency prices into domestic currency prices. As a result of an intricate system of taxes and subsidies, the so-called 'price equalization mechanism' (see Pryor, 1963), actual domestic prices were influenced only to a very limited degree by these domestic currency prices. In actual fact, a unified exchange rate did not exist. There were as many exchange rates as there were groups of products, that is, one for each group. The founding nations solved the problem by a proposal of the Soviet Union that the control of exchange rates should not apply to an exchange rate which had no effect on international transactions of Fund members. This proposal was accepted, but, of course, the exchange rate problem remained afterwards, especially with regard to balance-of-payments adjustment policies.[6] Since the exchange rate in a planned economy had an accounting rather than an allocative function, it could hardly be used as an instrument for balance-of-payments adjustments. In the case of rising world market prices, the 'price equalization mechanism' led to an overburdening of the state budget with excessively rising subsidies. As a consequence, in order to reduce the budget burden, the authorities of centrally planned economies were inclined to *re*value the currency. The revaluations of the Hungarian forint in the 1970s constitute an example of such a policy of neutralizing import prices by means of exchange rate adjustment. In a market economy, in similar circumstances, a *de*valuation to counter the worsening of the balance-of-payments situation would be more appropriate (see Wolf, 1985, 237).

The participation of centrally planned economies in the international monetary system was also complicated by the inconvertibility of their currencies. In line with the idea of a liberal international payments system, externally held balances of members' currencies, at least when resulting from current account transactions, should be freely convertible. This kind of convertibility is highly problematic for centrally planned economies. External ownership of a country's currency is useful only if foreigners are able freely to convert their balances into commodities and services supplied by the country. By the very nature of planning, current account convertibility is impossible to guarantee in centrally planned economies. Commodities and services will only be available on the basis of explicit decisions of the planning authorities. This characteristic of a planned economy is also referred to as 'commodity inconvertibility' (Holzman, 1966). The systemic problem of inconvertibility was circumvented in the Fund's articles by giving countries the opportunity to make use of a clause which allowed a 'transitional period' during which member-states could continue to apply exchange rate restrictions. By not defining the duration of that period, the clause made it possible to accommodate countries relying on exchange rate restrictions. A substantial number of Fund members, especially developing countries, make use of this clause up to the present day. However, for centrally planned economies, the need for a 'transitional period' was not just a matter of economic development; it was inherent to the system of central planning.

Besides problems associated with joining the international monetary and financial system, the centrally planned economies also experienced predicaments with participation in international trade forums, of which GATT was the most important. Although the GATT was a rudimentary remainder of what after the Second World War was supposed to become the International Trade Organization (ITO), and, therefore, did not become a global organization and remained a forum for consultations between government representatives, its impact as a forum for trade policy issues was beyond dispute. The primary aim of the countries which endorse the GATT is the mutual and non-discriminatory reduction of trade barriers. Besides Czechoslovakia, which was one of the founder-nations of the GATT, Poland (1967), Romania (1971), and Hungary (1973) were also accepted to participate before the collapse of their centrally planned economic systems. This implies that all the Central European countries under scrutiny participated in this global trade forum. The question remains, though, how were these countries able to do so?

The GATT regulations did not contain any specific article for the entry of centrally planned economies. Within the provisional concept of the ITO, the possible participation of the Soviet Union was explicitly acknowledged, since article 28 stated that centrally planned economies were allowed to make commitments in quantitative terms as a response to tariff concessions by market economies (Matejka, 1990, p. 142). However, since the Soviet Union withdrew from the negotiations on trade liberalization and the creation of the ITO failed to occur, the possibility of such commitments was no longer considered within the regulations of the GATT.

The basic principles of the GATT are those of most favoured nation and reciprocity. The most-favoured-nation clause implies that a bilaterally negotiated reduction in tariffs applies to all other GATT nations, whereas the principle of reciprocity indicates that each tariff-reducing proposal will have to be responded to by similar commitments. These two principles are very difficult to reconcile with foreign trade organization in a centrally planned economy, since the replacement of quantitative trade restrictions by tariffs is highly problematic. Within a centrally planned economy, there are no tariffs. After all, foreign trade is regulated administratively, not by applying exchange rates and tariffs. Henceforth, a centrally planned economy is not able to fulfil the conditions of most favoured nation and reciprocity.

The irreconcilable principles of the GATT and centrally planned foreign trade were differently taken care of with the assent of Eastern European countries at the time central planning still prevailed in these countries. With the accession of Poland and Romania, the GATT relied upon the special provision of the ITO. Instead of offering tariff concessions, these countries were allowed to respond with an increase in imports from GATT nations with a certain percentage per year and for a well-defined period of time. The import increase and time span were matters for negotiation. Both countries were treated as special cases, since they did not have an effective tariff system. Poland became a GATT partner in 1967 and was forced to increase imports from GATT nations by 7 per cent in the period 1967–70. After 1970, the figures were somewhat relaxed and average import increases over a number of years were prescribed (GATT, 1972, p. 54). Similar arrangements were made for Romania's accession in 1971. It was agreed that the country's imports from GATT nations would at least be equal to the growth of total Romanian imports as decreed in the Five Year Plan 1971–75 (*ibid.*, p. 55).

Czechoslovakia and Hungary, the other Eastern European countries which became GATT nations before the 'annus mirabilis' 1989, were not subject to these special entry conditions. As already mentioned, Czechoslovakia belonged to the founder-nations of the GATT. At that time, communist assumption of power could not be foreseen, and hence there was no reason to require special commitments. After the communist takeover, Czechoslovakia remained a GATT partner, although, during the communist era, the country never actively participated in the various negotiations. The country was a 'sleeping partner' (Pissula, 1990, p. 193). As a consequence, at the start of the economic transformation in 1989, the country was confronted with a large number of 'bound tariffs'. Hungary was also able to avoid special requirements at the time its foreign trade was still subject to central planning. In the summer of 1973, the GATT nations unanimously agreed to Hungary's entry into the GATT and, unlike the entry of Poland and Romania, there were no special commitments required. The GATT nations believed, or pretended to believe, that Hungary could rely on an appropriate tariff system. Unconditional entry was a reward for the Hungarian reform attempts within the framework of the so-called 'New Economic Mechanism'. This comprehensive reform programme will be extensively dealt with in Chapter 5. Suffice it to say here that the economic reforms certainly did not meet expectations, although the relationship to some extent served as an external constraint that speeded up economic reforms. That is to say, reformist communist leaders were to some extent better able to defend reform measures internally by stressing the fact that international organizations left them no choice.

Inadequate Integration Within the Council for Mutual Economic Assistance

The above analysis illustrated that the state monopoly on foreign trade entailed systemic foreign trade behaviour which totally neglected comparative advantages and which appeared to be insensitive to exchange rates and tariffs in foreign trade decisions. But that was not all. It also led to a segmentation of foreign markets, since external economic relations with the West completely differed from the mutual trade relations of the Central and Eastern European countries. The latter were organized within the framework of the Council for Mutual Economic Assistance (CMEA), which organization had to foster regional economic integration in Eastern Europe. This section will address the extent to which regional integration could supply a reasonable alternative to integration with the West.

The founding of the CMEA in 1947 was initially meant as Stalin's response to the Marshall Plan, but afterwards became perceived as the counterpart of the European Economic Community (EEC).[7] In the West, therefore, the CMEA has been referred to as 'the common market of the East' (Lavigne, 1995), but given the fact that mutual trade relations were exclusively based upon bilateral agreements, this qualification is rather misleading. Regional cooperation within the CMEA was at most aiming at the 'coordination of national economic plans', but the organization of the CMEA was not even able to achieve this modest goal. The question remains as to how CMEA trade was conducted.

Trade agreements were the result of bilateral negotiations at the ministerial level. The desire to arrange external trade in such a way that a country's balance of payments will be in equilibrium not only *vis-à-vis* the total group of countries with which trade is conducted, but also *vis-à-vis* each country separately, facilitated the dovetailing of domestic economic planning and external economic relations. External economic relations are surrounded by uncertainty and therefore cause apprehension on the part of the planner. Bilateral trade agreements which are arranged before the start of a planning period will reduce trade volumes. Moreover, bilateral trade agreements were often propagated as a fair means of exchange. In practice, however, this orthodoxy of Marxism proved to be a willing instrument of political oppression by the stronger of the two bargaining nations.

But there were more disadvantages of bilateral trade. It reduced the total volume of trade and therefore impeded specialization (see Ausch, 1972). Moreover, it provoked a concentration in the commodity structure of foreign trade, implying not only that a country's balance of payments should be in equilibrium *vis-à-vis* trading partner, but that equilibrium should also to be attained within commodity groups. Low quality goods, that is soft commodities, were ideally not to be exchanged for hard currency commodities. This 'structural bilateralism' (Van Brabant, 1973) once more reduced total trade volumes and hampered specialization. Finally, it has to be noted that bilateral trade caused stabilization problems as well, since a country was forced to renegotiate, or to import from the West, in cases of non-delivery. Given the fact that the centrally planned economies were supply-constrained (Kornai, 1980), these problems were far from hypothetical.

With the accomplishment of bilateral trade agreements, two rules served for guidance. Firstly, prices were needed in order to conclude a contract. In this regard, world market prices were used as a yardstick. In the 1960s, the average of world market prices in the preceding five years was used, and, therefore, prices were fixed for a period of five years. Consequently, price developments in the world market were transferred with an enormous delay. After the oil crisis in 1973, the CMEA decided to change prices every year by means of a moving average of world market prices in the preceding five years. This brought some improvement, but still CMEA prices, of course, did not reflect global relative scarcities. Secondly, the bilaterally negotiated contracts had to be expressed in money. In 1963, the 'transferable rouble' was introduced for this purpose. There were, however, no actual payments in transferable roubles, but a special bank was erected for registration of trade flows and, if necessary and to a limited extent, for clearing imbalances (see for example Van Brabant, 1995, Chapter 3).

The consequence of the two rules was that trade surpluses were carefully avoided. Since foreign trade was planned and bilaterally negotiated by the ministries of the respective partners, there was commodity inconvertibility. A debt position automatically resulted in a credit, whereas a trade surplus could not be used for purchase of commodities outside the CMEA, neither could it be converted into the currency of other CMEA members (see Holzman, 1966; Lavigne, 1995; Van Brabant, 1995). Despite its connotation, the transferable rouble was not convertible into currencies of member nations of the CMEA, let alone into those of countries which did not belong to the CMEA.

After the collapse of the communist regimes, the CMEA severely languished and the organization was finally relinquished in the summer of 1991. The decisive steps which had triggered this event were taken in January 1990, during the 45th CMEA meeting in Sofia, at which comprehensive reform proposals dominated the agenda. But the new political leaders of the Central European countries believed that none of them was comprehensive enough, and therefore already proposed to dismantle the organization. However, since the parties could not agree on the dissolution of the CMEA, a provisional compromise was made. From January 1991, contracts were to be settled at current world market prices and in US dollars.[8] This was the straw which broke the camel's back and induced the organization's final dissolution in the summer of 1991.

EAST–WEST INTEGRATION

Following the Sofia decision to set mutual trade relations in US dollars at current world market prices, intra-CMEA trade completely collapsed. In 1991, trade volume fell by more than 30 per cent, while a significant decrease had already been registered for 1989 and 1990. It should be emphasized, however, that for the Central European countries, CMEA trade had already been declining since 1985. In the twilight of the communist regime, improvements in East–West trade relations were an important part of the economic reforms, especially for Hungary and Poland.

After the formal abolition of the CMEA, mutual trade relations in Central and Eastern Europe further declined. All efforts were focused on integration with the West. For this purpose, the Central European countries even decided to cooperate. The externally motivated cooperation influenced the EU in its attitude to treat the Central European countries as one geo-political unity, namely the 'Visegrád region'. Since the cooperation within the Visegrád framework had a major impact on the accomplishment of the formal agreement these Central European countries were able to reach with the EU, this section on East–West integration will start with a short introduction on the genesis and the further development of 'Visegrád'.

Accomplishment of the Europe Agreements and the Follow-up

On 15 February 1991 the leaders of Czechoslovakia, Hungary and Poland signed a declaration in Visegrád, a Hungarian town about 40 kilometres from Budapest.[9] The Visegrád summit focused on three main issues. Firstly, it was meant to mobilize common efforts to join West European institutions. Secondly, possibilities for closer economic and political cooperation were on the agenda. Thirdly, relations with the Soviet Union were discussed. The summit's declaration was very brief on all three topics, and its contents were not very concrete either (De Weydenthal, 1991).

As far as relations with the Soviet Union were concerned, vagueness in the document was not so much due to lack of ideas, but as the Warsaw Pact and the CMEA had not yet been dissolved, the Visegrád declaration carefully avoided being specific about the dissolution of military and economic structures (Tőkés, 1991). It did not imply that the political leaders lacked concrete views on stopping Soviet dominance, which was mainly institutionalized in the Warsaw Pact and the CMEA, and, thus, could be blocked most quickly by dismantling them. Contrary to the reasons for the document's lack of concreteness on relations with the Soviet Union, vagueness on intra-regional cooperation was based on different opinions about this. Severe trade and travel restrictions hindered active attempts to support regional economic cooperation. Besides, as has been shown above, the diverging pace and sequencing methods of transformation immediately after the collapse of communism, hampered the initiation of economic cooperation on a regional level. Therefore, the document stated only that the three countries would 'promote economic cooperation' (De Weydenthal, 1991, p. 30), without specifying what concrete steps this entailed.

The summit's declaration was most firm and determined on external political and economic relations. The underlying motives were joint aspirations to gain access to Western (European) institutions (Vachudova, 1993). The idea was to increase bargaining leverage in negotiations with NATO and the European Communities (EC). Although initially different opinions were to be found as far as their security was concerned,[10] at that time there was a common interest in talks with the EC in order to replace their trade agreements with the EEC and the 'European Coal and Steel Community' (ECSC) with EC Association Agreements.[11] Without relying on bureaucratic institutions, but restricting themselves to inter-governmental consultations, the Central European countries strove for recognition of similar goals and problems within the Visegrád countries. The Visegrád declaration defined the common goal as 'the restoration of each state's independence, democracy and freedom, and the dismantling of the structures of the totalitarian regimes, as well as the total integration into the Western European political, economic, security, and legislative order' (De Weydenthal, 1991, p. 29). Therefore, regional cooperation was purely externally motivated. At the Visegrád summit, possible welfare gains through dismantling mutual trade restrictions were hardly taken into consideration.

This attitude remained essentially unaltered during the period immediately afterwards. The Cracow meeting in October 1991 once more restated the priority of security objectives and the importance of intensifying relations with the EC (Tőkés, 1991). In this respect cooperation appeared quite successful. For instance, in negotiating the

Association Agreements the EC more or less treated them alike and all the agreements were completed in December 1991.[12] They focused on the same issues and differed only in small details. The EC was reluctant to be specific on the future EC membership of the Visegrád countries, but in the agreements it is explicitly stated that the Association Agreements are meant to create a framework for integration with the Community. However, the Association Agreements must not be confused with some kind of associate membership of the EC. Either a country is a member of EC, or it is not a member (Hedri, 1993, p. 154).

The Association Agreements to a large extent served as publicity gestures intended to stress EC involvement in the transition process. The agreements were veiled in unusual terminology to suggest that their impact went beyond earlier Association Agreements. They have, for example, often been referred to as 'Europe Agreements'. On the one hand, this simply meant that cooperation was not restricted to economic affairs, but extended to other spheres outside the competence of the community as well. Therefore, the individual EC countries had to ratify the agreements. On the other hand, the Central European countries were somehow to be treated as special cases for which the agreements served as a kind of ante-chamber for membership. Although no time-path has been settled in this respect, the Visegrád cooperation certainly has to be credited with the fact that the contracting parties realized they must explicitly state the ultimate goal of future EC membership of the Central European countries in the respective agreements.

As ratification by individual EC members would take rather a long time, it was agreed that the trade policy implications of the Association Agreements would be in force from March 1992. What did these entail? Essentially, they tried to arrange a free trade area by lowering customs duties and dismantling quantitative restrictions on industrial products. Within a period of ten years industrial free trade was to be achieved. As the level of economic development diverged between the contracting parties, the reductions of trade barriers were asymmetrical. Thus, the EC committed itself to reducing restrictions more quickly than the Visegrád nations.

The full liberalization of industrial products did not relate to the so-called 'sensitive' products, namely, textiles, ores and steel, for which special schemes were set up. For some of these products tariff reductions and/or enlargement of quota would be postponed for several years (steel), while for other sensitive products protectionism might be permanent (clothing and textiles). Besides, trade restrictions in agricultural products were to be maintained. Taking the importance of these commodities in the export structure of the four Central European countries into consideration, this implied a substantial loss of the agreements' impact (see Messerlin, 1992; OECD, 1994(c)).

The disappointing trade offers reinforced the attitude of the Central European countries regarding EU membership, although the EU summits in Copenhagen (1993) and Essen (1994) gave some impetus to the integration process. At the Copenhagen summit, the EU decided to expedite the lifting of trade barriers as agreed in the Association Agreements. More important, however, was the fact that accession of the associated countries was on the agenda for the very first time. In Copenhagen, the political leaders of the EU formulated criteria to be fulfilled for entry by the Central and Eastern European countries. These nebulously formulated economic and political criteria were (i) the preservation of democratic principles and the implementation of institutions to guarantee human rights, especially those of minorities, (ii) the willingness and the ability to accept EU laws, (iii) the display of a well-functioning market economy, (iv) the willingness to sustain EU competition, and (v) the ability of the EU to accommodate the entry of the Central and Eastern European countries in transition (see Csaba, 1996). As noted, the criteria (i) to (iv) were rather vague, whereas the countries involved were waiting for precise statements regarding inflation, budget deficits, the extent of the contribution of private economic activity to the country's gross domestic product (GDP), and so forth. But it really came as no surprise that the criteria lacked these kinds of indicators of the extent to which the economic transformation to a market economy was proceeding. Most revealing and meaningful was the fifth criterion. It has become quite clear that entry of the Central European countries, let alone entry of all the associated Central and Eastern European countries, would not only require necessary economic reforms within these countries, but would also require major adjustment within the EU. Without structural adjustments of the latter, accession would be too costly (Baldwin, 1994). The decisive factors for the financial consequences were the regional and structural funds and, of course, the Common Agricultural Policy (CAP) of the EU (see Hartmann, 1995).

The Essen summit was largely dominated by the formulation of strategies of 'pre-accession'. A matter of concern was the fact that the Association Agreements were only bilateral, whereas an eventual entry needed intensive dialogue with all the EU institutions, in a multilateral framework, as well.[13] The summit sparked off the EU Commission's White Paper on the 'preparation of the associated countries of Central and Eastern Europe for integration into the internal market of the Union' (Commission of the European Union, 1995). Since the White Paper aimed at assistance to fulfil the criteria of the internal market of the Union, it was only part of the 'pre-accession' strategy. The conditions for accession and the internal market were certainly not equivalent. Entry into the EU, of course, requires the approval of the entire 'acquis communautaire'. Consequently, and much to the discontent of the associated countries, no timetable for entry into the EU was fixed.

Meanwhile, the Czech Republic, Hungary, Poland and Slovakia have all officially applied for EU membership. Hungary was the first 'associated' country to do so in April 1994, followed within one week by Poland. The Czech Republic waited a relatively long time and requested membership in January 1996. In doing so, it followed the Baltic states, Bulgaria and Romania.[14]

Durable Affiliation to Other Prominent International Organizations

In order to achieve integration into the world economy, the Central European countries did not exclusively focus on membership of the EU. The Czech Republic, Hungary, Poland and Slovakia also renewed or tightened relations with international organizations with which, as described above, for systemic reasons they had so many problems in cooperating at the time when central planning in whatever form still existed.

Immediately after the collapse of the communist system, the countries facing the legacy of a monetary overhang, notably Poland and to a lesser extent Hungary, needed the IMF to help them endure the hardship of macroeconomic stabilization. Both Poland and Hungary were already members of this Bretton Woods institution and both were able to receive IMF loans. After more than forty years' absence, Czechoslovakia's renewed membership of the IMF and the World Bank was officially approved in October 1990. The membership was automatically passed over to the successor states after the Czechoslovak federation was split after January 1993. As will be shown in the next chapter, after the independence of the Czech and Slovak Republics, these Bretton Woods institutions were particularly important to Slovakia. It is interesting to note that the IMF set up special drawing rights for countries in transition. A so-called 'systemic transformation facility' was created as a new credit to support those countries in transformation which were not yet able to meet the IMF conditions for 'stand-by credits'. Regarding the World Bank, no special arrangements were set for countries in transformation. As other member-nations, the reforming countries could apply for 'structural adjustment loans' and were able to participate in World Bank projects in third countries. It has to be added, though, that the special problems due to the transformation from a centrally planned to a market economy were taken into account with the implementation of the European Bank for Reconstruction and Development (EBRD). At the Strasbourg summit of the EU in December 1989, it was decided to set up this bank. Its headquarters were located in London and the bank was operational from April 1991 (see Senior Nello, 1991).

When observing the relations with the GATT, there was no need to renew participation, since GATT partnership was settled for all the Central European countries under consideration from 1973. But as a consequence of several years of participation in this platform for international trade issues, the countries in transformation faced many 'bound tariffs' which were not easily disregarded when considering transient trade restrictions. In order to protect domestic industry during the period of transformation, Czechoslovakia especially, having participated in the GATT from the very beginning, had to rely upon special import surcharges. WTO membership for the Central European countries started without significant delay, that is coinciding with or immediately following the start of this global organization on international trade issues from December 1994. OECD membership took somewhat longer and is still not available to Slovakia.

In order to enable further appraisal of the extent to which global integration materialized for the Central European countries, Table 2.1 summarizes the main achievements of these countries in their attempts to join Western institutions.

Table 2.1   *Relations of the Czech Republic, Hungary, Poland and Slovakia with Western economic and political organizations (month/year)*

	Czech Rep.	Hungary	Poland	Slovakia
European Union				
Association Agreement				
- signed*	10/1993	12/1991	12/1991	10/1993
- in force	2/1995	2/1994	2/1994	2/1995
Interim Agreement				
on trade aspects				
- in force[†]	3/1992	3/1992	3/1992	3/1992
Application for				
membership	1/1996	4/1994	4/1994	6/1995

Table 2.1   continued

	Czech Rep.	Hungary	Poland	Slovakia
GATT partnership[†]	1/1948	9/1973	10/1967	1/1948
WTO membership	12/1994	12/1994	7/1995	12/1994
IMF membership[†]	1945–54		1945–50	1945–54
	10/1990	5/1982	6/1986	10/1990
World Bank	1945–54		1945–50	1945–54
membership[†]	10/1990	7/1982	7/1986	10/1990
OECD membership	11/1995	3/1996	7/1996	—

Notes: * Regarding the Czech and Slovak Republics, the data refer to a replacement of the previous Agreement with former Czechoslovakia, signed 12/1991.

† Regarding the Czech and Slovak Republics, data refer to former Czechoslovakia.

Sources: European Bank for Reconstruction and Development (1996(a); Fink (1996); *OECD Transition Brief* (various issues).

It has to be stressed that the legal status of 'associate partner of the EU', or *de jure* membership of leading organizations in the field of international trade and finance, does not imply that the Central European countries were in practice treated alike. Owing to diverse legacies in the realm of external economic relations, as well as to current diverse domestic policies, the Central European countries experienced different kind of problems. These will be examined in subsequent chapters. Moreover, especially when considering the follow-up of the Association Agreements, disappointment emerged regarding the date at which full membership of the EU would become known. Economic integration within the region of Central Europe, initially being one of the least important items in the Visegrád declaration, returned the political agenda. Therefore, the next section will intends to consider this item first.

REGIONAL ECONOMIC INTEGRATION IN CENTRAL EUROPE

The Painful Birth of the Central European Free Trade Area[15]

After the Association Agreements with the EC had been concluded, the Visegrád countries reconsidered intra-regional integration (see Sereghyová, 1995). Externally motivated cooperation gradually moved inwards, although several problems had to be solved before the Central European countries agreed in December 1992 to implement a free trade area (see Vachodova, 1993). The Czech Republic, Hungary, Poland and Slovakia decided to abolish import restriction on industrial products within eight years.[16] In this section the motives for creating a 'Central European Free Trade Association' (CEFTA) are examined, as are the problems that surrounded its implementation.

Apart from the fact that regional cooperation raised bargaining leverage with the EC, the Central European countries had to prove that they would be ready for EC membership. This has also been referred to as the 'image of maturity' (Richter and Tóth, 1993, p. 16). It would be ridiculous if the respective nations pretended to be able to lift trade and factor barriers with EC member states in the immediate future, while not being able to dissolve trade restrictions among themselves. It more or less follows from this line of argument that the phasing of trade reductions to a large extent resembles the contents of the EC agreements. Although the implementation of CEFTA is purely symmetrical, whereas the Association Agreements are not, the same groups of products are responsible for delay in reaching the final goal of free trade. In order to protect certain sectors for a limited number of years, among them textiles, clothing and metallurgy, a three-stage reduction of tariffs was proposed. As was the case with the EC, negotiations on agricultural products appeared to be highly problematic. Eventually it was agreed that tariff barriers would be dissolved within five years, but no concessions were being made with respect to non-tariff barriers. Thus, in order to avoid unnecessary trade diversion, the countries of the Visegrád triangle (quadrangle since 1993) tried to tune trade barrier reductions to those with the EC. This once again affirms the idea that regional integration in Central Europe follows integration with the West.

If the motives for regional economic integration are clear, the question remains, 'why was it so difficult to reach agreement on the CEFTA?' At the Cracow summit in October 1991 the signing of the agreement on the establishment of the CEFTA was scheduled for the summer of 1992, but this was postponed. The reasons were manifold, but two items dominated the disputes. The first was that the Central European countries implemented new trade barriers against each other. The second problem was that the leaders of the countries involved disagreed on the institutionalization of Visegrád cooperation, which so far entailed only consultation of presidents and prime ministers. Both aspects will be dealt with briefly in the following.

Apart from the often enumerated facts that led to the collapse of CMEA trade, bilateral Central European trade also declined because of newly implemented trade barriers, quantitative as well as tariff barriers.

The emergence of tariff barriers was obviously to be expected from the fact that these countries had to convert their foreign trade system. It essentially implied the replacement of planned foreign trade, that is implicit quantitative trade restrictions, by tariffs. Abandoning the old foreign system without introducing market-conforming tariffs could lead to a development in which viable Central European industries would not survive the transition period in which a certain distortion of central planning still prevailed. What counts here, of course, is the infant-industry argument, although, following the line of reasoning behind a 'shock therapy' approach, one could also argue that promising industries are deprived of necessary world market conditions, and therefore lack efficiency incentives.

The newly implemented non-tariff barriers towards each other did not, however, directly follow from the collapse of the communist system. But these partly emerged because the transition crisis was deeper than expected. In order to save jobs, to diminish the fall in production, and to allow certain state enterprises to restructure before they were privatized, there was some leeway allowed for protectionism. Ironically, those in the best position to strive successfully for protectionist measures were Western investors, notably car producers. As the Central European countries badly needed direct foreign investments, their governments were very vulnerable to Western rent-seekers. These temptations were also hard to resist during negotiations about the Association Agreements with the EC. For example, Poland implemented quantitative restrictions on Hungarian wine, while quotas for Portuguese wine were substantially enlarged in order to appeal to the EC (Richter, 1992).

A free trade area cannot function without proper institutions. Within CEFTA the Czech Republic, Hungary, Poland and Slovakia will be allowed to maintain their own tariffs *vis-à-vis* non-member states, which at least necessitates registering the origin of trade flows. Discussion of the matter of institutionalization actually started at the Prague summit in May 1992. Security motives for cooperation no longer dominated the agenda for cooperation, but discussion of economic matters gained momentum. At this summit the Visegrád leaders were quite optimistic about the establishment of a free trade area. Statements on institutions, however, were diplomatically avoided. Until then, President Václav Havel of Czechoslovakia and Prime Minister József Antall of Hungary were reluctant in this respect, while the Polish President Lech Wałęsa thought it useful to have certain Visegrád institutions (Vachudova, 1993). As ideas on the establishment of CEFTA became more concrete, confrontation on this matter became unavoidable.

In particular the Czech leader Václav Klaus, who became prime minister after the elections of July 1992, was strongly opposed to intensifying cooperation among the Visegrád triangle (quadrangle since 1993). Klaus's arguments were not so much related to fear of restoration of some kind of CMEA-like cooperation, but were based on the idea that the Czech Republic would be able to enter the EC more quickly without having to take cooperation with the other Central European countries into account. The lower levels of economic development in these countries would hinder early access. The split of the federation only strengthened this attitude. It implied that the authorities of the Czech Republic believed that Visegrád cooperation was only to be used as a valuable tool in relations with the EC. Thus, there were no Czech motives for intensifying economic cooperation among the Visegrád quadrangle. Time and again Klaus tried to loosen economic integration in the Central European region, and suggested sticking to regular consultative meetings of the countries' leaders. Thus, with respect to the Czech Republic's position there is some ambivalence. On the one hand, the Visegrád agreement was believed to enlarge the possibilities of EC membership, since it raised bargaining power. On the other hand, (perceived) lower economic development levels of the other Visegrád partners was interpreted as an important barrier to joining the EC in the near future. Be that as it may, in any event the Czechs rejected part of the Visegrád agreement to apply jointly for EC membership.

The Hungarian and Polish authorities have repeatedly proposed the encouragement of intensification of regional economic integration (see Guzek, 1993; Sereghyová, 1995). Neither were they strictly opposed to some kind of institutionalization, so long as it did not imply bureaucratization. During the second half of 1992, when the splitting of Czechoslovakia was under negotiation, they warned Czech and Slovak leaders that Hungary and Poland were even willing to establish a free trade area without them. But since with the split of the federation a customs union was maintained between the Czech Republic and Slovakia, the sky cleared. Moreover, Slovakia expressed itself to be in favour of cooperative action.

The differences in the strategic behaviour of the four Central European countries is difficult to understand within the framework of standard theory on regional economic integration. A bargaining approach seems to be more appropriate in this respect, as behaviour of the political leaders relied upon the divergent interests of the partners. However, it once more confirms the fact that regional integration in Central Europe is to follow integration with the West, from which the highest possible welfare gains are expected.

Expanding the Central European Free Trade Area?

The above-mentioned dispute on possible loss of strength due to different welfare levels of the participating countries is well known in other regions, notably the EC. The Czech arguments against far-reaching regional cooperation appear quite differently within economically weaker nations, which hope to climb on the bandwagon. The question that will be addressed in this section is related to matters of intensifying or extending regional economic integration in Central Europe. Or to put it differently, 'to what extent are there possibilities to expand the CEFTA?'

In 1996, Slovenia became a member of CEFTA and Romania will join the Association from January 1998. But there exists a loose form of regional cooperation in Central Europe as well, the so-called 'Central European Initiative' (CEI). This group of countries was originally set up in the autumn of 1989 by Austria, Hungary, Italy and Yugoslavia. Czechoslovakia subsequently joined in May 1990, after which the cooperation became to be known as the 'Pentagonale'. The extension to a 'Hexagonale' followed with the admission of Poland in July 1991. Since in the meantime several countries in this region have been split, the CEI now comprises ten states, among them Slovenia, Croatia, Bosnia-Herzegovina and Macedonia. Contrary to the motives which led to the emergence of CEFTA, the reasons behind CEI merely relied upon the notion that they share common historical features, which entitles them to be characterized as belonging to Central Europe. The initiative stemmed from the Italian Minister of Foreign Affairs Giovanni De Michelis, who wanted to counterbalance increasing German dominance within Europe. The CEI was first and foremost a political gesture (see Senior Nello, 1991).

The initiatives in the field of regional economic cooperation so far have been very modest, mainly because the functioning of the CEI has been overshadowed by the break-up of Yugoslavia and the splitting of Czechoslovakia. Thus, so far processes of disintegration seem to be the common factor that identifies the *differentia specifica* of Central Europe. Although there have been economic projects in the field of transport, energy, environmental protection and tourism, proposals to establish a free trade area that would even include the Baltic States have not been further elaborated (Reich, 1993). Apart from problems related to national minority issues, underlying differences in economic development also hinder effective regional economic cooperation. Taking the above-mentioned arguments into account, it is no wonder that at the Budapest summit in July 1993 it was again the Czech Prime Minister Klaus who lowered the ambitions of the CEI. Regional cooperation within the Visegrád region is difficult enough, let alone integration of a much larger area.

For the Central European countries, the welfare gains are mostly to be expected by looking westward. Anchoring to the agreements between the EC and the European Free Trade Association (EFTA) on forming a 'European Economic Area' (EEA), comprising an enormous free trade area in industrial goods, is much more promising. Regional economic integration in Central Europe will more probably induce trade-creating effects if external barriers are limited, especially because the four countries comprise a region that is too small to generate these effects without considering external trade relations with Western Europe.

CONCLUSION

During the communist era, fully-fledged integration into the world economic system was impossible for the Central European countries under scrutiny in this book. Systemic factors underlay this exclusion. Central planning as the leading principle of economic coordination induced an entirely different organization and function of these countries' external economic relations. Exports did not serve as an engine of economic growth, as is the case in an economic order dominated by market coordination, but came to the fore as a residual of the central planners' domestic production targets. Foreign trade was completely subordinated to these plans. Imports remained restricted to commodities and services which the country was unable to produce or deliver itself, or not at a minimally required quality level, whereas exports served merely to finance necessary imports. Total volume, destination and region of origin, as well as commodity composition of foreign trade, were completely designed to that end. A state monopoly on foreign trade ensured that market-oriented steering of a country's external economic relations was excluded. In centrally planned economies, exchange rates and tariffs did not exist, or were meaningless. Regional economic integration within the framework of the CMEA appeared to be a vain alternative, since external economic relations required coordination of national plans and, therefore, were unable to escape their bilateral character.

The state monopoly on foreign trade also hampered the Central European countries' participation in leading international organizations in the fields of trade policy and financial issues, such as the GATT, IMF and the World Bank, which based their policies predominantly on principles of market coordination. In order to prevent the total exclusion of centrally planned economies, special provisions were made. For example, with the establishment of the IMF, the Soviet Union succeeded in securing the inclusion of an article which facilitated the postponement of currency convertibility for current account transactions for an indefinite period. Ultimately, the Soviet Union did not join the Fund, but other countries, including Western European nations during the period after the Second World War, were able to benefit from this article in the IMF agreement. For participation in the GATT, special arrangements were devised as well. These were designed as a substitute for tariff concessions which, given the very nature of central planning, these countries were unable to offer. These examples illustrate that eminent global forums and organizations for international issues in the field of trade and finance to a certain extent adjusted to the special characteristics of external economic relations under a system of central planning.

Influence and adjustment between the international organizations and the Central European countries, however, was and is a mutual process. The organizations are clearly visible in the current process of transformation from a centrally planned to a market economy. Firstly, there is a legacy of the communist past. All the Central European countries under examination, in different forms and with different provisions, participated in the GATT. This had a profound impact on the manner in which these countries were able to temporarily protect their domestic economy in the first years of the transformation, since, to a different extent, tariffs were bound by GATT agreements. Secondly, IMF loans are conditional. The Fund's 'seal of approval' may severely restrain domestic politics when loans are postponed or when the Fund threatens such actions. Thirdly, in the case of delayed loan disbursement, or in a situation close to that, the politicians responsible for economic reform may use the threat to pursue their policy. In this respect, events in Hungary in 1992 may serve as an instructive example. The current functioning of the Central European countries in the world economic order clearly shows that transformation and integration are interdependent.

NOTES

1. In this sense, it was often laid down in the constitution of the people's republics. 'All foreign and wholesale trade is carried out by state enterprises' and 'all trade is directed by the state', were the usual phrases in this context (Matejka, 1986, p. 250, note 3).

2. This balancing could lead to quite extreme cases in which even a ball-bearing factory was to keep pigs for a year.

3. In preparing this section, the author is highly indebted to Ger Lanjouw and Beppo van Leeuwen.

4. It has been suggested that the Soviet Union was more interested in membership of the World Bank, but Bank membership was made conditional on IMF membership. The envisaged task of the World Bank was to supply loan guarantees for postwar reconstruction and the development of less-developed countries. During the negotiations

on the creation of the Bank, the Soviet Union, together with a number of European countries, tried to rank the reconstruction objective first. In the final Articles of Agreement, this question of priority of purposes was, however, left to the discretion of the Bank (Mason and Asher, 1973, pp. 21–4).

5. In this way, of course, the founder-nations hoped to prevent competitive depreciations of the kind that caused so much damage in the 1930s.

6. The problem led for example to the expulsion of Czechoslovakia in 1954. The country was forced to withdraw from the Fund – unique in the history of this organization – after disputes over a devaluation of the koruna without consultation with the Fund. According to Czechoslovakia, the change of the *par value* had no consequences for international transactions of Fund members, since its trade was subject to central planning. This argument was rejected because Czechoslovakia refused to supply the information that was thought to be necessary to determine whether the *par value* change was indeed of that nature (see Horsefield, 1969, pp. 359–64).

7. In the West, the CMEA was better known as COMECON. The Soviet Union, Bulgaria, Czechoslovakia, Hungary, Poland and Romania were founder-nations of this organization. Albania and the German Democratic Republic (GDR) joined in 1949 and 1950, respectively. Afterwards, Mongolia (1962), Cuba (1972) and Vietnam (1978) were admitted. Albania never officially retired as a member, but ceased any active participation since its support for China in the Sino-Soviet dispute in 1961 (see Van Brabant, 1995).

8. The inability to dissolve the CMEA in Sofia was due to the fact that financial arrangements had to be made for bilateral debt and credit positions which had emerged in the 1980s. These had to be converted into dollars and, therefore, were subject to negotiations. Some of these bilateral relations were set quite quickly, but others took years to be settled, especially after the Soviet Union ceased to exist (see Lavigne, 1995, pp. 103–5).

9. This city was chosen because, in 1335, it had been the site of a meeting of Bohemian King John of Luxembourg, King Charles-Robert of Hungary, and King Casimir the Great of Poland. That meeting facilitated close and lasting economic and political co-operation among their kingdoms.

10. The Hungarians, right from the beginning, were in favour of strengthening ties with the North Atlantic Treaty Organization (NATO), whereas the Czechoslovak and Polish authorities believed it would be more promising to have security guaranteed by the Conference on Security and Cooperation in Europe (CSCE), an option which in the long run was meant to by-pass NATO as well.

11. The term EC is ambiguous. With the entering into force of the treaty on the European Union (EU), as of 1 November 1993, the European Economic Community (EEC) was converted into the European Community (EC). However, before the inauguration of the EU, it was common to refer to the three communities, namely the European Economic Community (EEC), the European Coal and Steel Community (ECSC) and the European Atomic Energy Community (EURATOM), as the European Communities, also shortened to EC. In the context of this chapter, the EC refers to the European Communities.

12. Meanwhile, other Association Agreements have been endorsed with Bulgaria (1993), Romania (1993), Estonia (1995) Latvia (1995), Lithuania (1995) and Slovenia (1996). All these associated countries have also officially requested membership of the EU.

13. In this respect, there was an attempt to align with the PHARE programme. PHARE is the acronym for 'Pologne et Hongrie: Aide pour la Réconstruction des Economies'. This multilateral aid programme was an initiative of the European Commission and it became operational in 1989. Soon after the implementation of the PHARE, the programme was extended to other countries in Central and Eastern Europe. An important element of the PHARE was the technical assistance to revise and adjust legislation to the standards of

the European Community. Though not important in the context of this book, it should be noted that a similar programme was launched for the region of the former Soviet Union, namely the Technical Assistance for the Commonwealth of Independent States (TACIS).

14. Latvia, Estonia and Lithuania requested EU membership in October, November and December 1995, respectively. Romania and Bulgaria applied in June and December 1995.

15. Part of this section is based upon the author's article in *Most-Moct* (Hoen, 1994). I am grateful to the publisher for the permission to rely upon this writing.

16. Although the agreement was signed before the splitting of Czechoslovakia, it was separately approved by the authorities of the Czech Republic and Slovakia. Since these two republics decided to set up a customs union after dissolution of the Czechoslovak federation, the split itself did not hamper implementation of the CEFTA (Okolichanyi, 1993).

3. Transformation in the Czech and Slovak Republics: Liberal Rhetoric versus Populist Disgrace

INTRODUCTION

From 1 January 1993, Czechoslovakia ceased to exist. The federal republic was separated into two sovereign states, the Czech Republic and Slovakia. Since the break-up, paths of transition to a market economy in the newly independent republics have been conceived as largely diverging. On the one hand, the creation of a market economy in the Czech Republic is frequently believed to be an outstanding example of successful transformation (Raiser, 1994). The achievements are often attributed to a genuine liberal government policy conducted by Prime Minister Václav Klaus, chairing a coalition of conservative and Christian democratic parties. On the other hand, current reforms in Slovakia are supposed to reveal a slowdown of the initial steps of the transformation as set in motion after the political turmoil in 1989. Owing to political and economic problems, partly a result of the separation, a negative attitude developed towards Slovakia's transformation to a market economy.

This chapter focuses on the transformation from mandatory planning to a market economy in the Czech and Slovak Republics and attempts to combat the generally expressed ideas on the transformation in these new Central European countries. Following the tasks of transformation identified in the preceding chapters, it will be shown that the Czech case certainly does not stand as a textbook example of liberally inspired shock treatment, whereas populist disgrace often appears to be a hindrance in appropriately assessing Slovakia's economic transformation. The chapter seeks to distil common and diverging components in macroeconomic stabilization and microeconomic restructuring in the two republics, and focuses particularly on the reform measures aimed at enlargement and improvement of external economic relations, including the mutual economic relations between the Czech Republic and Slovakia.

The chapter is organized as follows. In order to assess the relative starting conditions for the transformation, the next section explores the legacy of communism and the costs and benefits of independence for the Czech and Slovak Republics. Subsequently, the transformation strategies in the respective countries will be scrutinized. The section on the Czech transformation to a market economy is to a large extent dedicated to an explanation of strikingly low unemployment figures, whereas the analysis of the Slovak transformation is dominated by the political instability of the country. Both sections, however, try to dispel the confusion with respect to the strategies and the economic performances of the two countries. The penultimate section explores reforms of the foreign trade organizations in the two republics. Special emphasis will be placed on the measures designed to overcome inter-republican trade and payments problems resulting from the break-up of Czechoslovakia. The final section summarizes the main findings.

THE LEGACY OF COMMUNISM AND THE END OF CZECHOSLOVAKIA

The Communist Inheritance

Considering the total period of post-war communism in Eastern Europe and the Soviet Union, the Communist Party of Czechoslovakia (KSČ) has always been amongst the most conservative in the region. When comparing reform policies with those in Hungary and Poland, differences are manifest.[1] In the 1980s, these Central European countries were to a far greater extent characterized by decentralized economic decision making, whereas Czechoslovak authorities neither initiated economic reforms – rather than following Soviet-dominated agreements within the framework of the CMEA – nor stated political intentions to do so. Even the 'Prague Spring', during which political changes attended economic reforms, did not have enduring effects. On the contrary, in the 1970s, the policy of the Czechoslovak communists was aimed at the normalization of political power and the stabilization of the economy by means of strengthening direct state intervention (see Košta, 1978; Myant, 1989).

The question is to what extent this conservative policy of the KSČ had a negative or positive impact on the starting conditions for the transformation to a fully-fledged market economy. The answer is ambiguous. On the one hand, there are obvious disadvantages to be noted. The negative inheritance of the communist era concentrates on structural inadequacies in the economy. The production structure was obsolete and inefficient, certainly when compared to Hungary and Poland, since it was to a greater extent set up to supply the Soviet Union. Furthermore, the emphasis on heavy industry went even beyond the proportions the other Central European countries were familiar with, although it has to be noted that heavy industry was skewed towards Slovakia (OECD, 1994(b), pp. 29–31).

On the other hand, communist conservatism led to favourable prospects as well. Firstly, Czechoslovakia had a good record in macroeconomic stability. In the twilight of the communist regime, there was low inflation and the balance of payments and the state budget were – by and large – in equilibrium. These macroeconomic conditions strongly contrasted with those prevailing in Hungary and Poland, which both faced severe disequilibria due to past reforms, since hardening of the budget constraints did not attend decentralization of economic decision making. It has to be noted, though, that in Poland these stability problems were many times greater than in Hungary. Secondly, and following from the previous point, strongly centralized decision-making power at the beginning of transformation created a clear political set-up. There were for instance no claims to be lodged with respect to the transfer of ownership rights, either from the workforce or from the management. Decentralization of economic decision making in Hungary and Poland, though, did create opportunities to moderate the speed of privatization, since its future implications were obviously not always in the interest of management and workforce. This is a sequencing argument focusing on interest-group behaviour. Decentralization of economic decision making before privatization may appear more difficult than the other way around (Nunnenkamp, 1997). In Czechoslovakia, all privatization decisions were centralized before spontaneous privatization could occur. Thirdly, despite extreme communist conservatism, which resulted in economic growth persistently lagging behind that of the OECD countries since the 1970s, Czechoslovakia remained one of the most prosperous countries in Eastern Europe. Calculations show that at the initial stages of the transformation, Czechoslovakia had approximately a 30 per cent higher than average Eastern European GDP (see *PlanEcon Report*, 1993, No. 13–14).[2]

So, there is no unambiguous conclusion to be drawn on the relative impact of the communist legacy on the starting conditions for the creation of a market economy. In terms of macroeconomic stability, prospects were relatively favourable, whereas microeconomic structural deficits put Czechoslovakia in arrears. However, in this respect, regional differences between the Czech lands and Slovakia are to be taken very seriously.

The Anatomy of Independence

The gap between the Bohemian and Moravian Czech lands, on the one hand, and Slovakia, on the other, is deeply rooted in history. Until 1918, Slovakia belonged to the Hungarian part of the Austro-Hungarian monarchy, whereas Moravia and Bohemia were Austrian. At the time Czechoslovakia was created – immediately after the First World War – the Czech lands were highly industrialized and prosperous, whereas Slovakia was predominantly agricultural and poor (see Košta, 1978). It may be that differences in welfare and standards of education have been more or less levelled out during nearly 75 years of Czechoslovakia's existence, but the emancipation of Slovaks in the Czechoslovak Republic was never completed. Notwithstanding the creation of a federal constitution – one of the few lasting results of the 'Prague Spring' in 1968 – the Czech capital remained the pivotal power in political and economic decision making.

In November 1989, the KSČ was forced to renounce its dominant role in society, which until then had been legally established. The 'velvet revolution' was a fact and the former dissident and writer Václav Havel, one of the eminent leaders of Civic Forum (OF), became president of a new Czechoslovakia. After the euphoria at regaining political freedom had evaporated, the dormant contrasts between Slovakia and the centre of power – Prague – were awoken. One of the first measures taken by the new federal government entailed the closing down of heavy weapons production. Although a nice gesture, the halt to production meant an economic setback to Slovakia, which was heavily dependent upon this part of the military sector. The production of light weapons, mainly located in the Czech lands, proceeded as before. In Slovakia, this measure stimulated requests to delegate federal competence to the respective local authorities of the Czech and Slovak Republics. Furthermore, the authorities applied a policy which closely followed the arguments of adherents of shock treatment, as set out in Chapter 1. This resulted in a restrictive monetary and fiscal policy and a complete liberalization of prices and foreign trade. Domestic enterprises were protected only by a substantial devaluation of the Czechoslovak crown (Hrnčíř, 1991). The instruments of the central bank to conduct a restrictive monetary policy entailed high interest rates, the prescription of minimal financial reserves for commercial banks, and the implementation of administrative burdens with regard to credit accommodation (Levcik *et al.*, 1994). Since the Slovaks were in a relatively backward position, they claimed to be harder hit by the stabilization policy applied by the federal authorities and therefore expressed the desire to delay or postpone certain painful reforms. Greater political independence would increase the opportunity to adjust the shock approach which so far had been conducted in Prague.

In the Czech media, these Slovak desires encountered much incomprehension and condescending attitudes. In particular Vladimír Mečiar was made fun of. Since 1990, he had been Prime Minister of the local Slovak government, which gained support from the Slovak counterpart of the Czech OF, the 'Public against Violence' (VPN), a party which had emerged during the velvet revolution of November 1989. At the beginning of 1991, the VPN fell apart and Mečiar had to resign as Prime Minister. However, during his premiership, he had won popular support from the Slovak people and since his resignation took place under obscure circumstances, Mečiar was able to present himself as an underdog in the campaign for Czechoslovak elections which were to be held in June 1992. These elections brought a clear victory to Mečiar's newly founded 'Movement for a Democratic Slovakia' (HZDS), which adopted a more nationalistic stance and stressed much greater Slovak autonomy.

In the Czech Republic, Václav Klaus won the elections. He headed the Civic Democratic Party (ODS) and became Prime Minister of a government in which his party formed a coalition with the Civic Democratic Alliance (ODA), the joint Christian Democratic Union–Czechoslovak People's Party (KDU–ČSL), and the Conservative Democratic Party (KDS). Klaus strongly adhered to the maintenance of central control, whereas Mečiar favoured delegating authority to the local governments. In the subsequent talks between Klaus and Mečiar, the latter, time and again, proposed constitutional alternatives of confederacy, but none of these were acceptable to Klaus. Therefore, there was no choice left but to dissolve the Czechoslovak federation, and from 1 January 1993, the Czech and Slovak Republics became fully independent states.

Is the break-up of Czechoslovakia solely due to Slovak nationalism? This is highly questionable (see Musil, 1995). Full independence was not an item in the programme of Mečiar's HZDS. The only party for which separatism appeared pivotal was the 'Slovak National Party' (SNS). But at the time of the negotiations, this party was not yet in government. Other factors should be seriously taken into account, especially with regard to Slovakia's weaker economic structure. In order to completely resolve differences, enormous financial transfers from Prague to Bratislava were necessary. Therefore, Slovakia hindered rapid economic reforms such as Klaus would ideally have implemented. Since the legal constitutions of 1969 guaranteed veto power to both federal houses of parliament, this implied that Mečiar was able to wreck Klaus's reform plans and *vice versa*. So, it may well have been the case that Mečiar overplayed his hand by threatening separation, a hypothesis which forces us to make a cost–benefit analysis of the separation.

Economically, the separation was a serious blow for Slovakia. Political independence had to be bought at a high price. Table 3.1 provides some information on the relative economic positions of the Czech and Slovak Republics in the twilight of the federation. The figures support the view that the costs of independence were substantially higher for Slovakia.

Table 3.1   Relative positions of the Czech and Slovak Republics in the twilight of the federation (percentages)

	Czech Republic	Slovakia
Share (1992):		
in federal population	66	34
in federal GDP	72	28
in federal exports	74	26
in federal foreign direct investments	92	8
of inter-republican deliveries		
in total republican sales	11	27
of private sector		
in republican GDP	16	6

Source: Křovák *et al.* (1993), pp. 6–7

With a share of 66 per cent of total population and 72 per cent of GDP, labour productivity in the Czech Republic was significantly above that in Slovakia. In 1992, Slovakia's GDP was approximately a quarter below the Czech level (see *PlanEcon Report*, 1993, No. 13–14). The vulnerability of the Slovak economy can also be derived from the fact that the percentage share of mutual Czech and Slovak deliveries in total sales was considerable higher in the case of Slovakia. Apparently, the Czech Republic was less dependent upon Slovakia than *vice versa*. The other indicators also point to Slovakia's relative weak position, although with respect to a more than 90 per cent share in foreign direct investment, it has to be noted that many Slovak companies had their headquarters located in Prague, indicating that the figures may underestimate Slovakia's share of foreign investments. Notwithstanding this slight modification, the lower share in federal exports clearly shows the more autarkic nature of Slovakia, which can also be revealed by taking the regional composition of exports into consideration.

The regional composition of exports, presented in Table 3.2, definitely puts Slovakia behind the Czech Republic, since the figures indicate that Slovak export flows were less directed to Western markets. In the twilight of the federal republic, 70 to 80 per cent of exports were conducted with formerly centrally planned economies, whereas the Czech figures reveal a more Western orientation. In 1991 and 1992, the share of Western exports in total Czech exports amounted to over 35 and nearly 45 per cent, respectively. The collapse of trade among the former communist economies in Eastern Europe and the Soviet Union from 1990 had a larger negative impact on Slovakia.

Table 3.2   *Regional structure of Czech and Slovak exports, percentage shares in total exports, 1991–92*

| | Czech Republic | | Slovakia | | |
	1991	1992		1991	1992
Slovakia	33.0	31.5	Czech Rep.	51.5	46.6
CIS*	11.9	5.9	CIS	12.1	8.9
E. Europe†	11.8	8.7	E. Europe	10.1	8.9
EU	29.5	36.8	EU	16.6	22.3
EFTA‡	6.2	7.5	EFTA	4.0	5.7

Notes: * From 1 January 1992 the Soviet Union no longer existed and was replaced by the Commonwealth of Independent States (CIS), a loose association of the former constituent republics, excluding the Baltic States. For 1991, the figures refer to the Soviet Union, whereas for 1992 they include trade with the region of the former Soviet Union without Estonia, Latvia and Lithuania.
   † Eastern Europe refers to Bulgaria, Hungary, Poland and Romania, but does not include trade with Slovakia or the Czech Republic.
   ‡ In 1991–92, the European Free Trade Association (EFTA) comprised Austria, Finland, Norway, Sweden and Switzerland.
Source: *PlanEcon Report* (1993), No. 22–4

The relative backwardness of Slovakia implied the transfer of substantial financial flows from Prague to Bratislava. Several estimates for the 1980s set this at 7 per cent of Slovakia's GDP, corresponding to roughly 3 per cent of the Czech GDP at that time. Although these estimates reveal a significant decrease compared to the flows in the 1950s, 1960s and 1970s, which were within the range of 10 to 15 per cent of Sovakia's GDP, transfers were still substantial (see Křovák *et al.*, 1993).

The conclusions are quite straightforward. Slovakia being more heavily burdened with a negative communist inheritance, the expected costs of an independent transition to a market economy were to be correspondingly higher. To argue against purely nationalistic reasons for the splitting of the country, one could add that the economic gap between the two parts of the federation forced the Czech and Slovak authorities to make a choice between two scenarios for the transformation. Either the survival of the federation would involve increasing financial transfers from Prague to Bratislava in order to maintain the course initially set in motion, or strategies would have to be more differentiated, which would put at stake the continued existence of the federal republic of Czechoslovakia.

After negotiations on these two basic alternatives gained momentum and the split eventually became inevitable, it became clear that Mečiar had overplayed his hand, since a dissolution of the federation was not in Slovakia's economic interest. Internally, Mečiar could only defend the split by playing along with latent nationalistic feelings. The suggestion that economic rather than populist forces triggered the events that led to the divorce does not, of course, alter the fact that the nature of political restraints largely determines the policy for economic transformation. In the remainder of this chapter, it will be seen to what extent the policies applied in the successor states indeed diverged as a result of differing starting conditions and changing political circumstances.

THE RHETORIC OF CZECH LIBERALISM

The Czech policy of transformation enjoys wholehearted support. There is not only general approval in the written and visual media, but full endorsement can also be found in leading economic and financial institutions, such as the OECD, the IMF, the World Bank and the EBRD (see Aghion and Blanchard, 1993; Blejer *et al.*, 1993; Fries and Lane, 1994, OECD, 1994(a)). The Czech transformation is often presented as a textbook example to other countries which try to create a market economy. The yardstick for the achievements is generally found in unadulterated liberalism, especially as proclaimed by Prime Minister Klaus (see for example Klaus, 1992).

There is no reason to deny the relative success of Czech policy makers in regard to the transformation from mandatory planning to a market economy. Table 3.3 shows that the country is not confronted by large internal and external disequilibria and the level of unemployment not only is the lowest among the Central and Eastern European countries in transition, but the less than 5 per cent unemployed is also far below the West European average. It has to be added, though, that the total decline in economic activity was no less than in Poland or Hungary, since, independently of the strategy applied, declining economic activity manifested itself in all countries in transition. But the remarkable combination of transformation without massive unemployment prompts further scrutiny of the concept of a Czech road to a market economy.

Table 3.3   *Development of important economic indicators in the Czech Republic, 1990–95*

	1990	1991	1992	1993	1994	1995
GDP growth (%)	-0.4	-14.2	-6.4	-0.9	2.6	5.2
consumer prices (%)	10.8	56.7	11.1	20.8	10.0	9.1
government budget (% of GDP)*	0.1	-2.0	-3.3	0.5	1.3	1.0
unemployment (% active pop.)	0.8	4.1	2.6	3.5	3.2	2.9
current account (bln. $)†	-1.1	0.4	-1.0	-0.3	-0.4	-3.8
foreign direct investment (mln. $)	120	511	983	517	850	2500

Notes: * Data for 1990, 1991 and 1992 refer to the federal budget of Czechoslovakia.
† Data for 1990, 1991 and 1992, exclude trade with Slovakia and comprise only payments in convertible currency.
Sources: European Bank for Reconstruction and Development (1996(a), 1996(b))

The analysis focuses in particular on the question of the extent to which the astonishingly low unemployment can be ascribed to a genuine *laissez-faire* policy, or to the maintenance of inefficiently producing state enterprises, or to the relatively favourable economic conditions at the start of the transformation. As mentioned above, at the time the federation still existed, a tough stabilization policy based upon a shock approach towards the creation of a market economy was applied. After the splitting of the federation, the Czech authorities initially maintained a restrictive monetary and fiscal policy, but in the second half of 1993, a path of transformation emerged which strongly relied upon direct state interference. State intervention focused on the tuning of demand and supply on the labour market and on the prevention of a 'credit crunch' in financial markets. The policy was rooted in a strong belief that the as yet insufficiently functioning markets in production factors need strong government guidance. The Czech course, therefore, to an increasing extent deviates from a genuine liberal shock approach as discussed in Chapter 1. A government retreat in all relevant fields of the economy is beyond dispute. This can best be shown by elaborating government policy aimed at the development of the factor markets.

Financial Markets and Budget Constraints

Financial markets are essential to an efficient allocation of resources. With respect to the transition, Stiglitz has argued that 'if capital is at the heart of capitalism, then well-functioning capital markets are at the heart of a well-functioning capitalist economy' (Stiglitz, 1992, p. 161). Because of the lack of well-developed stock and bond markets, the formerly centrally planned economies have to rely primarily on banks for fund raising and allocation. For that, the banking system needs to be thoroughly reformed. Under the system of mandatory planning, the banks only register financial transactions for book-keeping purposes, that is, the monetary reporting of real plan directives. Within this passive banking system, there was no relationship between savings and fund raising, while incentives for an efficient allocation of resources were ineffective owing to the soft budget constraints of enterprises as well as banks (see Kornai, 1980).

A first step towards a Western-oriented banking system involves the separation of monetary and commercial tasks through the introduction of a so-called 'two-tier banking system', in which the national bank is split into a central bank and a number of commercial banks. Following Hungary and Poland, which had already reformed their banking system along these lines in the second half of the 1980s, Czechoslovakia implemented a two-tier system in the spring of 1990 (Raiser, 1994).[3] Three commercial banks were set up, which, as in the Polish and Hungarian cases, were burdened by a bad portfolio as a result of dubious lending during the communist past. The total amount of bad debts was estimated at more than 100 billion Czechoslovak crowns (Dittus, 1994). This heavily restrained the possibilities for the commercial banks to supply credits to newly emerging enterprises. However, in comparison with what happened in Hungary and Poland, the Czechoslovak – and after the dissolution of the federation especially the Czech – authorities were better able to prevent a so-called 'credit crunch' (Schmieding, 1993). This was due to a number of specific governmental policy measures.

In 1991, the Klaus government set a maximum to the amount of total credit available for state enterprises. This gave leeway for credit accommodation on the part of private firms. Contrary to the situation in Hungary and Poland, the private sector was not so much crowded out by the reduction of the total real credit volumes to half their previous amount. Besides, the government took additional measures aimed at the recapitalization of banks. The Czech authorities introduced a centralized consolidation programme. In order to relieve the inherited financial burdens of commercial banks and enterprises, a 'Konsolidační Banka' was set up as early as February 1991. For 80 per cent of the nominal value of bad loans, this consolidation bank bought risky bank claims on Czech and Slovak enterprises, and thereby gave them financial injections at a very crucial moment (Orenstein, 1994). In due course, the consolidation bank developed from being a large supplier of credits to an institute heavily involved in the restructuring of large state enterprises. Finally, extra regulations were issued to relax the ratio of credit accommodation to dubious financial liabilities with regard to funding new private enterprises (see for example Dittus, 1994; Kouba, 1994).

Thanks to this policy, the classic problem of 'adverse selection' could to a large extent be avoided. Developments were quite the other way around: well-aimed financial injections supported the evolution of a private sector. In addition, bankruptcy legislation was introduced rather late. It dates from April 1993 and, so far, appears to be rather ineffective. The fact that only a very limited number of enterprises are adjudged bankrupt can be ascribed to legislation which had been approved in 1992 (Act on Bankruptcy and Competition 328/1992), officially recording that state enterprises may not fail during the process of privatization (Orenstein, 1994). This might indicate a continuation of subsidizing loss-making firms. Political considerations may have persuaded Czech policy makers not to carry through too tough a policy. As a result, the restructuring of production may have been delayed and inefficient allocation may have taken place. Levcik *et al.* (1994) and Kouba (1994) seem to subscribe to this view. Both papers stress that it is true that voucher privatization brought about a successful transfer of ownership rights, but that the restructuring of privatized firms remained problematic. Effective restructuring was postponed not so much by the feared scattered structure of ownership rights as a result of the free distribution of coupons among the population at large – this did not emerge, due to the spontaneous emergence of bank-led investments funds – but rather by conflicting interests between a bank as owner and a bank as supplier of credits. Other sources acknowledge these problems of 'corporate governance', but at the same time mask the critique by focusing on achievements in deconcentration of industrial production (OECD, 1994(b), Chapter 13; Charap and Zemplinerova, 1993). Moreover, another part of the explanation for the limited number of bankruptcies with subsequent large-scale dismissals is to be found in wage control (Raiser, 1994). In comparison with Hungary and Poland, the Czech authorities were very keen to keep control over labour market development and therefore they directly intervened on a large scale.

Labour Market Policy

In the Czech Republic, liberalization of the labour market has been rather limited and, at the start of the process of transformation, real wages declined substantially, certainly when compared with Hungary and Poland. In Poland, stabilization policy had to be paid for in a restriction of real wage increases, but attempts to tax away wage rises which exceeded inflation ('popiwek') enjoyed no lasting success. For Hungary, in none of the first five years following the collapse of communism did the decline in real wages exceed 5 per cent. As a legacy of reforms during the 1980s, wage formation was most liberal in this country and it was beyond the government's power to regain effective control over wage development.[4]

However, more interesting than the fact that the Czechoslovak government applied tough wage controls – it was not unique in that – was the reason why the wage freeze was so easily accepted by trade unions and employees. Wage restraint was a recurrent topic in 'tripartite' consultations between the government, trade unions and employers (Adam, 1993). The authorities took the opportunity to use those instruments which were at their disposal during central planning. During the communist era, all wages were administratively decreed on a yearly basis. This remained the case in 1990, after which, in 1991, in combination with the freeing of prices, there was a limited liberalization in the labour market. In 1991, an agreement was reached within the context of the tripartite talks, after which the maximum wage rises would be prescribed to state enterprises as well as to private firms (decree 15/1991). The agreement was based upon inflationary expectations of less than 10 per cent for 1991. In reality, inflation was much higher, resulting in a real wage decline of approximately 25 per cent (Nunnenkamp, 1997). In the following years, the policy remained in principle unaltered. The Czechoslovak – and later on especially the Czech – government kept intervening directly: at least it reserved the right to decree the results negotiated within the tripartite talks. The liberalization was to be found in the fact that the decrees were no longer applied to private firms, although during 1994 conditions became more restrictive and the wage decrees also affected private enterprises with more than 24 employees. From 1993, real wage increases became negotiable again within the tripartite consultations, but five years after the communists were forced to resign power, real wages were still below the level of 1990, and during that period, the real wage decline far surpassed the decline in labour productivity.

The Czech labour market policy was not aimed at wage control alone. In a broader perspective, labour market policy focuses on 'matching', that is, allocating those searching for a job to available vacancies (Burda,

1993). In comparison with Hungary and Poland, a lot of money has been spent on finding employment. Of all the available financial means reserved for the re-placement of unemployed in 1992, 60 per cent was allocated to occupational resettlement and employment packages, whereas for Hungary and Poland this amounted to only 14 and 11 per cent, respectively (Raiser, 1994). District labour offices played a pivotal role in matching demand and supply in the Czechoslovak – and later the Czech – Republic. In February 1991, legislation was enacted which mandated the newly set-up district labour offices to provide jobs for the unemployed. Persons in search of employment could be accommodated within different programmes, such as those designed to create long-term jobs by assisting the newly started employers for a maximum of half a year, short-term jobs for a maximum of half a year aimed at public work, jobs for new graduates and jobs available for a period of retraining. The local labour districts were given great autonomy in regard to the allocation of the funds provided by the Ministry of Labour and Social Affairs. In the period 1992–93, the number of jobs involved was between 100,000 and 140,000 at any given time, corresponding to approximately 2 per cent of total employment (Orenstein, 1994).

Regarding the active labour market policy in the Czech Republic, it is important to emphasize again that occupational resettlements and employment packages were agreed upon within the framework of the tripartite discussions. Thanks to the programmes, it became easier to commit trade unions to wage control. As part of the tripartite consultations, many efforts have also been made to create a social safety net. In this regard, legislation was agreed upon in November 1991 and came into force in 1992. The negotiating parties agreed to define a socially acceptable minimum level of welfare. Depending on the family composition, legislation has been approved which guarantees that all those unable to earn a living are entitled to benefit. The allowances are not far below the level of minimum wages (Adam, 1993).

It is extremely difficult to assess the extent to which the Czech labour market policy contributed to the low unemployment figures. Orenstein (1994) estimates that unemployment figures would have been twice as high in the absence of the measures. Taking the magnitude of unemployment in Hungary, Poland and Slovakia into consideration, these calculations leave a significant part of the unemployment figures unexplained.[5] Other plausible explanations are based on the large absorption capacity of the service sector in the Czech economy (OECD, 1994(a)), while the larger decline in the number of female workers participating in the labour market also had an impact on employment figures. An assessment of tripartite consultations in the Czech Republic, however, should be measured not only by unemployment rates, but rather in terms of popular support for far-reaching reforms.

Consensus in the framework of corporatist tripartite consultations is not usually connected with a liberal policy. It seems more appropriate to characterize the Klaus government as pragmatic. The intention is to keep unions' power within acceptable limits by making them partly responsible for social policy and not by trying to rule this out along Thatcherite lines. Although Prime Minister Klaus did not wholeheartedly support the idea of a guided labour policy at the time the tripartite consultations were being established in October 1990, the corporatist structure brought him major political advantage in terms of policy legitimacy. The carefully designed strategy aimed at a modest level of unemployment and a sound social safety net generally contributed to political stability. Contrary to the political developments in Hungary and Poland, where former communist parties resumed power, Czech citizens remained satisfied with the ruling Klaus government (Juchler, 1994).

On 31 May and 1 June 1996, there were parliamentary elections with sixteen competing parties and the results displayed relative stability. Klaus's party remained the largest with nearly 30 per cent of the popular vote, although, contrary to the expectations shortly before the elections, the Czech Party for Social Democracy (ČSSD) lost the election by very small margins (*Report on the Czech and Slovak Republics*, No. 5, 1996). Moreover, in contrast with the social democratic parties in Hungary and Poland, the ČSSD – chaired by Miloš Zeman – did not have communist roots. Arduous coalition talks followed the elections, and on 4 July a new government was appointed. For the sake of the national interest and in return for the acceptance of Zeman's position as chairman of parliament, ČSSD approved the programme of the Klaus government. With the exception of the conservative KDS, which was merged with ODS, the government proceeded with the same coalition.

The relative stability can be seen as a necessary precondition for the creation of a well-functioning market economy. But so long as markets are not fully developed, the Czech authorities are strongly relying on direct government intervention. They certainly believe that the task of government goes far beyond the simple recommendation to withdraw from economic life. In the institutional vacuum that would emerge, chaos has to be feared. So, despite all the rhetoric, the Czechs perfectly understood that a market economy cannot be created by a pure *laissez-faire* policy.

THE MEČIAR FACTOR IN SLOVAK TRANSFORMATION

The Political Scene[6]

In the foregoing section on the forces which led to the dissolution of the federation, economic rather than nationalistic factors have been stressed. Political independence for Slovakia was believed to give leeway to modify the shock treatment conducted in Prague in the period immediately following the political turmoil. In order to ease the pain which attended this transformation policy, the Slovak authorities proposed to follow a more gradual strategy of transformation. The question to be addressed here is to what extent the Slovak authorities have been able to do so.

While Klaus dominated policy making in the Czech Republic, Mečiar stamped his presence on Slovakia's political face. He became Prime Minister of the federal Republic of Slovakia following the elections of December 1989, but had to resign after his party, the VPN, fell apart in the spring of 1991. Mečiar founded the HZDS, which won the elections held in June 1992. Mečiar became Prime Minister again. Initially, his cabinet consisted only of HZDS members, but since many leading members later left the party, Mečiar was forced to form a coalition with the SNS at the end of 1993.

Michal Kováč belonged to those leading HZDS members who joined the exodus from Mečiar's party. At the beginning of 1993, he was elected President of the Slovak Republic with the support of Mečiar, but in the course of that year, Kováč became Mečiar's most important political opponent and triggered the events which led to the fall of the government. In February 1994, Mečiar's coalition party split, as a result of which the government lost its majority in parliament. In a speech addressed to the parliament, Kováč encouraged the members to demand Mečiar's resignation. He succeeded and, within a matter of days, there was a new government headed by the former Minister of Foreign Affairs, Jozef Moravčík (ex-HZDS). This government, which was supported by the Party of the Democratic Left (SDĽ), the Christian Democratic Party (KDH), and disloyal HZDS members, had to prepare for general elections to be held in the autumn of 1994. These elections brought victory again to Mečiar. So, with the exception of the spring and summer of 1994, he ruled Slovak governments during the first four years of independence. The question is whether he and his government were able to delay the reforms and, if so, to what extent they succeeded.

Table 3.4 illustrates the development of the main economic indicators for Slovakia. It can be seen that during the first year of independence the country suffered hard times. But afterwards, a remarkable recovery in economic activity took place, while the monetary authorities were also quite successful in regaining control over inflation. GDP growth in 1994 and 1995 even surpassed the Czech performance. Although, when comparing the development in unemployment and foreign investments with the Czech Republic, the picture is more complex, the general perception of Slovakia's economic performance remains brighter than one would expect on the basis of information about the political scene.

Table 3.4 Development of important economic indicators in Slovakia, 1990–95

	1990	1991	1992	1993	1994	1995
GDP growth (%)	-0.4	-14.5	-7.0	-4.1	4.8	6.6
consumer prices (%)	18.4	61.2	10.1	23.2	13.5	9.9
government budget (% of GDP)*	0.1	-2.0	-12.3	-7.6	-1.4	0.4
unemployment (% active pop.)	1.5	11.8	10.3	14.4	14.8	13.1
current account (bln. $)†	-1.1	0.4	0.2	-0.4	0.7	0.3
foreign direct investment (mln. $)	52	74	130	163	310	44

Notes: * Data for 1990, 1991 and 1992 refer to the federal budget of Czechoslovakia.
         † Data for 1990, 1991 and 1992 exclude trade with the Czech Republic and comprise only payments in convertible currency.
Sources: European Bank for Reconstruction and Development (1996(a), 1996(b))

In order to assess the Mečiar factor in the current Slovak transformation from a centrally planned to a market economy, it is necessary to explore the starting conditions as well as the external constraints the Slovak government has to cope with. In the following, therefore, the Czech-made framework for transformation and the degrees of freedom regarding an independent policy will be scrutinized.

The Czech-made Framework for the Slovak Transformation and Evolving Policy Resolutions

Although Slovakia's contribution was not voluntary, as a constituent republic of the Czechoslovak federation the Slovak Republic had fully taken part in the transformation policy applied during the period 1990–92. In the foregoing sections, this policy was described as quite successful. So, despite disproportionately heavier sacrifices relative to the Czech

Republic, the independent Slovak Republic started with a high degree of macroeconomic stability and inherited an institutional framework to create a fully-fledged market economy.

The centrepiece of the reform package, set to go into effect on 1 January 1991, was a plan to achieve price liberalization, import liberalization and commercial currency convertibility. The principal architect of these reforms was Finance Minister Klaus, later appointed prime minister, who was dedicated to a rapid and well-monitored transformation to a market economy in which macroeconomic stabilization was to be established with restrictive monetary and fiscal shock treatment. In the period immediately following independence, print and electronic media revealed an intended policy change towards a more gradual economic transformation (Fisher, 1993). But it has to be noted that during the first year of independence there was no resolute policy course officially worked out on paper. Regarding macroeconomic stabilization in practice, the aims of the Slovak monetary policy may not have been as conclusively defined as in the Czech Republic, but stabilization of prices and exchange rate by means of money supply and credit restrictions remained the principal objective.

Besides the fact that *de facto* the transformation policy remained restrictive, official statements regarding the desirability of a more gradual approach towards the transformation also evaporated after half a year of independence. During the summer of 1993, a more pragmatic view emerged. This was mainly due to external political constraints set by important international organizations, notably the EU and the IMF. These institutions exerted pressure on Slovakia not to delay transformation to the extent that market development would fall behind that in the neighbouring Central European countries.

After the splitting of Czechoslovakia, the successor nations had to renegotiate the Association Agreement which the EC and the federation had signed in December 1991, but which was never ratified. New negotiations started and led to a new agreement with Slovakia in October 1993. In the period between the date of independence and the achievement of a new agreement, the trade sections of the agreement with Czechoslovakia applied. The new Association Agreements with the Czech Republic and Slovakia closely resembled the one with Czechoslovakia, but special safeguards had been included in the field of democratization and the violation of human rights (Fink, 1996). It almost goes without saying that Slovakia was forced to make strong commitments regarding the process of democratization and the implementation of a market economy. But the strong similarities between the agreements of the Central European countries indicate that the EC – since November 1993 the EU – did not lose confidence in the progress of Slovakia's economic transformation.

Even more important than the concessions for the achievement of a new Association Agreement with the EC were the negotiations with the IMF on a first tranche of credit for overcoming balance-of-payments difficulties. Talks with the IMF started in February 1993, but were immediately abandoned. The IMF-proposed devaluation of the Slovak crown by 30 per cent, followed by the introduction of free floating against a number of important Western currencies, was rejected by the Mečiar government. In the summer of 1993, negotiations were resumed on a new credit facility for systemic transformation. In June 1993, an agreement was reached on a systemic-transformation facility of 90 million dollars. The IMF did not demand a devaluation of the Slovak currency to the extent initially proposed in February 1993. Instead, the introduction of import surcharges was accepted. However, the Fund dictated that the budget deficits had to remain within the limit of 5 per cent of GDP.

The credit facility placed Slovakia in a somewhat backward position when compared with the Czech Republic, Hungary and Poland, since none of these countries had to rely on the systemic-transformation facility, but were all able to receive normal stand-by loans. This implied that the IMF had more confidence in their ability to rely on market-conforming instruments to combat balance-of-payments difficulties. And since the IMF has a so-called 'seal of approval' for private financiers, the chosen type of credit facility had a far-reaching impact. Furthermore, the conditionality of the IMF loan did enforce a policy switch by the Mečiar government. In the summer of 1993, the desire to decrease the speed of transformation after independence was settled made leeway for pragmatism.

The most eye-catching item which illustrates this shift in Mečiar's transformation policy was the effort to keep budget deficits within the IMF-set boundaries. In July 1993, important cuts in government expenditures to the tune of 4 billion Slovak crowns were announced and it was notable that the Ministry of Labour and Social Affairs was forced to contribute to these reductions. In an effort to increase government income, value-added taxes were increased on a wide range of commodities and services. Given the fact that Slovakia could no longer count on financial compensations from the Czech Republic, the efforts to keep budget deficits within the limits set by the Fund were quite successful and certainly did not reveal any delay in the reforms. Besides, the Mečiar government decided to devalue the national currency by 10 per cent. Slovak citizens perceived this reform package as a clear intensification of transformation policy. Although the policy switch led to a temporary decrease in Mečiar's popularity, it convinced the IMF that Slovakia was ready to rely on the 'normal' credit facility of stand-by loans.

This leads to the provisional conclusion that policy resolutions were evolving during 1993. External constraints forced the Mečiar government to reconsider the intentions to slow down Czech-made reforms. At least, this holds true for macroeconomic stabilization. The most important and striking deviation regarding the creation of a market economy was revealed in privatization.

Privatization as an Instrument of Political Patronage

The major policy shift from the Czech-made framework for transformation was not in the field of macroeconomic stabilization, but in privatization. Since 1990, large-scale privatization in the Czechoslovak Republic was very thoroughly considered and well prepared. Privatization legislation was set in place with the foundation of the Privatization Ministry (1990) and, at the level of the republics, National Property Funds (1991). Following the establishment of these institutions, the laws on small-scale and large-scale privatization were approved in October 1990 and February 1991, respectively (Takla, 1994).

Thus, the basic framework which facilitated the divestiture of state-owned enterprises was completed before the splitting of the federation. Since Slovakia became an independent nation, small-scale privatization has been nearly completed: almost 10,000 small and medium-sized business have been auctioned off. Large-scale privatization has not been completed and has become subject to important changes in policy. Until the split of the federation, large-scale privatization was conducted by means of vouchers, a method which ensured that vouchers were distributed among citizens almost free of charge. The vouchers represented assets which could be exchanged for company shares, sold for cash, or lodged with an investment fund. Each round of privatization comprised a number of auctions. If the amount of submitted tenders exceeded the number of available shares of a certain enterprise, the price of the shares would rise in a subsequent auction and would fall with a shortage of tenders.

The first wave of privatization was quite successfully completed and the ownership rights of more than 600 enterprises were wholly or partially transferred from the state to the public (*Deutsche Bank Research*, 1993). But since the type of privatization did not generate state revenues, the Mečiar government decided in 1993 to postpone voucher privatization indefinitely. Furthermore, the postponement was meant to maintain control over certain industries which were believed to be of strategic importance and to monitor the already gloomy employment outlook. The measures resulted in a significant decrease in private-sector growth. In the first year of independence, private economic activity only expanded from 20 to 21 per cent of GDP (*PlanEcon Report*, 1994, No. 4).

The Moravčík government, after gaining power in the spring of 1994, tried to revive voucher-based large-scale privatization and initiated the second wave in September 1994 by distributing vouchers. However, with the change of government towards the end of 1994, the programme was delayed. A new debate started on the most appropriate method of privatization. In the summer of 1995, new privatization legislation was passed in parliament and, consequently, the second wave of voucher privatization was officially cancelled. In addition, restrictive amendments were made regarding the competence of investment funds and a law concerning state interests in enterprises was approved, following a veto by President Kováč.

From July 1995, voucher privatization was officially abandoned with the introduction of state bonds (European Bank for Reconstruction and Development, 1996(a)). The government decreed that each of the 3.5 million voucher holders would be given a five-year state bond, which afterwards could be converted into state-property shares. So, Slovak citizens will obtain a return on their money, but, at the same time, will be deprived of the right to invest directly in companies or in investment funds. The original idea of voucher privatization has been completely abandoned, since the Slovak authorities will be able to keep control on state companies at least until the turn of the century, and the development of a capital market will be hampered.

There are solid arguments which support the view that Slovak privatization is subject to political patronage. While citizens received five-year bonds, the government meanwhile sold state enterprises directly to the ruling management. It is commonly believed that the prices paid for ownership transfers were far below what, as a proxy for market value, foreign investors would have been willing to pay, and the procedures for transfer of state ownership are rather obscure and, therefore, hard to control (*Business Central Europe*, 1995).

Regarding foreign investments in Slovak enterprises, developments seem to reflect the political constraints in the country. With the notable exception of 1994, that is, during the short period of the Moravčík government, the development in foreign direct investment appeared to be rather gloomy (see Table 3.4). Because, so long as the federal republic of Czechoslovakia still existed, the Prague region was the most attractive to foreign investors, the per capita value of direct foreign investment in Slovakia was relatively low from the very beginning of the transformation process. But foreign activities even diminished after Prime Minister Mečiar became the decisive factor in Slovakia's image to the outside world.

FOREIGN TRADE REFORMS IN THE CZECH AND SLOVAK REPUBLICS

Liberalization of External Economic Relations

In Czechoslovakia, the state monopoly on foreign trade as the constituent element of external economic relations had been preserved until the very end of the communist era. Certainly, there was some legislation implemented during the 'Prague Spring', but most of it was abrogated in the period following the military intervention by the Warsaw Pact.[7] In this period of normalization of political power and stabilization of the economy, there was a recentralization of the foreign trade organization. This led to the revival of an almost classic example of a communist state monopoly on foreign trade, as described in, for example, Holzman (1966), Matejka (1986), and Pryor (1963).

First of all, the limited number of foreign trade licences for production enterprises, which could be seen as the legacy of the 1968 events, were almost completely withdrawn in the first half of the 1970s and were never extensively issued again afterwards.[8] Consequently, until the end of the communist era, the strict separation of foreign trade from domestic production by means of sectoral specialized FTOs was sustained. Foreign trade had a residual status, implying that it accomplished only internal production purposes. Only those commodities which could not be produced domestically, or not at a sufficient quality standard, were imported from other countries and exports served merely to finance necessary imports.

Secondly, despite the fact that the Czechoslovak authorities never annulled the 'valuta multiplicator', which was introduced in 1968 as an embryonic stage in the creation of a unified exchange rate system, the isolation of fixed domestic prices from constantly fluctuating world market prices by means of an intricate system of subsidies and taxes, the so-called 'price equalization mechanism', regained its normal practice in the 1970s and 1980s. This meant that exchange rates were non-existent, or that there were as many exchange rates as there were commodities.

Finally, the state monopoly on foreign trade ensured strict control over currency exchange. Of course, the balance-of-payments argument with respect to a state monopoly on foreign trade was already considered important at the time when the system of central planning had not even been fully worked out, but when it had, the two factors were dovetailed. In fact, currency control became increasingly important in the twilight of Czechoslovak communist leadership. Whereas, in the years 1970–72, the recentralization focused on limiting independent trading rights, the currency restrictions played a central role in the remainder of the 1970s, and, especially due to the hard currency debts of neighbouring countries, the 1980s. The FTOs could no longer apply for hard currency at the National Bank, but the currency was made available to the FTOs only at the written request of the central authority responsible for investment projects (Altmann, 1988, pp. 134–5 and Csaba, 1983, p. 83).

The decreasing economic power of the FTOs was symptomatic for the Czechoslovak economic organization in which industrial Associations of Enterprises (VHJs) became the basic economic unit.[9] The VHJs could involve a horizontal integration of one or a few large enterprises linked with smaller ones (a concern), or a merger of enterprises of comparable size (a trust). But, following experiences in the GDR, it could also imply the vertical integration of enterprises responsible for different stages in the process of production (a 'Kombinat'). The emergence of VHJs ensured a concentration of decision-making power at the intermediate level in the planning hierarchy, at the expense of single enterprises participating in a VHJ. FTOs never took part in any of the VHJs, but acquired subsidiary status.

Owing to this organizational structure, all foreign-trade reforms implemented in the late 1980s lost their impact. Contrary to Hungarian and Polish experiences at that time – the issuing of foreign-trading licences to production enterprises – harmonization of trade and production took place under the umbrella of the VHJ. Consequently, there was no increase in independent decision making in foreign trade whatsoever, since these came within the realm of the VHJ. Moreover, these reforms in the twilight of the Czechoslovak communist era were limited to a few enterprises and had only an experimental status. There are good reasons to assume that these reforms were purely cosmetic and were merely introduced to appeal to Mikhail Sergeyevich Gorbachev after he became Secretary General of the Communist Party of the Soviet Union in March 1985.

The institutional setting led to a systemic foreign-trade behaviour that totally neglected comparative advantages, appeared to be insensitive to exchange rates and tariffs in foreign-trade decisions, and led to a segmentation of foreign markets into the world market and the CMEA. Within the latter, trade was conducted on a purely bilateral basis. It was obvious, therefore, that, after the fall of communism, the new political leaders would want to dispose of the foreign-trade organization as soon as possible. So they did, but without jeopardizing the country's macroeconomic stability.

An important step towards liberalization of foreign trade was the dismantling of the monopoly of FTOs and the simplification of the exchange rate mechanism. In 1990, there was an enormous increase in foreign-trading rights issued to producing enterprises, while competition emerged among FTOs, since their trading rights were no longer restricted to certain commodity groups.[10] Of course, the liberalization implied a radical break with the past, since exports were no longer considered as a means to pay for imports required by domestic shortages, but were perceived as a catalyst for the transformation instead. None the less, the adoption of a licensing system was partly used as a transitional measure aimed at keeping import surges within acceptable margins. In 1991, the licensing system became more transparent and generalized. For a number of commodities, permits to conduct foreign trade were automatically issued, whereas for crucial imports and exports, authorization was not automatic. Regarding sensitive products, the practice of non-automatic licensing is also practised in fully-fledged market economies, but in the Czechoslovak case it also covered products which remained under some price regulation and therefore was meant as a measure serving to govern the transformation to a market economy.

The liberalization of imports was firmly implemented, but important steps to avoid depletion of hard currency reserves and too severe competition for domestic producers were also taken. The *de facto* quantitative restrictions inherited from the foreign-trade organization under central planning were converted into tariffs. However, an import surcharge of 20 per cent coincided with the elimination of the vast majority of trade restrictions in early 1991. The import surcharge was an attempt not to violate GATT rules. Because Czechoslovakia had participated in the GATT since 1947, and despite the implementation of mandatory planning, the country had maintained its GATT partnership status, the vast majority of tariffs was 'bound' and could only be modified in agreement with other GATT partners.[11] Therefore, the country had to rely on this temporary import surcharge to compensate for the impact of an extraordinarily low level of tariff protection at the start of the liberalization of foreign trade.

During this period of GATT-approved import surcharges, Czechoslovakia had to implement a sound tariff system. At the end of 1991, the modification of the system was completed. It implied a limited increase in average tariffs. Consequently, the import surcharge introduced the year before was reduced to 10 per cent; however, contrary to the general expectations and recommendations of experts in the field, it was not abolished. The import surcharge remained until 1992. It can be concluded that, although foreign-trade liberalization was quick and decisive, there was no question of an entire liberalization at once.

The path of reform regarding external economic relations was also shaped by Czechoslovakia's regained membership of the IMF and the Word Bank in September 1990.[12] Besides indirect effects stemming from a so-called 'seal of approval', IMF membership in particular had also had a direct influence on Czechoslovakia's exchange rate policy. Regarding the exchange rate mechanism, the federal government had already started in January 1990 with its simplification. The commercial and non-commercial rates were merged to a unified rate, combined with a devaluation against the US dollar. After several devaluations of the Czechoslovak crown, internal convertibility conforming with article 8 of the IMF charter was introduced for current account transactions from January 1991. The official rate was pegged to a basket of currencies of Czechoslovakia's most important trading partners in the West. Subsequently, the nominal exchange rate was kept anchored until the dissolution of the federation.

The Czechoslovak exchange rate policy was generally perceived as successful. During the period of the nominal peg, the real appreciation of the Czechoslovak crown did not erode the country's competitiveness, indicating that the chosen exchange rate was 'accepted' by the market. However, regarding the free access to foreign exchange for import purposes, practice remained initially rather restrictive. The National Bank introduced special regulations, whereby for certain import commodities the bank required finance through trade credits. In the autumn of 1991, these requirements were abrogated, but still the resident convertibility remained limited: for example, the National Bank did not permit foreign exchange accounts.

Liberalization of external economic relations was continued by the successor states of Czechoslovakia. The Czech Republic was most determined in this respect, but Slovakia took decisive steps as well. Although the latter country introduced a 10 per cent import surcharge on consumer goods in March 1994, resembling the Czechoslovak practice in the period 1990–92, licensing procedures for foreign-trade activities were practically abandoned in the course of that year (see Fidrmuc *et al.*, 1994). Having abandoned the practice of state trading nations, both countries became members of the WTO in December 1994. Since the main framework for external trade relations was already set at the beginning of the transformation, developments in the field of currency convertibility were more striking.

The requirement that EU investors in the Czech Republic should apply for a foreign exchange licence was abandoned during 1995, and a new law on foreign exchange became effective as from October that year, which provided full current account and limited capital account convertibility. Direct investment and real estate purchases were permitted, but regarding the inflow of capital, restrictions apply to the purchase of real estate in the Czech Republic by non-residents. Moreover, foreigners are free to repatriate profits and income from investments. Finally, Czech companies were no longer obliged to convert their foreign exchange revenues immediately into domestic currency, but became free to deposit these in foreign currency accounts. The liberalization coincided with pressure on the Czech currency, despite a recent devaluation in May 1997.

Regarding currency policy, Slovakia initiated similar measures, even though the country was not in a position to follow the Czech reforms to the full extent. Limited current account convertibility already existed, resulting from the above-mentioned Czechoslovak legislation implemented in 1991. Consequently, the main restrictions on foreign exchange related to capital flows. Simultaneously with the Czech initiative in legislation, the Slovak parliament approved a new foreign exchange law, also valid from October 1995. The further liberalization of foreign exchange mainly entailed the free circulation of Slovak currency in foreign countries. For the rest, the declaration of a convertible Slovak crown was unclear. It has been suggested that the Mečiar government is simply window-dressing to prove to the outside world that Slovakia is keeping up with the reforms of the Czech Republic rather than introducing anything of real economic substance. Given the foregoing analysis on privatization, indicating the tightening of state control, it is indeed questionable whether current and capital account transactions will be fully liberalized. But that may not be the whole story. Another reason for Slovakia more or less to follow the Czech Republic with respect to liberalization of foreign trade to the extent that the underlying economic conditions permit was the special inter-republican trade and payments arrangements between the two countries. These were agreed during the negotiations on the break-up of the federal republic. Since inter-republican trade and payments form a significant part of the external relations of both countries, these arrangements will be dealt with separately in the following section.

Inter-Republican Trade and Payments Arrangements

As pointed out above, the dissolution of Czechoslovakia appears to have proceeded relatively smoothly. To a large extent, this was due to a network of bilateral agreements designed to ensure that the Czech and Slovak Republics would continue to cooperate closely after the separation. With regard to mutual economic relations, the key arrangements provided for a temporary monetary union, which lasted only two months, followed by a clearing payments settlement. Furthermore, the Czech and Slovak Republics decided to set up a customs union. These accords will be elaborated in the remaining part of this section.

As early as in the autumn of 1992, that is, during the negotiations on the separation of the Czech Republic and Slovakia, it was agreed to create a customs union after the split was effected. This implied that no serious trade barriers between the nations were to be erected – in particular no quantitative restrictions – while equal treatment was to be applied to third parties in foreign trade. Given the attempts to foster regional economic integration in Central Europe, the customs union facilitated the further exploration of the creation of a free trade area in the region (see Chapter 2). But, once it was settled, the customs union of the Czech and Slovak Republics came under severe pressure. As mentioned above, Slovakia implemented a 10 per cent import surcharge from the spring of 1994. It was agreed with the IMF that the duties were to be reduced by 50 per cent from September 1994. The duties on consumer goods were meant to improve Slovakia's balance of payments, but the Czech Republic decided to retaliate by depreciating the Czech crown in the clearing account through which trade had been organized with the Slovak Republic since early 1993.

The clearing account was a legacy of the monetary union, which the two republics decided to implement. The monetary union was assumed to be effective until the summer of 1993, but it broke down after the first week in February 1993, since there were speculations stemming from an expected devaluation of the Slovak crown. Due to massive inter-country trade, the high amount of mutual transfers and the limited amount of foreign reserves, a clearing payments settlement was subsequently agreed upon. Funds were fixed through a clearing centre, which made financial transactions between both countries easier, since neither had enough hard currency at that time for a standard payment system. The payments agreement was valid until the end of 1993. Afterwards, the validity of the agreement was extended indefinitely. It could be abrogated by three months' notice in writing.

The basic accounting unit of payments agreement was the European Currency Unit (ECU). The system has been used for all transactions – either current or capital – with the exception of re-export transactions which were to be settled in convertible currencies.[13] Basically, there were two accounts, one for all obligations which originated before 8 February 1993 (old account), and one for the settlement of transactions following that date (new account). For the old account, a special 'clearing crown' was introduced, fixed at the value of one Czech and one Slovak crown. Furthermore, it was anchored to the ECU according to the exchange rate of the Czech crown to the ECU on 5 February 1993.

The new account, created for transfers from 8 February 1993, soon opened up space for exchange rate manoeuvring. The agreement entailed the introduction of a special 'accounting ECU'. The Czech and Slovak National Banks could independently determine the rate of the national currencies against the accounting ECU and were allowed to change the exchange rate of the accounting ECU against the ECU within bands of minus 5 to plus 5 per cent. Clearing was on a monthly basis, although it only implied a return to equilibrium from amounts in excess of 130 million ECU. Thus, the agreement specified a credit limit of 130 million ECU, above which obligations were to be settled in convertible currencies.

The balance of the old account finished with a Slovak deficit of 11.6 billion Slovak crowns in 1993, mainly ascribed to the developments in trade relations. The results for 1994 resembled those of the preceding year, after which the old account ceased to exist.[14] Regarding the evolution of receipts and payments on the new account, a completely different picture emerged. It showed Slovak surpluses right from the beginning and, time and again, the Czech Republic exceeded the 130 million ECU limit of the clearing agreement. In the spring of 1995, after having been forced several times to pay the excess amounts in dollars, the Czech Minister of Finance Iwán Kočárník suggested cancelling the agreement (*Report on the Czech and Slovak Republics*, 1995, no. 2). The termination of the agreement did not imply that the country was unable to guarantee full payment in convertible currencies, but was due rather to the introduction of Czech currency convertibility according to the IMF article and Czech membership of the OECD. Therefore, in June 1995, the Czech Republic officially declared the determination of the bilateral payments arrangement from October that year (European Bank for Reconstruction and Development, 1996(a), p. 39). Czech and Slovak banks had to devise a method for realizing trade and private payments among their clients after that date. The banks had to decide in which currency they would effect mutual payments and also had to set fees for these services. In this regard, there were some interesting offers being proposed by banks which had branches in both the Czech Republic and in Slovakia.

CONCLUSION

This chapter has addressed the issue of economic transformation in the Czech and Slovak Republics. It is a general belief that after the division of the federal Republic of Czechoslovakia, the Czech Republic consistently continued along a path of shock treatment, whereas the Slovak Republic started to slow down the Prague-initiated reforms. The above survey regarding the policy of transformation in the Czech and Slovak Republics does not confirm this opinion, however.

Regarding the transformation in the Czech Republic, it is found that the country certainly does not offer a textbook example of a liberal shock approach, as Prime Minister Klaus wants the world to believe. In the field of microeconomic reform (restructuring and privatization) and institution building, in particular, it can be asserted that there are important elements of a gradual approach to be found in the Czech model of transformation. The Czech authorities intervened extensively. In order to prevent a 'credit crunch', a policy of tight monitoring of banks supported by substantial capital injections was applied, whereas in the labour market, there were direct wage controls within the context of corporatist labour relations. The country's best performance was in macroeconomic stabilization. But it was precisely in this realm that the legacy of the communist past was positive. To sum up, the government budget was under control, inflation fell to an annual rate of below 10 per cent and the current account over the past five years was positive. However, with economic activity recovering recently, current account deficits are on the increase.

As far as the Slovak Republic is concerned, it can be asserted that political events do seem to hide the real economic performance of the country. In this chapter, this phenomenon has been referred to as the 'Mečiar factor'. It is beyond any doubt that, regarding the task of resuming economic growth, the split of the federal Republic of Czechoslovakia was most detrimental to Slovakia and therefore put pressure on policy makers to slow down and postpone certain painful economic reforms. But after approximately half a year of independence, external relations pressed policy makers to remain on the track which had initially been settled upon by 'Prague'.

Consequently, this chapter concludes that the divergence in the paths of economic transformation during the first three years of independence has been exaggerated, in both mass media and academic writings. Moreover, statistical indicators regarding economic activity, inflation and the current account certainly do not reveal any relative backwardness of Slovakia *vis-à-vis* the Czech Republic. In fact, higher unemployment rates than in the Czech Republic may even indicate more genuine efforts at restructuring. Regarding the economic transformation from a centrally planned to a market economy, there is, however, one important issue which may have a negative impact on the country's future development. This concerns privatization. Voucher privatization has been abandoned and replaced by a system of state bonds. Even though the restructuring of enterprises is far from easy in the Czech Republic as well, the Slovak policy changes will undoubtedly have a negative impact on microeconomic restructuring, since privatization has turned into a system of political patronage. This problem has already been manifested in the somewhat moderate enthusiasm of foreign investors.

NOTES

1. In the 1970s and 1980s, there were several waves of economic reform in these countries. These reforms, however, in no way affected the political system, but were rather implemented to avert political reform. Economic reform as an instrument to avoid the establishment of a pluralistic political system was most pronounced in Hungary (see Chapter 4).
2. Of course, GDP estimates are rather troublesome. Definition problems and varying relative prices frequently hindered us in making appropriate comparisons between economic welfare in East and West, since the latter were expressed in GDP, while centrally planned economies counted Net Material Product (NMP). Hence, GDP calculations for Eastern European countries were not very informative. Regarding the above-mentioned figures, problems have partly been circumvented by comparing a large package of commodities and services (purchasing power parities), which better enables us to produce a ranking.
3. Since, at least at that time, hardening of budget constraints did not attend these reforms of the banking system, there was no real improvement in portfolios.
4. Raiser (1994) estimated that average net wages in Czech industry for 1993 amounted to 146 US dollars. For Hungary and Poland, net wages in industry were 195 and 186 US dollars, respectively. Although these calculations do not express purchasing power parities, there is consensus regarding the magnitude of wage restraints for Czech employees in comparison with their Hungarian and Polish colleagues (see Adam, 1993; Orenstein, 1994; Švejnar *et al.*, 1994).
5. Unemployment in the countries which serve as a frame of reference exceeded 10 per cent of the workforce within a period of two and a half years after the collapse of communism. So far, Hungary and Poland have not been successful in reducing these figures to single-digit levels (see Chapters 4 and 5).
6. I am highly indebted to Sytse Knypstra for informing me of the recent political history in Slovakia.
7. Romania did not participate in this military intervention.
8. In August 1968, approximately 70 production enterprises had received foreign trading rights. In 1970, 50 of these enterprises lost their permits, after which, in 1971, the authorities stopped issuing new foreign trade licences (Matejka, 1986, pp. 266–7).
9. VHJ is an acronym of 'Vyrobni Hospodářské Jednotky', which may be translated as 'Association of Enterprises'.
10. This measure was an extension of the Law on External Economic Relations implemented in 1988, which in principle enabled the establishment of new FTOs (OECD, 1991(b), p. 84).
11. During the communist era, Czechoslovakia had maintained GATT partnership status, although it was clear that central planning was incompatible with the GATT principles of most favoured nation and reciprocity. But, since the country did not actively participate, but rather behaved as a sleeping partner, GATT nations did not think it necessary to require special conditions, as was the case with Poland in 1966 and Romania in 1971 (Pissula, 1990).
12. It has already been mentioned in Chapter 2 that Czechoslovakia belonged to the founder-nations of both Bretton Woods institutions, but it was forced to leave them in 1954. For the withdrawal from the IMF, the reader is referred to the chapter's note 6 on page 45. As far as the end of the World Bank membership was concerned, apart from a dispute about a loan, there was a conflict about payment of the country's capital subscription. This led to suspension and, subsequently, to formal termination of membership (Mason and Asher, 1973, p. 171).

13. Export of commodities imported from a third country was considered to be a re-exporting transaction.

14. Of course, arrangements had to be made about the balance of the old account. It was agreed to check the balance every three months, starting from May 1993, and to add it to the balance on the new account or to repay in convertible currencies. For this purpose, exchange rates had to be determined between the old and the new accounts.

4. The Hungarian Approach to Transformation: Was it Really Gradual?

INTRODUCTION

Many people in the West happen to know the names of the Czech President and Prime Minister – Václav Havel and Václav Klaus. But it is quite unusual for them to name Hungary's first post-communist leaders, such as President Árpád Göncz and Prime Minister József Antall, who led a conservative coalition from May 1990 until his death in December 1993. Apparently, since its economic transformation is perceived as less radical, Hungary does not attract attention to the same extent as the Czech Republic. Gradualism fails to appeal to the media.

In the 1970s and 1980s, it was the other way round. Relatively speaking, Hungary received a great deal of attention and, as far as Western countries are concerned, people were more familiar with the Hungarian communist leader János Kádár than with the Czechoslovak rulers Gustáv Husák and Míloš Jakeš. Again, this is related to striking changes. Thanks to a rather liberal climate, Hungary came to be known as the brightest shed in the Eastern European camp. Political constraints to some extent deviated from those in other countries of the Soviet-dominated region. In order to avoid a repetition of the revolutionary events in 1956, the political leaders changed attitudes. Kádár introduced 'those who are not against us are with us' as a new credo, indicating that the communist political leadership tolerated deviating opinions on the one condition that they would not lead to direct opposition (see Schöpflin, 1987).

This liberal atmosphere was extended to the system of economic planning. Hungary marched in the vanguard of reform attempts in Eastern Europe. In 1968, the Hungarian authorities launched a comprehensive reform programme. It was the so-called 'Új Gazdasági Mechanizmus' (New Economic Mechanism, in the remainder of this chapter abbreviated as ÚGM). This programme entailed the abolition of mandatory planning and implied the start of a modest development of a private sector (see Bauer, 1983; Friss, 1978). The ÚGM is often referred to as a silent agreement between the people of Hungary and the communist party under Kádár's leadership. In order to make them refrain from demands for political reform, the communist party promised the Hungarian population more welfare. At any price, the communists wanted to prevent a repetition of the 1956 events.[1] Since the ÚGM focused especially focused upon the availability of consumer goods, the programme also came to be known as 'goulash communism'.

Following the basic theoretical notions of path-dependency and hysteresis outlined in Chapter 1, the underlying idea is that the rather moderate interest following the political events in 1989 and the relative familiarity with Hungary's policy during the 1970s and 1980s are interrelated. Owing to the ÚGM, the starting conditions for the transformation to a market economy varied and these were supposed to have a decisive impact on the strategy for economic reform. The general assumption is that, unlike the other Central European countries, Hungary presents an example of a gradual approach to the transformation (see Hare and Révész, 1992). The Antall government did not destroy the communist inheritance as soon as possible, but rather tried to build on it. Past reforms prescribed the alternatives to the creation of a fully-fledged market economy.

The main purpose of this chapter is to explore further the legacy of communism and its impact on policy alternatives for economic reform in Hungary. It intends to show that the perception of a gradual transformation to a market economy is not quite correct. Firstly, the inheritance was rather ambiguous. On the one hand, one could argue that the ÚGM partly realized important necessary preconditions for the creation of a fully-fledged market economy, such as a decentralization of economic decision making (see Székely and Newbery, 1993). On the other hand, decentralized economic decisions created interest groups at the enterprise level and their interests may have conflicted with the objectives of privatization and genuine marketization, that is, with efforts at making the income of enterprises solely dependent on performance in the market and not on bargaining power *vis-à-vis* state legal bodies. Secondly, the transformation policy was ambiguous too, and certainly did not stand as an example of gradualism. It will be shown that gradualism may have dominated stabilization policy, but shock-like measures prevailed in microeconomic restructuring, precisely that part of transformation which the political authorities in the Czech Republic – despite liberal rhetoric – tackled most cautiously by means of direct government intervention.

'How did the communist legacy and the transformation policy affect

Hungary's external economic relations?', is the subsequent question to be dealt with in this chapter. Here, one can observe the same ambiguity. One of the main goals of the ÚGM was to enhance Hungary's participation in the international division of labour, since mandatory planning appeared to be particularly detrimental to this small and poorly endowed country. Therefore, the foreign trade organization had to be reformed, but the opportunities for decentralizing foreign trade decisions were constrained by the differences between the trade mechanism for dealing with the West and that for commerce with the countries of the CMEA. CMEA trade continued to be conducted by means of bilateral negotiations at ministerial level (see Csaba, 1990). Hence, considering the external economic relations since the start of the transformation, it is important to take the legacy of split foreign markets into account and to analyse East–West and regional integration separately. But apart from that, the fact that, in the field of Western external economic relations, the ÚGM appeared to be a mixture of serious attempts to improve competitiveness on hard currency markets and successful window-dressing has to be taken into account. International financial and trade organizations accepted – or pretended to accept – Hungary's arguments for possible access to the GATT, the IMF and the World Bank, although it is hard to believe that Hungary could meet the conditions of these institutions. The aim is to scrutinize the extent to which this kind of window-dressing hampered or accelerated economic integration after the communist leadership ceased to hold power in May 1990.

THE KÁDÁR ERA: A CONSTRAINT ON TRANSFORMATION STRATEGIES?

Disappointing growth performance in the 1960s gave rise to a fundamental debate on the rationality of the economic mechanism based upon mandatory planning (see Szamuely, 1984). Reform proposals were prepared by a commission chaired by Resző Nyers. The commission, broadly composed of party members, bureaucrats, managers, scientists and journalists, officially started in the autumn of 1964 and the Central Committee of the Hungarian Socialist Workers' Party (MSzMP) was presented with a concept for major reforms in May 1966. This concept paved the way for the ÚGM, a comprehensive economic reform programme, which was to be implemented in January 1968.

The blueprint of the ÚGM did not deal with the abolition of central planning as such, but rather intended to reduce its scope and to change its instruments. Detailed plan instructions to enterprises were eliminated and on a micro-level direct government regulation was restricted to large investment projects, the defence industry, domestic supply of certain indispensable consumer goods, and commitments with respect to CMEA countries. On the macro-level, targets were to be realized by means of prices, interest rates, taxes and subsidies, so-called 'financial regulators' (see Friss, 1978).

Whereas the reform concept was based upon the idea of 'planning and market', the implementation of the ÚGM led to a system which, for example, Bauer (1983) characterized as 'neither planning nor market'. On the one hand, the mechanism which in the literature was referred to as central planning, namely disaggregation of the plan into detailed instructions for enterprises about what to produce and where to deliver, ceased to exist. On the other hand, well-functioning markets did not emerge, since there was bureaucratic rather than economic competition. Essentially, the ÚGM brought about a shift from 'plan bargaining' to 'regulator bargaining'. Before 1968, the bargains between enterprises, sectoral ministries and the SPC focused on how much to produce within a certain period of time and given a limited number of inputs. During the ÚGM period, enterprises constantly bargained on preferential prices, favourable tax conditions or subsidies, or on acquiring the status of a supplier of indispensable commodities. Hence, enterprises maximized profits, but their income was not solely dependent on market performance, but rather on hierarchical relations. There was no hardening of budget constraints (Kornai, 1980; 1986). Decision making was decentralized, but not commercialized. A system of diffuse property rights emerged, in which economic agents were able to gain specific profits at the expense of the efficiency of the economic system at large.

With respect to economic reform prior to the collapse of the communist era, it can be concluded that János Kádár, having implemented the ÚGM, intended to convert the traditional system of central planning into a more efficient 'third way', but the process he initiated ultimately worked counter to the goals originally set and finally led to his political defeat. The ÚGM proved to be an arduous process lasting two decades, showing a continuous oscillation of de- and recentralization in economic decision making. After János Kádár's political defeat in May 1988, matters changed rapidly. Within a few months, the opinion developed that economic reforms should no longer be politically restrained. Whereas in the 1960s a trade-off was supposed to exist between economic and political reform, that is, economic reform should enable the communist party to maintain its monopoly, at the end of the 1980s political pluralism appeared to be a *conditio sine qua non* for the creation of well-functioning markets. The communists realized their fate and officially approved the development of a plural political system, after which they dissolved the party in the autumn of 1989. Those in favour of speeding up economic reform subsequently founded a new democratic party, the 'Hungarian Socialist Party' (MSzP).

In March 1990, the first free elections for more than forty years decisively defeated the communist rulers (Barany, 1990). The conservative 'Hungarian Democratic Forum' (MDF) won the elections: on the basis of 24 per cent of the popular vote, it received 164 of the 386 parliamentary seats, or more than 42 per cent.[2] The liberal 'Alliance of Free Democrats' (SzDSz) became the second largest party. The party obtained 92 seats (25 per cent). The 'Independent Smallholders' Party' (FKgP), a pre-war farmers' party, which in 1945 received two-thirds of the votes, was now mandated for 44 seats (11 per cent), followed by the 'Federation of Young Democrats' (Fidesz) and the 'Christian Democratic People's Party' (KDNP) each obtaining 21 seats (5 per cent) in parliament as well.[3] Together with the FKgP and KDNP, the MDF formed a coalition government. It took office on 25 May 1990 and was led by József Antall, the political leader of the Forum. After his death in December 1993, six months before the new elections were to take place, Antall was succeeded by his Minister of the Interior, Péter Boross.[4]

Although Hungary did not have a monopoly on economic reforms during the 1970s and 1980s, it is still important to examine the extent to which the legacy of the ÚGM differed from those in the surrounding countries in Central and Eastern Europe and the way it influenced the strategy followed by the Antall–Boross government. The literature frequently suggests a positive inheritance, since the ÚGM realized profit-oriented management behaviour, good relations with Western financial organizations – also indicating an IMF 'seal of approval' – and a foreign trade structure which was more attached to Western markets than elsewhere in Central and Eastern Europe (see Csaba, 1994; Székely and Newbery, 1993). Hungary was well ahead of other Central and Eastern European countries. The enforcement of realizing profits in the market was perceived as the single most essential task for the transformation. It is highly questionable whether this line of thought can be fully sustained. There are strong arguments which point to relatively unfavourable conditions at the start of the transformation. Firstly, it can be argued that the ÚGM had reduced the degrees of freedom with respect to alternative transformation strategies, since relative prosperity lowered the political willingness to accept large costs of transformation. This is also partly a political argument pinpointing the fact that the Hungarian communist party acknowledged its political defeat to be irreversible and allowed opposition at a rather early stage, whereas in Czechoslovakia and Poland the opposition forced the communists to their knees. Contrary to what happened in Czechoslovakia and Poland, where opposition emerged from mass movements ('Civic Forum' and 'Solidarity') driven by the single goal of destroying communist rule, opposition in Hungary was organized into political parties, having different interests and objectives. Hence, the legitimacy of the new leaders varied somewhat. Whereas in Poland, the Mazowiecki government was able to implement the radical Balcerowicz Plan (see Chapter 5), since the communists were to blame for all its negative social consequences, the Antall–Boross government could not fully apply the shock treatment, as will be shown in the next section.

Secondly, the system of diffuse property rights hampered further economic reforms due to vested interests. This is a sequencing argument. It can be asserted that privatization after decentralization of economic decision making incurs higher costs of transformation than conducting it the other way around. Privatization is not always in the interest of managers and employees, because they may lose their jobs. Therefore, they will try to resist certain measures and, owing to decentralized decision making, will be able to do so successfully. Thus, it takes more effort to proceed with privatization than was the case in Czechoslovakia, where it was less easy for employees and managers collectively to look after their common interests, since decision making was still fully centralized.

To conclude, one could suggest that, in the case of Hungary, path-dependency implied a winner's curse, identifying the Kádár era as a constraint on transformation strategies rather than as a favourable start. Politically speaking, the post-communist leaders were confronted with vested interests organized into parliamentary parties. In the field of economics, a system of diffuse property rights hindered radical reform measures. Now, given these constraints, the question presents itself of how far the Antall–Boross government was able to advance towards a fully-fledged market economy. Can we confirm the commonly held view that Hungary has fallen behind, or are there misconceptions with respect to the speed and sequencing of reform measures, as was the case with above-mentioned changes during the ÚGM?

MACROECONOMIC STABILIZATION: MINIMIZING OR EXTENDING THE CRISIS?

Immediately after the collapse of the communist system, a radical platform of economists emerged. It was inspired in particular by a club of Harvard economists, among them Jeffrey Sachs. He made an important contribution to Polish shock therapy implemented in January 1990. As has been elaborated in Chapter 1, these thoughts on the economic transformation from a centrally planned to a market economy were characterized by a strong belief in pragmatic constructivism. The system of mandatory planning could be reversed by changing the rules of the game. Economic agents were supposed to adjust immediately and a hoped-for supply response was believed to depend simply on a successful macroeconomic stabilization scheme, namely a cold turkey policy. This line of thought also inspired the 'Blue Ribbon Commission', an occasional commission consisting of leading Hungarian and international scholars who wished to advise the post-communist leaders in Hungary (Blue Ribbon Commission, 1990). Swift and radical change also appeared to be János Kornai's advice (Kornai, 1990). His pamphlet was more or less an emotional appeal to the new Hungarian rulers not to repeat the mistakes of the ÚGM. This section addresses the macroeconomic policy applied in Hungary since the start of the transformation, and, following the discussion outlined in Chapter 1, includes stabilization and liberalization issues. The section is divided into two parts, the first focusing on the policy and the performance of the Antall–Boross government, the second scrutinizing that of the first years of its successor from June 1994, the government headed by the socialist Gyula Horn. Although external economic relations will be dealt with in a separate section, they will inevitably be raised in the context of macroeconomic stabilization as well.

The Antall–Boross Government

With respect to macroeconomic stabilization, the Antall–Boross government did not lend a willing ear to this scholarly platform. The government waited nearly a year to present its Economic Policy and Action Programme, which outlined Antall's economic policy for the period 1991–94, and the plan itself bore witness to steadiness. What were the constituent elements of this stabilization scheme?

External relations are pivotal in stabilizing the economy. These will be more extensively dealt with in the remainder of this chapter. Suffice it to note at this stage that in the Economic Policy and Action Programme a choice was made of an adjustable peg to manage the Hungarian currency and not to restrain fiscal and monetary policy by introducing a 'nominal anchor'. But if exchange rates were not to guide monetary and fiscal policy, the question remains which measures were to replace these restraints. In the first place, the IMF remained an important external constraint, since the Fund issues only conditional credits, whereas other credit suppliers focus on IMF findings – the so-called 'seal of approval'.

Hungary, in trying to avoid a restructuring of its twenty-billion-dollar foreign debt, was eager to take appropriate measures to keep budget deficits within acceptable margins. The Antall–Boross government proposed to change the system of financing the budget deficits. Since capital markets were almost non-existent until 1989, budget deficits were monetized by the National Bank of Hungary. Regarding direct credit from the National Bank of Hungary, changes were introduced to impose more stringent limits. A new Budget Law stipulated the maximum lending which the National Bank was compelled to provide. If budget targets were exceeded, parliament had to approve the increase in the ceiling, and subsequently had to find the concomitant financing (OECD, 1991(a). pp. 59ff). Although the introduction of this law generally restrained money increase, it seriously threatened the availability of credits to newly emerging private enterprises. As unemployment rose for subsequent years, the government had to finance budget deficits which exceeded the specified ceilings, thereby 'crowding out' private investments.

Notwithstanding the measures taken by the Antall–Boross government to limit budget deficits, it has to be noted that in comparison with Czechoslovakia and Poland the authorities applied a policy that secured the purchasing power of the citizenry. Contrary to what happened in Czechoslovakia and to a lesser extent in Poland, there were no successful attempts made to freeze nominal wages; rather the opposite happened. The government more or less continued the liberal wage policy of the ÚGM. In 1989, the communists had widened the margins for wage increases by no longer taxing such increases away. Taxation was dependent upon turnover increases in the respective enterprises. Although the Antall–Boross government decided to tax nominal wage increases which exceeded 20 per cent, it certainly did not directly intervene in wages, but maintained the liberal status of wage policy as it emerged during the ÚGM. As a result, Hungarian employees were among the best-paid within Central and Eastern Europe. Raiser (1994) calculated that at the end of the Antall–Boross government, monthly average wages in Hungary were approximately 195 US dollars, whereas in Poland and the Czech Republic they amounted 186 and 146 US dollars, respectively. One could argue that maintenance of purchasing power is inspired by Post-Keynesian arguments, which in a shock approach have been more or less denied. One can neither confirm nor deny such a statement. But it is quite obvious that a perceived lower acceptability of social costs which attend the transformation to a fully-fledged market economy urged the Hungarian authorities to be careful.

It can be seen from Table 4.1 that, after a yearly negative GDP growth performance since the start of the transformation, Hungary experienced a moderate recovery in 1994, which, as in the case of the other Central European countries under scrutiny, indicated the end of the transition crisis. But convalescence did not come without difficulties because, in consequence of the policy of the Antall–Boross government, large state budget imbalances and current account deficits emerged (see *PlanEcon Report*, 1996, No. 45–46). These imbalances came to be referred to as 'twin deficits' (World Bank, 1995). It is widely accepted in the literature that the imbalances had fiscal roots. The fiscal deficits which prevailed since the implementation of the Economic Policy Action Programme in 1991 were 6 to 7 per cent of GDP. The magnitude of these deficits could only partly be ascribed to the inevitable drop in output, the consequent rise in unemployment, decreasing revenues and increasing social expenditures during the first period of the transformation, but it was also due to the government's failure to keep the budget under control. The fact that parliament had to give its approval to government spending which exceeded a specified ceiling did change the expenditure procedures, but did not abolish the inert bureaucratic behaviour of payments of large amounts of money for public services.

Table 4.1   Development of important economic indicators in Hungary, 1990–95

	1990	1991	1992	1993	1994	1995
GDP growth (%)	-3.5	-11.9	-3.0	-0.9	2.6	2.0
consumer prices (%)	28.9	35.0	23.0	22.5	18.8	28.2
government budget (% of GDP)	0.4	-2.2	-5.5	-6.8	-8.3	-6.8
unemployment (% active pop.)	2.5	8.0	12.7	12.6	10.9	10.4
current account (bln. $)	0.1	0.3	0.3	-3.5	-3.9	-2.5
foreign direct investment (mln. $)	311	1459	1471	2339	1146	4512

Sources: European Bank for Reconstruction and Development (1996(a), 1996(b))

Besides the fiscal roots of the imbalances, the inability to keep wages under tight control had a detrimental impact on macroeconomic performance as well. Whereas at the beginning of the Antall–Boross government, the imbalances did not severely hamper macroeconomic performance, since there was an upward shift in household savings and inventories accumulated by enterprises under the previous regime were depleted, in 1993 they certainly did. The inertia of the Antall–Boross government in successfully terminating the 'twin deficit' played an important role in the 1994 elections. The Hungarian electorate perceived the policy of the Antall–Boross government more or less as an example of 'muddling through' (see Csaba, 1994; Dobszay, 1994).

The Horn Government

The elections held in May 1994 brought a huge victory to the MSzP. The socialist party, which to a large extent consisted of members of the former Hungarian communist party, won an absolute majority of 209 of the 386 parliamentary seats (54 per cent), where it had obtained only 33 (8 per cent) in 1990. Having secured 18 per cent of the parliamentary votes, SzDSz remained the second largest party in the Hungarian legislature, although it lost 22 of its 90 seats. Fidesz, the other party in opposition during the Antall–Boross government, was forced to accept significant losses as well: it was barely able to meet the minimally required 5 per cent of the votes to enter into parliament (20 seats). At the same time, the then outgoing coalition government, headed by Péter Boross, experienced a really devastating loss and was forced to return to opposition. It is no overstatement to suggest that it vanished from the political scene. The MDF fraction in the Hungarian parliament was reduced from 164 to 37 seats (less than 10 per cent). The FKgP was devastated as well: in fact, following several splits within the party and the resignation of important politicians from its membership, it was not even clear which faction should be seen as the genuine successor of the FKgP (26 seats, 7 per cent). The KDNP, though, managed to retain its parliamentary position (22 seats, 6 per cent).

Notwithstanding the absolute majority in parliament, the socialist leader Gyula Horn aspired to form a coalition with the SzDSz and eventually achieved this (see Dobszay, 1994). The return of former communists to the political spotlight in no way implied a revival of the communist era at whatever stage of Hungarian history. On the contrary, the Hungarian transformation into a market economy was beyond dispute. Moreover, the problem of the 'twin deficits', to a large extent caused by the inability of the Antall–Boross government to enforce a strict wage policy and to maintain control of public finances, compelled the Horn government to implement a restrictive macroeconomic stabilization scheme. This proposed scheme appeared to be a late version of shock treatment. Thus, the fact of the matter was that the initial general perception of a favourable outlook for the Hungarian transformation was turned into the complete opposite. Liberalization in the twilight of the ÚGM was a deliberate attempt to decentralize decision making and to diminish state control, but, at the same time, it had weakened the government's ability effectively to control the transformation after the system had finally collapsed.

It was clear that the Horn government had to counteract the imbalances. In addition, the IMF made it clear that it would resist further lending if the Hungarian authorities failed to keep the budget deficit within the limits of 5 per cent of its GDP. Thus, the IMF required genuine fiscal reforms and no longer accepted radical promises to cut back government spending, such as were made by the Finance Minister Mihály Kupa in 1993 (see Csaba, 1994). It took some time after the Horn government took office in June 1994, but a clear stabilization package was presented in March 1995. The package was a definitive attempt to apply restrictive monetary and fiscal policy and to align with IMF requirements. Drastic reductions in expenditures were announced, including highly controversial ones in sick pay and in family and child allowances. Furthermore, the package included a 9 per cent devaluation of the forint relative to a basket of foreign currencies and the arrangement of a monthly crawling peg for the remainder of 1995. In order to avoid these devaluations triggering a wage–price spiral, the Horn government resumed tight wage controls for employees in state-owned enterprises and public administration.

The implementation of the package did provoke some difficulties, since the legality of certain elements was challenged in the high court and this delayed enforcement. Notwithstanding the delay, the Horn government was quite successful in overcoming the 'twin deficits'. In 1995, the budget deficit still did not remain within the critical band of 5 per cent of GDP, but in comparison to 1994 (8.3 per cent) the improvement was substantial. It has to be noted in addition that the package was launched in March, that is, in the second quarter of that year, whereas projected deficits on the basis of the first quarter of 1995 indicated that the imbalance would exceed 10 per cent of GDP at the end of the year. The task of restoring equilibrium, of course, had its price. In the wake of tightening fiscal and monetary policy, there was a slowdown in consumption, as a consequence of which imports contracted and the current account deficit improved, but the recovery in economic activity decelerated. Whereas the other Central European countries under examination in this book achieved growth rates of approximately 5 per cent in 1995, which were higher than the year before (see Tables 3.3, 3.4 and 5.1), Hungary had to face a moderate performance of only 2.0 per cent.

The macroeconomic performance for 1996 is expected to align with the above-mentioned development. The budget deficit is likely to have fallen below the critical level of 5 per cent of GDP and the current account imbalance is significantly diminishing, whereas inflation seems better under control after consumer prices rose as a result of the budget deficits in the years before, with nearly 30 per cent in 1995. Unemployment is also slowly declining, although more than 10 per cent of the workforce is still without a job and, taking regional differences into account, unemployment in the north-eastern region of the country reaches critically high levels of nearly 20 per cent (*PlanEcon Report*, 1996, No. 45–46).

MICROECONOMIC RESTRUCTURING: A 'HIDDEN SHOCK'

In comparison with policies aimed at maintenance and recovery in economic activity, the performance in microeconomic restructuring is less easily revealed in statistics, but it is certainly not less important, since it deals with the creation of institutions and legislation which have to enforce efficient management at the enterprise level. In fact, microeconomic restructuring involves all the measures that provide a legal framework for the effective functioning of markets. The reforms within the realm of microeconomic restructuring are, first of all, closely linked to the transfer of state ownership to the public, but they also comprise institutional reforms which focus on the legal preservation of once established property rights, guarantee freedom of contract, and, most importantly, are required to ensure contractors' liability. They should, basically, underlie a consistent incentive structure. This section first surveys Hungary's privatization and restructuring process and, subsequently, elaborates incentive reforms.

Privatization and Restructuring

During the ÚGM, opportunities had been created to induce the development of small private enterprises, mainly in the field of housing and servicing. In the twilight of communist rule, approximately two-thirds of the working population, besides having a job in a state enterprise or a cooperative, earned additional income from private activity. This led to Hungary's reputation as a 'do-it-yourself' economy, indicating that these economic activities were in the twilight zone of what was legally allowed and what was officially forbidden. In the 1980s, the communist authorities issued several decrees in an attempt to legalize unofficial economic activities. The 'Act on Economic Association' and the 'Act on Foreign Investment' were the most important in this respect. These two decrees became pivotal in the judicial framework which guided the process of privatization.

The 'Act on Economic Association' was passed by parliament in

October 1988 and provided all the legal forms of companies that Western investors were familiar with. Given the broad scope of this company Act, it is not surprising that the Antall–Boross government used it as a point of departure and subsequently the Act was only marginally amended by parliament (see Estrin, 1994). It basically enabled state-owned enterprises to transform themselves into a limited liability or a joint stock company, after which the management or the employees were able to buy the shares at prices below the expected market rate (see Nuti, 1992). But this 'spontaneous privatization', as it came to be known, led to abuses and scandals, since it enriched old party nomenklatura and became a cloak for many fraudulent actions.

In January 1989, the Hungarian parliament approved the 'Act on Foreign Investment'. This supplemented the company act and served to enlarge possibilities to start joint ventures with Western participation, which so far were heavily constrained by judicial and administrative burdens (Kilényi and Lamm, 1990). This investment act also appeared to be a stimulus to privatization, since it significantly improved opportunities for Western enterprises to invest in Hungary, even without Hungarian participation. Furthermore, it allowed private Hungarian enterprises to participate in Western investments on Hungarian territory. In combination with the act on economic activity, it created an unprecedented legal framework, at least measured by Eastern European standards at that time.

The legal framework was extended with special institutions to regulate the process of privatization. In order to meet public dissatisfaction related to spontaneous privatization, the Németh government established the 'State Property Agency' (ÁVU) in March 1990, two months before the Antall–Boross government took office. The most important task of the ÁVU was to monitor privatization, since spontaneous privatization was hidden and, therefore, liable to fraud. The monitoring function of the ÁVU exclusively entailed the observance of the judicial rules in force.

Another important task of the ÁVU was the selection of state-owned enterprises for which the transfer of ownership rights was to be considered. Selection was based upon enterprise performance in the recent past and in September 1990, that is half a year after the Antall–Boross government came to power, the ÁVU introduced the first privatization programme (see Mihályi, 1993). The programme provided a list of twenty enterprises, mainly in the service sector.[5] It did not really succeed, since, more than a year after the scheme was introduced, only two companies had been sold. So far, the ÁVU has been more successful in the fulfilment of its monitoring task than in promoting large-scale privatization. As a matter of fact, the Hungarian privatization scheme has been much criticized for a variety of reasons. The ÁVU was believed to be too bureaucratic and its selection procedures were often characterized as 'trying to sell those companies that cannot be sold, while trying to hold the companies that buyers would like to buy' (Járai, 1993, p. 80). Therefore, time and again, it has been suggested that a voucher privatization should be considered as an alternative to this cumbersome and time-consuming procedure of selling. These proposals, however, did not take hold. With the exception of the privatization of plots, the distribution of state property among the population at large has never been widely applied, either by the Antall–Boross government, or by the Horn government. The arguments are fairly sound. Firstly, the state badly needs money to balance its budget; secondly, the state has invested in the enterprises and therefore expects money in return; and, thirdly, those paying the highest price are supposed to conduct the best management (see also Canning and Hare, 1994).

In order to improve the process of privatization, the Hungarian parliament decided in the summer of 1992 to create a State Holding Company Inc. (ÁV Rt), which was responsible for exploitation of that state property which was perceived to be ineligible for privatization. The ÁV Rt was meant to support the ÁVU by more clearly distinguishing privatization from exploitation of state enterprises, but it also implicitly set a maximum on the number of enterprises to be disposed of through privatization.

At that stage, many problems remained and it seemed that popular support for the privatization process had diminished to critical levels. Therefore, the Horn government wanted to give new impetus to the process of privatization and did so by countermanding the decision of the former government to split privatization and the exploitation of state-owned enterprises. An additional motive to do something was related to the macroeconomic conditions prevailing at the time, namely, the disappointing state revenues from privatization. A new privatization law was passed by parliament in May 1995, and the ÁVU and the ÁV Rt were merged into the 'State Privatization and Holding Company Inc.' (ÁPV Rt). Considering Hungarian privatization since the start of the transformation process, the policy seems to resemble the swing of a pendulum. After great dissatisfaction with the functioning of the ÁVU, the Antall–Borros government decided to establish a separate ÁV Rt, whereas the Horn administration took the initiative to terminate the distinction between privatization and exploitation by merging the ÁVU and the ÁV Rt into the ÁPV Rt. 'Did anything really change?', seems to be the obvious rhetorical question in this context. Yet, the answer is that the privatization process did indeed change: not so much the procedures, but rather the speed of ownership transfer and the extent to which companies were to remain state-owned companies.

The new privatization strategy included a division of the portfolio of the ÁPV Rt into three groups of companies, of which the first was expected to generate cash, whereas the second and third would not. The first group comprised approximately forty enterprises in the energy and enterprise areas. Under the previous privatization strategy, these companies were expected to remain state-owned and were managed by the ÁV Rt. The companies in the second and third groups were until then managed by the ÁVU and comprised medium-sized and small enterprises, respectively. The point is, however, that those companies which the Antall–Boross government wanted to keep under state control were, under the new privatization strategy, identified as the most promising for privatization. All in all, the number of companies with a majority of state ownership was to fall to 161, compared with 252 under the previous privatization law of the Antall–Borros government. In 1996, the Horn government indeed succeeded in significantly increasing cash revenues from privatization and hoped to complete the privatization of most of the remaining state-owned assets by the end of 1997 (*PlanEcon Report*, 1996, No. 45–6).

The Incentive Structure

As noted above, more than the other Central European countries, Hungary faced the necessity of reducing the magnitude of its budget deficit in order to achieve sustainable growth. This fiscal motive to a large extent even inspired the method of privatization. However, sustainable growth ultimately rests upon the elimination of loss-making activities and the guarantee that resources released by, for example, privatization are (re-) allocated to the most profitable enterprises and sectors. This reallocation of resources is an incentive problem and basically addresses the implementation of the rules of the market game. Following the line of reasoning put forward in Chapter 1 on the agenda of transformation, the questions to be raised in this context are the extent to which the two post-communist governments have been able to enforce competition and bankruptcies, and to build and support financial institutions which have to free money for new private activities instead of endlessly lending to loss-making companies.

The reform of the financial system is of crucial importance for an efficient mechanism of capital allocation. Hungary was the first country in Central and Eastern Europe to do this. In 1987, the communist government implemented a two-tier banking system and split the monetary and commercial functions of banks, whereas until then the two were carried out by the National Bank (see Estrin *et al.*, 1992; Várhegyi, 1993). The two-tier system implied that the business relations between the National Bank and the enterprises were terminated and were left to commercial banks. The modernization of the banking sector was an important element of the reforms in the framework of the ÚGM, but, as was the case with other parts of this comprehensive reform package, it could not alter the functioning and the performance of the economic order. No mechanisms to harden the budget constraints of the enterprises were simultaneously introduced. In one way or another, state-owned enterprises retained bargaining power, which allowed them to survive.

The Antall–Boross government introduced a further stage in the development of the banking system with the Law on Commercial Banks, which became operative from January 1992.[6] This Act prescribed a reduction of state ownership in all banks to less than 25 per cent and was an attempt to align the banking system with Western European principles, that is, the Basle standard, although some of the licensing procedures restricted the principle of universal banking and kept, for example, the separation of securities trading and investment fund management. The crucial problem, though, was not the extent to which licensing procedures resembled those of the Western European standard, but the way in which the problem of bad portfolios was to be solved. More than any other section in the economy, the banking sector was severely constrained by the legacy of the communist past. Under the system of central planning, banks merely fulfilled the function of registering financial flows after the event and, as was the case with producing and trading enterprises, lacked hard budget constraints, even though a large part of the outstanding loans were dubious and not repayable. Hence, the commercial banks, which had been operating autonomously since 1987, were not in a favourable position to lend money for new private activities, but, in order to survive, were rather inclined to keep financing loss-making state-owned enterprises.

As a consequence of the bad portfolios of the commercial banks, inter-enterprise debts had increased dramatically and, in fact, this was a continuation of enterprise behaviour under the former regime, namely acting under soft budget constraints. The credits were not the result of arrangements of credits made in advance, but in practice emerged if the receiving enterprise was unable to pay its debts and therefore resembled the passive financial structure under central planning (see Stiglitz, 1992). The Act on Commercial Banks was an attempt to stop this extremely undesirable development and therefore coincided with a series of capital injections to improve the balance sheets of the state-owned commercial banks. At the time the Horn government took office, the cumulative amount of the financial injections since the implementation of the Act on

Commercial Banks reached 8 per cent of Hungary's GDP (European Bank for Reconstruction and Development, 1996(a)).

Although following different procedures of recapitalization of the commercial banks, at first sight the Hungarian case seems to resemble the Czech reforms with the erection of the 'Konsolidačni Banka', as described in the previous chapter. In both countries, there was substantial financial support for heavily indebted commercial banks. However, one important difference remained. Whereas bankruptcy legislation was rather ineffective in the case of the Czech Republic, it had an enormous impact on the Hungarian economy after it passed through parliament more or less simultaneously with the Act on Commercial Banks in December 1991. The bankruptcy law became effective from January 1992. The law was far more restrictive than elsewhere in Central and Eastern Europe. It forced companies with overdue liabilities for more than 90 days to initiate bankruptcy proceedings themselves, depending, of course, on the magnitude of the outstanding debt; otherwise the company would be subject to criminal prosecution. Owing to the strict rules, as well as to the accounting principles it prescribed, this law had an enormous and unanticipated impact on the number of bankruptcies in 1992 and 1993. After it had been operative for 18 months, approximately five thousand enterprises were subjected to bankruptcy procedures and a further sixteen thousand companies had been filed for liquidation by their creditors (World Bank, 1995). The number of bankruptcies was far beyond the amount the adminstration was able to handle and this created queues.

While waiting for bankruptcy or liquidation, the enterprise's value diminished, since it was impossible to restructure enterprises during the bankruptcy procedure. This, of course, also had a detrimental effect upon the already bad portfolios of the banks. The bankruptcy legislation was meant as a kind of shock treatment to bring about the efficient allocation of scarce resources – more or less contrary to the Czech case in which bankruptcy was not allowed during the period of privatization – but the number of casualties forced the Antall–Boross government to respond. It did so in September 1993, when the bankruptcy law was substantially amended. The major difference was that the companies with overdue liabilities were no longer obliged to declare bankruptcy, but the creditors were to take the initiative and they were entitled to decide on restructuring without going to court (see Ábel and Prander, 1994). This legislation remained essentially unchanged and also became the leading principle for the Horn government. As a consequence, the number of bankruptcies steadily declined to less than one hundred in 1995.[7]

Besides implementing legislation for bankruptcy, the first post-communist governments tried to establish competition policy aimed at effective functioning of decision making by market participants. As became clear from the outline of the ÚGM, price regulation was already an important instrument to influence and monitor economic activities. When considering the transformation to a market economy, though, price control had to be replaced by genuine competition policy. Legislation followed half a year after the Antall–Boross government took office. The Law on Economic Competition was passed by parliament in autumn 1990. Quick implementation was required to overcome the institutional void and to align as soon as possible with European competition legislation. Thus, as outlined in Chapter 2, reforms were externally driven, so as to prepare and smooth negotiations for the Association Agreements. None the less, the Hungarian Law on Economic Competition included several features which in Western Europe fell under civil law.

The Law on Economic Competition comprised several parts, among which the prohibition of cartelization and the specification of conditions under which companies were allowed to merge were the most important.[8] The law specified that no agreement which could possibly restrict or rule out competition was permitted under any circumstances. Of course, price agreements among companies were the most obvious settlements this law tried to eliminate. The task of monitoring the extent to which enterprises observed these rules was given to a special competition agency. It was fully compatible with the development in Hungarian economic reform since the introduction of the ÚGM that this agency succeeded the former state office for price regulation. Initially the office dealt with commodities alone, but from the autumn of 1993, its scope was extended to insurance and banking. It is important to note here, though, that the new agency did not have any authority to demolish existing monopolies, set up under the former regime to facilitate the planning procedures. The rules were that, for any merger, the prior consent of the agency had to be acquired. The Law on Economic Competition was slightly amended in the summer of 1996 by more precisely aligning the text with EU standards.

Finally, as far as the reforms addressed to building the rules of the market are concerned, it can be concluded that Hungary certainly did not slow down the transformation to a market economy. Competition policy was adopted only half a year after the Antall–Boross government came to power and it was not substantially amended afterwards. In certain fields, such as bankruptcy legislation, the path was even too shock-like, and since it seemed to be counter-productive, because it led to too many bankruptcies, necessary measures were taken. At the same time, the above-mentioned provisions made to ensure that firms would have the right incentives to behave as closely as possible to the competitive ideal, also implied that the Hungarian authorities actively applied some kind of industrial policy. Finally, there are no basic differences to be discerned between the two governments that followed the collapse of the communist regime. At the time the Horn government took office, the rules of the game were basically set.

HUNGARY'S EXTERNAL ECONOMIC RELATIONS

The ambiguity of the ÚGM also had its impact on the organization of foreign trade and therefore the reforms failed to trigger off a genuine improvement in competitiveness on Western markets (see Hoen and Van Leeuwen, 1991). The initial purpose was a revision – not the abolition – of the state monopoly on foreign trade, an autarkic system, as described in Chapter 2, which was characterized by the separation of foreign trade from domestic production by means of specialized FTOs, an exclusive focus on domestic production targets as an appendix of the central plan, the isolation of fixed domestic prices from constantly changing world market prices by means of an intricate system of subsidies and taxes ('price equalization mechanism'), and strict control over foreign exchange. The constraints on organizational change were twofold. Firstly, in the preparation of the reform package, the abandonment of the foreign trade monopoly was never considered. On the contrary, the monopoly was explicitly adopted in the 'Foreign Trade Act' of 1974, after which the barrier between production and trade had to be lowered through cooperation – not competition – between producing enterprises and FTOs (see Náray, 1987; Salgó, 1986, 1989). During the 1980s foreign trade competition among Hungarian firms was introduced as a new element; an increasing number of producers were authorized to trade on their own account. Notwithstanding these reform attempts, liberalization remained conditional, since the right to trade did not guarantee the right freely to buy or sell foreign exchange. Throughout the period of ÚGM, the foreign exchange monopoly remained beyond the scope of reforms.

Secondly, foreign trade reforms during the ÚGM era were restricted to the hard currency area. CMEA trade continued to be conducted on a bilateral basis. In order to maintain a certain minimal room for reform manoeuvre without being confronted with a military threat, the Hungarian authorities had a strong interest in the non-violation of CMEA relations. Owing to this, a large part of the foreign trade system was excluded from market-oriented reform, which rendered reform efforts inconsistent as a whole, since CMEA trade remained an important rent-seeking opportunity for Hungarian enterprises.

The internal inconsistencies of the ÚGM forced the political authorities to react and, in the twilight of the Hungarian communist regime and consequently the ÚGM, the basic provisions for revising the organization of external economic relations were established. Two months after the withdrawal of János Kádár, genuine import liberalization was discussed at a meeting of the Central Committee of the MSzMP and, contrary to the expectations of many, the Németh government promptly decided to liberalize imports thoroughly from January 1989. Within a period of three years, 80 per cent of total imports were to be liberalized. The licensing system was replaced by a registration procedure, indicating that the separation of trade and production, one of the cornerstones of the state monopoly on foreign trade, had disappeared. The programme was heavily criticized, in particular by scholars who believed that the package of commodities which were to be freely imported was rather arbitrary and would make certain industries extremely vulnerable to competition from abroad (see Gács, 1994). The implementation was perceived as too rapid, especially since it did not envisage substantial devaluations of the Hungarian currency. Since the import liberalization programme proved to be a success soon after its implementation, criticism evaporated.

Both the Antall–Boross and the Horn governments based their policy on this import liberalization programme. In the context of the negotiations on the Association Agreements, the Antall–Boross government only shortened the time schedule for the liberalization process, but compared to Czechoslovakia and Poland, both of which introduced internal convertibility more or less overnight and relied upon the idea that devaluation of the currency was the only mechanism to protect domestic industries, import liberalization remained gradual. This implied that not all industrial sectors were exposed to world market conditions at once (Ábel and Bonin, 1993; Gács, 1994; Hanel, 1992). But, of course, the liberalization of imports attended the abolition of foreign currency restrictions with respect to these transactions, and, therefore, implied a break with the ÚGM era in which the separation of real and monetary sides of the economy – one of the essential features of central planning – had been preserved.

On the one hand, this speeding up was externally motivated by the accomplishment of the Association Agreement, but, on the other hand, it was also a constituent and intrinsic part of the transformation strategy. Regarding the external motivation, the Association Agreement permitted Hungary to protect a number of industrial and agricultural products only temporarily and, therefore, from the time it was implemented in March 1992, it forced Hungary towards further liberalization of its external economic relations. But, of course, liberalization also became an innate element of the transformation from a centrally planned system to a fully-fledged market economy. The intention was to introduce limited currency convertibility and thus to expose domestic producers to worldwide competition. A speedy introduction of currency convertibility was also perceived as pivotal since, at the dawn of the transformation, the domestic production structure was still extremely monopolistic.

As stated above regarding economic stabilization, the discussion focused sharply on the use of the exchange rate as a 'nominal anchor' (see Edwards, 1992). The idea is that by nominally fixing the exchange rate to a currency or a basket of currencies, correctly perceived relative prices, and also the rate of inflation in the country or region to which the currency is fixed, will be transmitted to the country which has to be stabilized. Credibility with respect to sustaining the anchor is of major importance to the success of this exchange-rate-based stabilization scheme. In order to maintain the fix, the authorities force themselves to conduct sound monetary and fiscal policy, which, as a result, reduces inflation expectations. It goes without saying that the credibility itself is highly dependent upon the consistency of the entire reform programme, as well as upon the institutional arrangements which force the authorities to maintain the nominal anchor. The Antall–Boross government did not fix the Hungarian forint to the US dollar or to a basket of hard currencies, but applied a 'crawling-peg' instead (Ábel and Bonin, 1993). This implied a search for an equilibrium rate to be attained by an iterative process of adjustments (devaluations) of the forint. In order to have a stable real exchange rate, there were frequent devaluations of the forint after inflationary upheavals due to phased price liberalization.

The perceived advantages of an adjustable peg were especially related to the problem of overshooting in the case of conducting a fixed nominal anchor. Since domestic inflation is higher than in the country or region to which the currency is fixed, a real appreciation of the exchange rate has to be anticipated. But an initial real undervaluation of the currency may itself have a destabilizing inflationary impact. As will be shown in the next chapter, the literature indeed suggests that this was exactly what happened in Poland after the introduction of the 'Balcerowicz Plan', indicating that the depth and the obstinacy of the crisis was partly due to an undervalued Polish złoty. The Hungarian authorities, bearing in mind the Polish experience and being confronted with less severe macroeconomic disequilibria, decided to opt for an adjustable pegging of the Hungarian forint. Hence, nominal adjustments of the currency were believed to reflect domestic price increases, rather than to transmit foreign price changes on to the Hungarian economy. It has to be added, though, that the forint remained overvalued in real terms and was not declared convertible overnight, as was the case in Czechoslovakia and Poland.

With respect to lifting foreign exchange restrictions, the Economic Policy Action Programme of the Antall–Boross government also indicated a gradual approach which would be completed only after the entire term of office of the Antall–Boross government ('Stabilization and Convertibility: Economic Policy Action Programme', 1991). Contrary to its Central European neighbours, though, Hungary did not *de jure* declare the forint convertible for current account transactions; but since nearly all domestic requests for foreign exchange purchases were authorized from autumn 1990, *de facto* it was. Producing and trading enterprises could freely import commodities from abroad and therefore competition was fully guaranteed. Private persons were not always permitted to change their forints into foreign currency. On the contrary, the Antall–Boross government felt that it had slightly to restrain travel possibilities established under the communist Németh government, since the current account deficit came under severe pressure.[9] The Horn government more or less continued the policy of its predecessor. Currency convertibility for transactions regarding the current account of the balance of payments was secured, but *de jure* convertibility for current account transaction according to the IMF article 8 was announced only from January 1996. Furthermore, restrictions on private activities were only reluctantly abolished. Citizens were allowed to keep dollar accounts, but the maximum amount which could be cashed annually was only moderately increased, to 250 US dollars, after the Horn government came to power. This also explains the fact that, for a quite long period of time, black market activities for foreign currency remained, whereas in, for example, the Czech Republic these had been practically eliminated.

Regarding trade liberalization, it should be recalled that Hungary had already participated in the GATT before the collapse of the communist system. Moreover, it had been able to convince the organization that the economic reforms of the ÚGM had made tariffs a meaningful instrument in trade policy. At the start of the transformation, the average tariff rate was somewhat higher than in the average OECD country, but it was significantly lower than the tariffs imposed by countries at a similar stage of economic development. In addition, over 80 per cent of its tariffs were bound, a level that certainly surpassed the level of other countries at comparable stages of economic development. Henceforth, as was the case with the Czech Republic, GATT partnership restrained the possibilities of protecting domestic industries, since tariffs were bound. Therefore, Hungary also had to rely upon special import surcharges. Moreover, in those areas in which it enjoyed GATT-approved exceptions, Hungary had to give up the privileges when it signed the Association Agreements. These agreements specified the reduction in most of the tariffs within a decade, whereas part of the GATT provisions were less restrictive.

The fact that tariffs were GATT-bound induced the Horn government to introduce special import surcharges as part of its stabilization programme. In March 1995, the Hungarian authorities introduced an 8 per cent import surcharge on all commodities. Energy sources and machinery for investments were exempted from this protection. These measures for domestic protection had to be complemented by a tight schedule for phasing out the surcharges. The schedule revealed that the surcharges were to be eliminated within two years. Also part of the stabilization programme of the Horn government was the slight change in exchange rate policy. Apart from a change in the basket of currencies to which the forint was pegged – the German Mark becoming more important at the expense of the US dollar and the ECU – the exchange rate was adjusted on a monthly basis at a pre-announced rate of 1.2 per cent. This was implemented to improve Hungary's balance of payments, which had so dramatically deteriorated in 1993 and 1994. It certainly had an impact and external trade relations improved in 1995.

In sum, it can be concluded that, contrary to its surrounding neighbours under examination in this book, Hungary started liberalizing its external economic relations before the collapse of the communist system. The Antall–Borross government somewhat accelerated the liberalization process. But regarding the exchange rate, current account convertibility of the forint was not declared. Moreover, no policy of nominal anchoring was applied. Facing the problem of the 'twin deficit', the Horn government thought it necessary to impose new temporary import surcharges and to announce in advance the monthly adjustment of the crawling peg rate of 1.2 per cent. *De jure* convertibility of the forint according to article 8 of the IMF was declared from January 1996. Hungary thereby followed the Czech and Slovak Republics as well as Poland, all of which converted at an earlier stage of the transformation process. Nevertheless, liberalization of external relations still has to be perceived as amazingly fast and almost without historical precedent.

CONCLUSION

In many surveys of the economic transformation in Central and Eastern Europe, two points about Hungary's process and performance generally come to the fore. Firstly, the country is presented as an example of gradual change from a planned economic order, in whatever form, to a market economy. Economic reforms during the communist era enabled post-communist political leaders to avoid too painful steps. As a pivotal element of the economic reforms initiated in 1968, liberalization of prices, trade and production had to a significant extent already materialized during the 1970s and, especially, the 1980s. Secondly, the country is exposed as a relative loser in the first years of the transformation. To put it differently, Hungary lost the favourable position which it had built up under Kádár. With respect to both the country's legacy and its current performance, this chapter concludes slightly differently.

The end of the communist era in Hungary clearly differed from that in the other countries in the region. In the late 1980s, the opposition parties, which *de facto* operated already for quite some time, became legalized. As a consequence, the Hungarian situation in the political turmoil was not characterized by mass movements, such as was the case in Czechoslovakia and Poland, but relative positions of interests were fairly quickly established. The idea that the political change was initiated from within the Hungarian communist party is not fully subscribed to in this chapter – it was rather that the Hungarian communist leaders, at an early stage, understood that changes were irreversible and, therefore, decided to cooperate – but it seems justified to conclude that the stage of opposition parties' common goal and joint efforts to dispose of the communist system had passed quickly. The free elections held in May 1990 did not completely destroy the legitimacy of the parliamentary presence of former communists who had transformed themselves into social democrats.

The impact of this political climate in the realm of economics was that the conservative coalition of the Antall–Boross government was unable to apply macroeconomic shock treatment as generally advocated by the IMF. A cold turkey policy aiming at a restriction of aggregate demand would too much undermine the government's position from the very beginning. This consideration confirms the legacy of preliminary political constraints as discussed in Chapter 1. The political situation undoubtedly had a negative impact on macroeconomic performance and the country quite soon was confronted with large and enduring deficits in the government budget and current account. At the same time, it shows that Hungary had not so much lost the lead during the first years of the transformation, but rather it questions Hungary's favourable position at the start of the transformation.

In other respects, the country's unfavourable position came to the fore as well. During the reforms in the framework of the 'New Economic Mechanism', liberalization was the pivotal issue. Instead of relying on a system of directive planning, the Hungarian economic order was reformed into a system of indicative planning, demonstrating that economic decisions were decentralized and were supposed to rely upon macroeconomic regulators. An economic order of regulator bargaining emerged and it appeared to be extremely difficult to monitor and control several issues in the transformation process. Privatization may serve as an example here. Given the fact that the reforms under Kádár created a system of diffuse property rights, the undesirable path of spontaneous privatization was a small but unavoidable step in the transfer of ownership rights. Whereas in Czechoslovakia strictly centralized decision making enabled them to circumvent this problem, the Hungarian authorities faced enormous difficulties in regaining control of the process of privatization.

The legacy of communist reform may certainly not always have been beneficial to Hungary's speed of transformation, but it should not be concluded that the country's path towards a market economy was gradual in all fields. Regarding several aspects of the transformation concerned with inducing the restructuring of enterprises, among which the introduction of a bankruptcy law was the most important, the reforms were much tougher than in Czechoslovakia and its successor nations. The same holds true for liberalization in (foreign) trade and prices. A perceived slower pace in these areas seems much more due to nominal, that is *de jure* differences. The facts do not justify such a statement. Even in the field of macroeconomics, the qualification of a gradual strategy is no longer valid. Regarding macroeconomic stabilization, as initiated by the coalition of socialists and leftist liberals and externally pushed forward by the IMF, the Hungarian experience was rather revealed as a late shock. The Horn government came into power after popular discontent with transformation, and promised to ease the pain of transformation. Horn appeared to be a wolf in sheep's clothing. With the monetary and fiscal policy severely restraining effective demand, the economic recovery was relatively moderate in 1994 and the following year. Now, the Hungarian population seems grudgingly to accept the social costs of the transformation.

NOTES

1. By contrast, the reforms during the 'Prague Spring' not only addressed economic, but also political organization. Consequently, and similar to the Hungarian revolution of 1956, the communist system could be sustained only by military force.
2. The Hungarian voting system is a complicated one. Given the combination of individual contests and regional constituencies, as well as the minimum requirement of a 5 per cent mandate, the percentage of popular votes in no way corresponds to the percentage of shares in parliamentary seats (see Arato, 1994). The percentages mentioned in the remainder of this chapter refer to shares in parliamentary seats and not to the popular vote.

3. The remaining parliamentary seats were taken by the MSzP and independent candidates. The new 'Hungarian Socialist Workers' Party' (MSzMP), set up by a conservative communist minority after the dissolution of the communist party, was not elected into parliament (see Barany, 1990; Tőkés, 1990).

4. The remainder of the chapter, therefore, refers to the coalition as the Antall–Boross government, though it is clear that Antall as prime minister was responsible for the major part of the policies between May 1990 and May 1994.

5. The best-known among these enterprises were 'IBUSZ' (travel and currency exchange agency) and 'HungarHotels' (Hotel and catering service).

6. The implementation of the law on commercial banks coincided with the National Banking Act, which was intended to guarantee the independence of the National Bank.

7. This figure excluded the liquidations, which were nearly ten times more numerous (European Bank for Reconstruction and Development, 1996(a)).

8. Other sections of the Law on Economic Competition addressed the protection of consumer interests and binding rules for producers, for example, not to link selling and purchasing within one transaction, or accurately describing a product and so on (see OECD, 1995; Stadler, 1993).

9. After relaxation of travel restrictions in 1989, Hungarian citizens, on a grand scale, went shopping in the West. The influx of Hungarians became so manifest that, for example, people from Vienna even referred to the *Maria Hilferstraße*, famous for its shopping facilities, as *Magyar Hilferstraße*.

5. The Creation of a Market Economy in Poland: From Shock to a Hands-off Approach

INTRODUCTION

Poland's transformation from a centrally planned to a market economy has become a frame of reference for all transition countries in the Central and Eastern European region. In January 1990, Poland was the first among these countries to inaugurate policy for the creation of a fully-fledged market economy. The package of reform measures was named after Poland's Finance Minister Leszek Balcerowicz in the first post-communist government headed by Prime Minister Tadeusz Mazowiecki: it was the 'Balcerowicz Plan'. Furthermore, once several policies were triggered during the remainder of 1990 and 1991, Poland was perceived as the most radical country. Poland's economic transformation became synonymous with shock treatment and the country's transformation policy was an example to many other transition countries, especially those which, like Poland, faced enormous macroeconomic problems at the start of the process.

Despite decisive steps taken in the field of economic transformation, Poland quite soon experienced a return to power by former socialist political leadership. In autumn 1993, there were new parliamentary elections and economic items concerning the transformation to a market economy dominated the campaigns. As in Hungary in 1994, the elections brought victory to a party governed by former communists, namely the 'Democratic Left Alliance' (SLD), accompanied by the 'Polish Peasant Party' (PSL), which during the communist era served as a block voter. The new political landscape led to a perpetual struggle between the parliament and president Lech Wałęsa, which impeded further implementation of economic reforms.

The interaction of economic and political developments constitutes the leading thread in this chapter on the creation of a market economy in

Poland. The questions to be addressed are, first of all, why Poland, rather than the other countries under examination in this book, had a radical platform at the start of the transformation. To this end, a historical survey is indispensable. It will focus on the immanent cyclical patterns of Polish history and their impact on the political climate at the dawn of the transformation.

Secondly, the initial reform package and its results will be scrutinized. The programme which was launched in January 1990 was predominantly a stabilization and liberalization package. It was fully supported by the IMF and the World Bank, but the question remains whether it was compatible with an economic order which was yet not fully coordinated by well-developed markets. Therefore, the discussion centres on the severity and the necessity of the collapse in economic activity in the period following the introduction of the reform package. Poland was the first among the four countries under scrutiny in which economic activity recuperated, but it remains to be seen whether the elements of shock treatment in Balcerowicz's stabilization and liberalization package were too damaging for the Polish economy in the first stages of the economic transformation.

Thirdly, after dealing with macroeconomic developments, the focus will shift towards microeconomic restructuring. In Poland, there has been extensive debate on the issue of privatization and restructuring, and also on institution building. But the factual implementation of various reforms in this field was time and again politically constrained. The question is to what extent this interdependency affected proposals and implementation of reforms in the field of microeconomic restructuring.

Fourthly, as a final theme to be tackled in this chapter, Poland's external economic relations will be addressed. The introduction of current account convertibility was a pivotal part of the Balcerowicz programme and, in fact, implied trade liberalization. The extent to which the liberalization proceeded afterwards is under scrutiny in the penultimate section. The final section summarizes and concludes the chapter.

WHY A RADICAL PLATFORM AT THE START OF THE TRANSFORMATION?

The Cyclical Pattern in the Contemporary Economic History of Poland

In the academic literature, Polish history is recurrently qualified by its cyclical nature (see Berend, 1996; Biessen, 1996; Gerrits, 1990). These cyclical patterns also seem to be valid when analysing contemporary economic history. This section briefly addresses the political and economic developments since the 1950s in an attempt to clarify why there existed such a radical platform at the start of the economic transformation from a centrally planned to a market economy. It is maintained that shortcomings in evolving reform attempts since the 1950s strongly influenced the design of a shock approach.

In 1956, for the first time since the implementation of a system of mandatory planning, social upheaval induced economic reforms. In June of that year, railway workers in Poznan started to strike as a protest against their poor economic condition and the government's policy. The strikes soon turned into genuine mass demonstrations and, in an attempt to restore order, the Polish army directly intervened, but the bloody suppression was unable to still the hunger for political change. At the end of that explosive summer, the leaders of the communist party saw no other option than to allow the return of Władysław Gomułka who, following his dismissal of rapid collectivization had been forced to resign as head of the communist party in 1949. Gomułka's membership of the communist party was re-established and at the eighth plenum of the Central Committee in October 1956 he was appointed leader of the party (see Berend, 1996, 109ff).

Economic reform was the obvious result of Gomułka's return to the political centre, although external political pressure from Moscow to stay in line with Soviet perceptions of socialism initially remained. The reforms consisted of three parts. Firstly, independent workers' councils were installed to check managerial decision making. Secondly, and contrary to all other Central and Eastern European countries, Polish agriculture was not collectivized. Finally, and again contrary to what happened in most of the other communist countries, in the policy Gomułka applied, a substantial societal influence of the Catholic church was brooked. Whereas the last two categories of reforms were able to survive for a longer period of time, the first and most pivotal aspect of Gomułka's plans was not. Soon after their implementation, the workers' councils fell within the realm of the party and were eventually entirely controlled by party officials. There was no way of independently operating workers' councils.

Whereas Gomułka re-entered the political stage as an advocate of economic reform, he left it fourteen years later in December 1970 as a conservative communist averse to genuine reform. History seemed to turn full circle. The Polish population lost confidence in Gomułka's rule and in December 1970 there was violent social upheaval. Shortly before he had to resign, Gomułka even asked for Soviet military support. He received 'no' for an answer and decided to repress mass demonstrations by military force. He succeeded, but his position as party leader was no longer sustainable, and he was succeeded by Edward Gierek.

Gierek's political leadership lasted nearly ten years and the period he was in power may illustrate the next cycle in Poland's economic history since the Second World War. As did the Hungarian leader Kádár, Gierek pragmatically relied upon the trade-off between political and economic reform. In an attempt to retard political reform, Gierek also promised to raise living standards. Gomułka's successor tried virtually to buy political support. At the beginning of the 1970s, almost all Eastern European countries faced the problem of low rates of economic growth. It became necessary to turn a process of extensive growth, which was based on higher input of labour and capital, into a process of intensive growth, that is, growth through more efficient use of the factors of production. Gierek was more extreme than Kádár in the way he tried to accomplish this new growth strategy without sacrificing current consumption, that is, still maintaining political support. Gierek, though, did not implement comprehensive economic reforms such as the Hungarian ÚGM, but mainly relied upon a shift in economic policy.

Under the Gierek government, Poland followed an 'import-led' growth strategy. Capital investments financed by foreign loans were expected substantially to improve the capacity to export, so that rising export earnings could be used for debt servicing. Moreover, external financing had to enable the restructuring of the economy without sacrificing current consumption and lengthen the upward phase in the investment cycle (see Winiecki, 1988).[1] Though several Central and Eastern European countries followed this kind of import-led policy, Poland was the most enthusiastic country to do so. Between 1970 and 1979, the nominal value of machinery and transport equipment imported from the OECD by the six smaller European CMEA countries, namely Bulgaria, Czechoslovakia, the GDR, Hungary, Poland and Romania, grew by an average annual rate of 16.8 per cent. Poland and Hungary exceeded the average with growth rates of approximately 21 per cent (Hanson, 1982). However, while Hungary showed a fairly evenly spread pattern, the rapid expansion of Polish imports was mainly concentrated in the first half of the 1970s.

In 1976, Gierek encountered the first problems due to his economic policy. The political leaders were forced to announce an immoderate increase in food prices, since Poland was living far beyond its means. As a result of the import-led policy, Polish hard currency debt rose enormously and there was incessant inflationary pressure. The government lacked political clout and legitimacy to combat effectively the dangers of emerging external and domestic disequilibria. Indispensable price rises were partly or sometimes even entirely compensated by wage increases (Biessen, 1996). Towards the end of the 1970s, the policy of import-led growth somehow had to be terminated, since credits increasingly had to be used for debt-service payments (see Zloch-Christy, 1987). The Gierek government made the 1970s a decade of opportunism and finally led Poland to the verge of an economic catastrophe, one which marked the beginning of a new cycle.

The Polish Crisis of 1980–82 and Ensuing Economic Reforms

During 1980, Poland's economy seriously deteriorated. Import restrictions were announced in conjunction with wage restraints. A politically volatile situation emerged. Poland became once more the scene of labour unrest and mass demonstrations, events which in reality implied the failure of Gierek's policy based on rapid growth and modernization of the Polish economy as prerequisites for political stability. The formal resignation of Gierek followed within months, immediately after the Gdansk Agreement between Lech Wałęsa, leader of 'Solidarity', the trade union whose right to exist had just been politically accepted, and the Gierek government's deputy prime minister, were reached on 31 August 1980. The Agreement was a major political and economic concession, but Gierek's departure did not completely satisfy Solidarity's demands, and therefore strikes went on during 1980 and 1981.

The demonstrations themselves had a bad impact on the already gloomy economic situation in Poland. Shortages on domestic markets increased and further destabilized the macroeconomic situation. For a wide range of commodities, among them important food products, rationing was introduced (Berend, 1996, p. 259). In the first quarter of 1981, the Soviet Union was still willing to guarantee Polish debt-servicing obligations *vis-à-vis* Western creditors, but quite soon the Soviet umbrella stopped functioning.[2] In March 1981, Poland had to declare that it was unable further to service its debts (see Cline, 1984, 273ff; Zloch-Christy, 1987). The financiers did not declare Poland's default, but were willing to restructure the country's debt. Meanwhile, it was clear, though, that the country had to implement economic reforms in an attempt to restore domestic and external economic equilibrium. There was no option left to rely further upon direct instruments of central planning, since these had proven to be unacceptable to the Solidarity movement.

Proposals for economic reform were accepted by the Polish parliament, the Sejm, in the course of 1981. The package very much resembled that of the Hungarian ÚGM, which has been described in the preceding chapter. Consequently, it also suffered from the same drawbacks. The main points of the Polish reform package can, therefore, very briefly be summarized. Firstly, there was a decentralization in economic decision making. This implied that the mandatory character of planning had to be abolished. With the notable exception of CMEA deliveries, enterprises were allowed autonomy regarding the decision about what, how many, and for whom to produce. The central plan had to be maintained, but it was no longer imperative. Secondly, in order to fulfil the plan, financial regulators were introduced. Most important in this regard was the establishment of a new price system. To a far greater extent, prices had to reflect conditions of demand and supply. But, as was the case in Hungary, there was a shift from plan bargaining to regulator bargaining. Thirdly, and to a certain extent deviating from the Hungarian ÚGM, workers' councils were given wider powers. For example, they received the ultimate right to dismiss management. This was due to the bargaining power of Solidarity. A weak point of this self-managerial system was that it significantly loosened wage restraints and, therefore, further threatened to destabilize the economy (Balcerowicz, 1995).

The implementation of the reforms was scheduled for January 1982. Meanwhile, the situation remained volatile and, on 13 December 1981, General Wojciech Jaruzelski, Prime Minister since January 1981, declared martial law in an ultimate attempt to restore law and order. Martial law did not delay the introduction of the reform package, but, of course, had a significant impact on its content and design. Trade unions, including Solidarity, were first suspended and then dissolved. Furthermore, the authority of the workers' councils became severely restricted or temporarily suspended. Reforms in the field of indicative planning, though, were implemented as scheduled.

Jaruzelski succeeded in his attempts to stabilize the economy. In 1983 and 1984, there was economic recuperation. It remains questionable how far this could be attributed to the economic reforms. Most of the literature points out that regained economic stabilization was due to military repression which restored labour discipline. The cessation of social upheaval and nation-wide strikes had a positive impact on the level of production itself (see Biessen, 1996). However, the simple restoration of labour discipline, combined with the relative ineffectiveness of the economic reforms, meant that the structural economic problems surfaced again and, hence, the emergence of a new cycle. In 1987, the Polish economy faced new and chronic shortages of basic consumer goods. A policy response was needed and came in October with the implementation of follow-up reforms, the so-called 'second stage' (Balcerowicz, 1995).

Key elements in these reforms were price corrections to fight chronic shortages on consumer markets. By means of a more extensive liberalization of prices, disequilibria had to be resolved. As anticipated, price increases occurred, but since the government compensated for losses in real income, the policy led to a disaster. Inflation was boosted, while the shortage problem became aggravated. This presaged the final collapse of the communist system: in other words, it was the last short-lived cycle. Mieczysław Rakowski headed the government which had to implement these reforms. He was a pro-reformist communist and the leaders of the communist party hoped this prime minister would be able to secure the political system. Rakowski indeed liberalized prices, notably in agriculture and, as a result, mass protests engulfed the country. The straw which broke the camel's back was the announcement of the closure of the Gdansk shipyard by the end of 1990. Gdansk was the birthplace of Solidarity and instead of preserving communist leadership, the government was forced to re-enter negotiations with that trade union.

The Accomplishments of the Mazowiecki Government

After failing negotiations between the Polish government and Solidarity representatives in the autumn of 1988, the so-called 'Round Table' talks started in February 1989. Agreement was reached on 5 April. Solidarity regained the status of a legal trade union and partially free elections were scheduled for June 1989. In the Sejm, 65 per cent of the seats were allotted to the Polish United Workers' Party (PZPR) and the remaining seats were to be contested by the opposition alone. Solidarity won all these contested 161 seats.[3] After the elections, there was at first an attempt by the communist Czesław Kiszcak to form a government. Unable to do so, he resigned as prime minister within two weeks. Subsequently, Tadeusz Mazowiecki, a leading intellectual within Solidarity, was asked to become prime minister. He was the first post-communist leader in Poland and his coalition government, consisting of members of Solidarity, the PZPR and those of the former block-voting PSL and 'Democratic Party' (SD), took office in September 1989.

In the new government, Solidarity acquired a large majority in ministerial positions. With the exception of the ministries of foreign and domestic trade, it administered nearly all the pivotal departments involved with the transformation from a centrally planned to a market economy. So, despite the fact that the political changes were quite gradual, there was room for radical political manoeuvre to liberalize trade, prices and production, to implement sound and restrictive monetary and fiscal policy for stabilizing the economy, and to initiate reforms which intended to underpin privatization and marketization. The gloomy economic situation at the time of the political change-over required far-reaching reforms and after so many cycles of social upheaval and subsequent inadequate economic reform – a pattern in which the frequency and the amplitude of evolving events increased over time – a radical platform emerged.

The government rejected proposals for economic reform as accepted in the follow-up to the Round Table contracts in the summer of 1989. Within a matter of months after it was installed and with the assistance of the Harvard economist Jeffrey Sachs, a plan for economic transformation was designed. On 1 January 1990, the Mazowiecki government implemented the 'Balcerowicz Plan', named after its initiator, finance minister and deputy prime minister. The plan was perceived as a genuine shock approach and received enormous support in the West. In particular the IMF wholeheartedly supported the reform package, though it was not imposed on Poland by IMF officials (Sachs, 1993, p. 42).

The main ingredients of the 'Balcerowicz Plan' were the following (see Biessen, 1996; Jeffries, 1993; Sachs, 1993). Firstly, there was a far-reaching liberalization of prices, production and trade. Bureaucratic restrictions on the private sector were removed and after an anticipated price jump which was needed to clear the monetary overhang, prices were to reflect relative scarcities in the market. Secondly, tight wage control was implemented. In the state sector, wage increases which exceeded productivity gains and inflation rates became subject to high and progressive taxes, the so-called 'popiwek'. The previous month's consumer price index became the decisive norm for wage taxation. Thirdly, the plan comprised a series of reforms to balance the budget. Apart from the implementation of new taxes, of which the corporate profits tax with a uniform rate of 40 per cent was the most important at that time, it basically entailed that subsidies for loss-making companies were drastically cut.[4] Fourthly, the plan was based upon a restrictive monetary policy. Tight credit ceilings were implemented and the monetary authorities tried to effect positive real interest rates. Fifthly, the Polish złoty underwent a draconian devaluation and was, subsequently, nominally anchored to the US dollar at a competitive rate. From January 1990, the currency was also declared convertible for current account transactions, implying that imports were liberalized and that Polish enterprises were forced to adjust to world market conditions.

The 'Balcerowicz Plan' was first and foremost a stabilization package. Structural reforms had to follow and were envisaged as a phased introduction after harsh stabilization. This sequencing in the 'Balcerowicz Plan', though partly, because of inevitable technical as well as time constraints, inherent in microeconomic reforms, was heavily criticized. The harsh stabilization package was designed with the idea in mind that the failure of the gradual reforms in the 1980s had resulted in a large degree of 'political capital', as Balcerowicz put it (Balcerowicz, 1995). In other words, people were willing to accept the high costs of the transformation and this attitude paved the way for irreversible reforms. However, the ultimate proof of successful stabilization is the effectuation of the hoped-for supply response. Critics pointed out that supply responses ultimately depended upon the structural reforms, especially in the labour and capital markets. Since these were yet to follow, stabilization implied merely a reduction in real incomes (see Brainard, 1991, p. 98). The next section will further scrutinize this claim and address the Polish economic performance since the introduction of the 'Balcerowicz Plan'. Of course, for an appropriate assessment in this respect, it is important to indicate subsequent policy shifts as well.

WAS THE CRISIS REALLY NECESSARY?

The Reverberation of the 'Balcerowicz Plan' through the Polish Economy

The immediate impact of the reforms was enormous. After prices were liberalized, the inflation rate soared. Consumer prices rose by nearly 80 per cent in January, whereas a 45 per cent increase was envisaged. However, supply bottlenecks very soon disappeared in consumer markets – indicating the disappearance of the monetary overhang – after which inflation fell back rapidly. The first months after the introduction of the stabilization package were to a very large extent determined by the inflation rate for 1990. As indicated in Table 5.1, consumer prices rose in 1990 by approximately 600 per cent.

Table 5.1   Development of important economic indicators in Poland, 1990–95

	1990	1991	1992	1993	1994	1995
GDP growth (%)	-11.6	-7.6	1.0	2.5	3.8	5.2
consumer prices (%)	586.0	70.3	43.0	60.0	32.2	29.4
government budget (% of GDP)	-0.7	7.0	6.9	3.4	2.5	2.8
unemployment (% active pop.)	6.3	11.8	13.6	15.3	16.8	14.9
current account (bln. $)	0.7	-2.2	-0.3	-2.3	-1.1	-2.4
foreign direct investment (mln. $)	11	117	284	300	542	1134

Sources: European Bank for Reconstruction and Development (1996(a), 1996(b))

Since anticipated price rises were much lower, the 'popiwek' norm for nominal wage increases for employees in state enterprises was below the necessary level as well. State enterprises assumed a permitted wage increase for January of somewhat less than 15 per cent, whereas subsequent inflationary developments showed room for a 25 per cent wage rise. As a consequence, real wages declined dramatically: within one month, real wages dropped more than 40 per cent. Afterwards, the enforcement of the 'popiwek' was somewhat relaxed. It was decided that the tax authorities should no longer observe wage increases on a monthly basis, but consider a longer period of time.

The sharp decline in real incomes initiated a deep and long-lasting economic recession. In January alone, industrial production declined by 20 per cent compared with the month before and the whole decrease in 1990 was 25 per cent. In the year following the introduction of the 'Balcerowicz Plan', there was negative GDP growth of nearly 12 per cent, far more than the anticipated 5 per cent. With the total economic activity declining, unemployment rose. Table 5.1 indicates that within two years, more than 15 per cent of the active population faced the problem of being jobless, a percentage which despite recent growth in GDP is still above 10 per cent of the workforce.

The necessity of a transition crisis has always been beyond dispute, but the question whether the social costs may have been unnecessarily high to a large extent dominated economic literature on stabilization in Poland (see Blejer *et al.*, 1993; Bruno, 1992; Ellman, 1993; Winiecki, 1993). A majority – by and large corresponding to neo-classical Anglo-Saxon literature – emphasized that the achievements of the 'Balcerowicz Plan' were impressive. Critics most generally pointed out that IMF-approved stabilization was ill-suited to an economy which was in a state between central planning and a market economy and proved to be counter-productive. In a more specific and technical sense, arguments referred to the 'nominal anchor' of the złoty to the US dollar and later to a basket of Western currencies.

The exchange rate anchor was introduced from January 1990. As applied elsewhere, the general intention was to impose discipline on the fiscal and monetary authorities and to reduce expectations of inflation. By doing this, the notion was to import inflation from the region possessing the currency to which the złoty was fixed. However, since domestic inflation was much higher than in the anchor region, a tremendous real appreciation of the złoty was expected, making the country less competitive on world markets. Therefore, a large devaluation of the złoty was to precede the nominal anchoring. Now, serious doubts have been expressed regarding the extent of devaluation. Many authors point out that it was too much. As a consequence of the 'over-shooting', inflation rose rather than moderated and needlessly deepened the crisis.[5]

The 'Balcerowicz Plan' as Scorched-Earth Policy

Owing to the enormous economic consequences of the 'Balcerowicz Plan', the first post-communist government very soon lost popular support and Prime Minister Mazowiecki resigned before the end of 1990. The presidential elections in November 1990 were the straw which broke the camel's back. In these elections in November 1990, Mazowiecki was humiliated, since he was defeated in the first round. The second position was taken by the relative outsider Stanisław Tymiński, a Canadian businessman of Polish origin, who lost the elections from Wałęsa in the second round. Jan Olszewski was nominated as Mazowiecki's successor, but the newly elected president blocked the formation of a government presided over by an outspoken critic of the Balcerowicz reforms (see Brown, 1994, p. 75). Wałęsa won and enabled the liberal Jan Kryzstof Bielecki to become prime minister in January 1991.

With the notable exception of two ministers, none of those who served under Mazowiecki took a position in the new government. However, Balcerowicz was one of the two persons and he consolidated his position as finance and deputy prime minister. This implied a continuation of the main ingredients of the shock approach. As one of the very few who continued, Balcerowicz's relative influence was even extended. The temporary relaxation of the austerity programme, which emerged in the summer of 1990 in an attempt to reduce the social costs of the transformation, was terminated after the Bielecki government took office. For example, despite strong political pressure from trade unions, it refused a further relaxation of the wage increase tax. Furthermore, the Bielecki government maintained a restrictive monetary policy by further increasing interest rates on the złoty.

An important shift in the direction of a relaxation in economic policy after the introduction of the 'Balcerowicz Plan' was likely to occur following the general elections in October 1991. Since the Solidarity movement had completely split into a large number of rival parties, Polish citizens had completely lost confidence in politics and were not interested in the elections. A mere two years after the collapse of communism, less than half of the electorate took the opportunity to vote in the first entirely free election (see Juchler, 1994, p. 262). The elections resulted in a completely fragmented political landscape, since there was no minimum threshold for entry. Nearly thirty parties appeared in the Sejm. With the exception of Mazowiecki's Democratic Union (UD) and the Democratic

Left Alliance (SLD), mainly consisting of former communists, none of these parties received 10 per cent of the votes. Without clear winners, of course, the establishing of a new government proved extremely difficult. After his failed attempts to become prime minister, Olszewski now succeeded.

The Olszewski government basically rejected the 'Balcerowicz Plan' and favoured a slower pace of economic reform and higher social security benefits. But in actual fact, this coalition consisting of seven parties was unable completely to follow these principles during the short period it was in office. Moreover, entirely in line with the liberal approaches of preceding governments, it approved steep price rises in the field of energy products and fully accepted the budget proposals as drafted by the Bielecki government for the first quarter of 1992 (see Jeffries, 1993, p. 437). The government's desire to relax monetary and fiscal policy for the remainder of 1992 failed to materialize. So did the efforts aimed at increasing social benefits. The failure to achieve these goals was due to the absence of parliamentary and presidential support.

In the summer of 1992, Olszewski had to resign after a 'no confidence' vote of parliament in a debate concerning the communist past of important civil servants. In the following parliamentary session, Waldemar Pawlak of the PSL was asked to preside over the government, but as the political leader of a smaller fraction which did not have its roots in Solidarity but had been a block voting party during the communist era instead, he failed in his attempt to form a majority coalition.

Regarding the anti-Balcerowicz strands of the Olszewski government, it has to be concluded that the administration was unable to ease the social costs of the transformation. The 'Balcerowicz Plan' had turned out to be a kind of 'scorched-earth policy', such as was described in Chapter 1 on the nature of political restrictions and the transformation policy applied. In an atmosphere of complete lack of confidence in 'piecemeal reforms' and one in which the former political opposition was united in its aim to deplore the communist system of central planning, a harsh policy was a likely option. This has been referred to as a case of '*ex post*' political constraints (Roländ, 1994). Given the political fragmentation after the implementation of the stabilization package, the costs of returning became insuperable.

From Misery to Recovery

Following several weeks of political struggle, Hanna Suchocka of the UD became the new prime minister. Although she lacked political clout as well, since the government she presided over faced similar problems of fragmentation in parliament and continuing rivalry with President Wałęsa, she commanded far more confidence than her predecessor Olszewski. Western observers in particular showed approval, since she displayed her support for further tightening the budget. The start of the Suchocka government was encouraging. Despite the fact that it could only count on 189 of the 460 members of the Sejm, and therefore was continuously forced to find support and cooperation among non-coalition parties, it achieved important goals.[6] It amended the 1992 budget and managed to win parliamentary approval for the 1993 budget. The latter appeared to be extremely important, since it enabled Poland to receive a substantial amount of IMF credits, which until then were blocked because of the delays in further economic reform. Besides, public approval also slowly emerged, since, at the end of 1992, the Polish economy appeared to be recovering slightly. Poland was the first among the countries in transition to experience an increase in economic activity since the start of the transformation from a centrally planned to a market economy. As indicated in Table 5.1, GDP growth in 1992 was a modest 1 per cent.

Economic recovery at that time was not enough, though, to assert that Poland would immediately enter a period of political stability. On the contrary, despite elegantly manoeuvring in parliament after it took office, the Suchocka government faced many strikes. During winter 1992/93, the authorities were able to resist the social upheaval, but in May demonstrations reached a climax, induced the coalition's surrender and the organization of new parliamentary elections.

The campaigns in the 1993 election were entirely dominated by a single theme: the inordinately high costs of transformation. The election on 19 September 1993 brought victory to the parties most critical to the results of the transformation process. The SLD won almost two-thirds of the seats in both chambers and the ruling coalition was defeated. Waldemar Pawlak, the leader of the other winning party in the elections, became prime minister. Experts associated with the outgoing and earlier governments predicted that the accession to power of the ex-communists and former block voters would lead to a breakdown of financial discipline and, consequently, thwart economic recovery. But these fears did not materialize. On the contrary, the basic reform process remained more or less on course, while the country's macroeconomic performance in 1994 and after was definitely encouraging. Moreover, the SLD–PSL coalition appeared to cope quite easily with social unrest and the resignation of the Pawlak government in February 1995 was not so much due to social unrest or to friction within the coalition, but to a very large extent resulted from conflicts with President Wałęsa. Confronted with a drastic drop in popularity and a presidential election planned for the end of 1995, Wałęsa tried to destabilize politics in an attempt to come forward as the man to count on. Among other things, the President refused to sign the 1995 budget, even though the proposals had been passed by two-thirds majorities in both chambers.

After Pawlak's withdrawal, the coalition remained unaltered, even though the former communist Jozef Oleksy of the SLD became prime minister.[7] But when looking at the year 1995, of course, that was not the most eye-catching political event in Poland. In two rounds of polling, Wałęsa lost the presidential elections in November 1995 and the SLD leader and former nomenklatura career man of the PZPR, Aleksander Kwaśniewski, became Wałęsa's successor. Yet again, despite these important political changes in favour of former communists, macro-economic policy was by and large maintained according to the path paved at the beginning of 1990.

Given the fact that the Polish economy was the first among those of the countries in transition which showed clear signs of recovery, the question of the necessity of the costs of transformation slowly evaporated and was replaced by that of whether the liberally inspired governments of Mazowiecki, Bielecki and Suchocka were to be credited with this success or whether the recovery was due to more moderate strands in the recent coalition in which the SLD plays a dominant role. The answer, of course, is ambiguous. The economic conditions in 1989 demanded restrictive monetary and fiscal policy. But the preceding analysis has also shown that the recent governments never relaxed the harshness of economic policy to the extent promised. So, the claim that SLD-dominated coalitions are just reaping the fruits of former coalitions, especially those which carried out the Balcerowicz reforms, seems unjustified. As is often the case, the truth lies somewhere in between.

The Polish way of economic stabilization seems to fit perfectly in the above-mentioned perception of '*ex post*' political constraints on transformation strategies. Quite soon after the implementation of the 'cold turkey policy' by Balcerowicz and his collaborators, there was no return. An exception may have been the moment at which the Mazowiecki government decided to withdraw, within a year of the implementation of the stabilization package. But in December 1990, President Wałęsa blocked the formation of a government presided over by Olszewski, which would have been strongly against the Balcerowicz type of further stabilization. In that respect, the liberal Bielecki government, which succeeded the Mazowiecki government instead, might have been the necessary force to make costs of return indeed insuperable, *i.e.* passing the point of 'no return'. Or as Brown put it, 'He [Jan Krysztof Bielecki] gave Poland several crucial months more of economic reform than it might otherwise have received' and 'is the unsung hero' (Brown, 1994, p. 75).

This argument strongly hinges on the fact that the Polish population was initially willing to accept large costs of transformation, since the post-communist governments could to a large extent blame the former regimes for these. The costs of transformation were perceived as due to the legacy of the past.

These considerations regarding the nature of political constraints leave unanswered the question of the necessity of the social costs of transformation. Even ignoring political constraints, the authors maintaining that these have indeed been too high seem to have a good case. However, estimations regarding the nature and the severity of the political constraints are extremely difficult if not impossible to make, leaving the question of the inevitability of the deep and long-lasting crisis basically unanswered. Moreover, many authors claim that part of the output decline was only administrative, since in a supply-constrained economy non-existent output was registered, whereas in a demand-constrained economy there is a systemic, fiscally driven underestimation of total production (see Winiecki, 1993). What is absolutely clear, though, is that, irrespective of any real economic decline and subsequent convalescence, the transition crisis was far more severe than expected and it also lasted longer than envisaged. The general idea behind the 'Balcerowicz Plan' was to reach welfare levels of 1989 – measured by GDP per capita – within two years. In actual fact, it appeared that the first half-decade following the victory over communism had to be celebrated with a cumulative 15 per cent loss in GDP.

POLITICAL INSTABILITY HAMPERING MICRO-ECONOMIC REFORM

As already pointed out in the foregoing survey, Poland's transformation can be characterized by its profound pattern of sequencing: harsh and immediate stabilization and liberalization followed by phased microeconomic restructuring and institutional reform (see Falk and Funke, 1993). Since the parliamentary positions shifted enormously within a period of two years after the introduction of the 'Balcerowicz Plan', the second stage of the transformation became vulnerable to the changed political scene. This section examines the interplay between the political conditions and the microeconomic reforms in Poland after stabilization and liberalization had basically been set. As in the preceding chapters on Hungary and the Czech and Slovak Republics, microeconomic reform will be split into privatization and restructuring on the one hand and institution building on the other.

Privatization and Restructuring

Whatever the final judgement of Polish stabilization may be, privatization appeared to be a far more problematic and complex aspect of transformation and so far has made only moderate progress. It was hampered by the fragmentation of political forces in parliament, but there were other factors involved as well. Due to the comprehensive power of workers' councils, which had far-reaching managerial rights and for which privatization did not always serve their interests, important obstacles to privatization very soon emerged after the Mazowiecki government took office. Solidarity's influence as the Polish legacy of the 1980s worked against the aim of quick privatization (see Berend, 1996, p. 329). To put it differently, despite its indisputably positive role regarding Poland's political transformation, Solidarity was above all a trade union, and consequently self-management rather than the capitalist principle of private ownership dominated its political agenda. Whether the post-communist governments were pleased or not, they were all forced to design privatization schemes in such a way that the ownership transfers would not damage workers' interests too much. This consideration to a large extent meant that privatization was initially to be carried out on a voluntary basis.

Another partly related problem was the fact that, at a very moderate pace, privatization had already begun before the political transformation (see Ciechocińska, 1992). In sharp contrast to the situation in Czechoslovakia, but similar to Hungary's practice of spontaneous privatization in the late 1980s, the transfer of ownership from the state to the public had started on the basis of communist legislation. In Poland, it was not referred to as 'spontaneous privatization', which was believed to be too polite a term of Hungarian origin. The appropriate phrase to be applied was 'nomenklatura privatization' (Gomułka and Jasiński, 1994, p. 221). Irrespective of the chosen typology, the practice of this kind of privatization was above all to be kept under control in order not to destroy popular support for economic reform. As was the case in Hungary, it was an attempt to monitor, not to forbid, since on the basis of legislation of 1981 on the independence of state-owned enterprises, companies had the legal right to initiate privatization by 'corporatizing' the state-owned enterprise, that is, transferring it into a joint stock company. As the Privatization Act also arranged the position of workers' councils, the Solidarity-led coalition did not see a feasible option in outlawing the practice. The problem the new policy makers faced was to maintain control over the path of privatization. The forced sequence of limited decentralization of economic decision making preceding the transfer of ownership was an undesired legacy of reformist activities under communism and had to be taken care of. The solution was looked for in temporary centralization of ownership rights at the intermediate level (see Jasiński, 1990 and 1992; Jermakowicz, 1992), a step which at the dawn of the democratic regime in Czechoslovakia was not required as ownership rights were already centralized.

Quite soon after it took office, the Mazowiecki government presented privatization proposals for parliamentary approval. The basic idea of these was to convert all state-owned enterprises into joint stock companies and to create intermediary bodies which were to handle the transfer of the shares to the public. These bodies were to be subordinate to a Ministry of Privatization and were to hold the ownership rights. Whatever the exact obligations to and responsibilities of the intermediaries, the idea was to privatize these intermediate legal bodies, either by selling or by distributing shares free of charge. This was a political matter still under dispute at that time (see Gomułka and Jasiński, 1994).

The Mazowiecki government faced gigantic difficulties in setting up these intermediary bodies; it was not even certain whether it had the capacity to transfer all ownership rights into one state body, for example a Ministry of Privatization. Bearing in mind the above-mentioned path-dependent institutional barriers to privatization, the government decided first to design a frame of reference for privatization and to postpone decisions with regard to the specific methods to be applied. After lengthy political debate, the implementation of a Privatization Law in July 1990 and the creation of a Ministry of Privatization in September 1990 were the first formal steps to prepare this frame of reference for transferring ownership from the state to the public (see Frydman *et al.*, 1993).[8] The role of the Ministry of Privatization was perceived as one based on approval of enterprises' privatization plans rather than on the selection of enterprises for privatization. Furthermore, the ministry had to advise on problems related to the conversion of enterprises into joint stock companies, that is the 'pre-privatization', such as valuation of assets, decisions on definite legal status, and arrangements regarding financial obligations towards creditors, and so forth.

The agreement on the Act on Privatization and the implementation of the Ministry of Privatization facilitated the evolution of a multi-track privatization scheme. The basic principles of the scheme were that privatization should be voluntary and that intermediate bodies in whatever form were to be established for effective corporate governance. Basically four methods have been applied. Firstly, as elsewhere in Central and Eastern Europe, there has been so-called 'small privatization'. This started even before the Privatization Law was passed, but was speeded up afterwards (see Ciechocińska, 1992; Gomułka and Jasiński, 1994). The local authorities have been the pivotal intermediary in this respect. Following the implementation of local self-administration in the autumn of 1990, municipal authorities received the ownership rights. By the end of 1992, approximately 90 per cent of retail businesses and other small-sized companies were privatized.

Secondly, a programme of capital privatization has been designed for medium-sized and large companies. This programme very much resembles the Hungarian approach of ownership transfers by first converting a state-owned enterprise into a joint stock company and then selling the shares. The conversion implied that the state initially received ownership rights and became the single shareholder. In this respect, the Ministry of Privatization was the principal intermediary which had to sell the shares, although the initiative for 'corporatization' belonged to the enterprises involved. The Act on Privatization required that 20 per cent of the shares had to be reserved for employees at substantially reduced prices. This method of privatization was based upon experiences with privatization in the West and was perceived as a promising method for large and viable firms, but it appeared to be a highly problematic approach. A lack of domestic capital, to a large extent a result of high inflation in the years following the 'Balcerowicz Plan', and problems with the appropriate valuation of shares in the absence of fully-fledged capital markets, hindered this method of privatization. At the end of 1993, not even a hundred enterprises were converted into joint stock companies and subsequently sold (Gomułka and Jasiński, 1994, p. 231). In fact, the failure underpins the claim of those economists who identified the weakness in the particular sequence of harsh stabilization and gradual institutional reform (Brainard, 1991).

Thirdly, liquidation has evolved as an attractive and important method of privatizing state companies. More than in any of the other countries under scrutiny in this study, privatization by liquidation has been very appealing in Poland. Liquidation could be effected in two ways (Frydman *et al.*, 1993). Either it was applied in accordance with article 37 of the Privatization Act of 1990, or it was based upon article 19 of the above-mentioned Law regarding the Independence of State-Owned Companies. The latter provided for transfer of the ownership rights of non-viable enterprises and in no way suited the framework initiated by the Mazowiecki government. This Act – already introduced in 1981 – which specified circumstances under which an enterprise could be declared bankrupt, was ineffective during the remainder of the 1980s, but offered a suitable framework after the political change-over and the introduction of a market environment. In fact, during the first five years of Poland's economic transformation, it was the basis for the lion's share of privatization (see OECD, 1994(d)). Since it was applied without special use of the privatization framework settled in 1990, intermediate bodies were more or less passed by.

Liquidation according to Article 37 of the Privatization Act did not imply bankruptcy, but made it possible to dissolve companies which were solvent, but were expected to become more competitive after the liquidation, reorganization and privatization of certain divisions. The liquidation needed final approval of the Ministry of Privatization in order to ensure that liabilities towards creditors were adequately taken care of. The management and/or employee buy-out has been the most popular form of liquidation under Article 37. In these circumstances, however, the management and/or employees most of the time leased from the intermediate body and, therefore, it remains problematic to identify the procedure as real transfer of ownership. Although an attractive method, privatization by liquidation also undermined the position of the intermediary and therefore ran counter to the initial ideas of the Mazowiecki government. It has been suggested, for example, that the monitoring was better than with 'nomenklatura privatization', but it still remained a symptom of decentralized methods of privatization and its consequent drawbacks (Frydman *et al.*, 1993).

Fourthly, several programmes for mass privatization have been designed. Initiatives in the field were taken to speed up the whole process and covered some 600 large enterprises responsible for roughly one quarter of industrial output. The plans for mass privatization were to resemble the Czech approach, but they appeared to be highly sensitive political issues. The first proposal was presented in spring 1990. Afterwards, nearly all subsequent governments tried to find parliamentary approval for mass privatization.

The basic idea of the plans presented in spring 1990 was to create approximately twenty competing investment funds. These intermediate bodies would receive the majority of shares of the 'corporatized' state-owned enterprises. Subsequently, adult Polish citizens were to be allowed to buy fund shares for a small fee which would only cover the administrative costs of the mass privatization. The shares not to be transferred to the investment fund were partly to remain in state hands and partly to be distributed among the employees of the relevant enterprise.

Advocates of this type of privatization claimed that it would be a quick procedure, not demanding huge amounts of domestic capital, and, above all, could induce simultaneously the development of capital markets. Since the method of privatization aroused great controversy, advocates of mass privatization through the creation investment funds were especially wrong about the speed. It took several years for the programme of mass privatization to be passed by the Sejm. After lengthy discussions in parliament, subsequent rejections, compromises, and stripping of initial proposals, the Suchocka government ultimately received parliamentary approval in April 1993 and the programme was planned to start from 1994, but actually commenced in July 1995.[9] None the less, problems remained. The prominent conflict touches upon the tension between the government-appointed supervisory boards and the private fund managers. (European Bank for Reconstruction and Development, 1996(a)).

Considering the whole process of Polish privatization, it has to be concluded that it suffers from awkwardness, even under the left-of-centre government. Political fragmentation following the initial shock approach almost impeded the implementation of sound privatization practices and to a certain extent necessitated a 'hands-off approach' as the only feasible option with regard to pivotal microeconomic aspects of the transformation from a centrally planned to a market economy.

So far, liquidation has proven to be the most important instrument, although its relevance has been declining since 1995. As a consequence, the ideas on intermediate bodies for corporate governance have largely been circumvented. As was the case in Hungary, the legacy of limited decentralization in economic decision making before the collapse of the communist system thwarted the process of privatization. On top of that, the typical Polish inheritance of workers' councils delayed and complicated privatization as well. The fact that privatization by liquidation was most successful before 1995 illustrates an interesting phenomenon regarding the sequence of transfer of ownership and restructuring. The method of liquidation implies that restructuring precedes transfer of ownership rights. This marks a sharp contrast with voucher privatization in the Czech Republic, which is based upon the idea of restructuring by the market following the privatization. But it also differs from the dominant Hungarian practice of capital privatization, a method which is an example of an attempt at simultaneously transferring ownership and restructuring the enterprise.

Institutional Reform

The transfer of ownership from the state to the public is not an aim in itself. The ultimate goal is an improvement in allocative and productive efficiency as a consequence of restructuring the enterprise, irrespective of whether this restructuring precedes, coincides with or follows privatization. In this respect, it is at least remarkable that, whereas in Western experience corporate governance has always dominated the decision regarding the method of privatization, this has not been the case to such an extent in Central and Eastern Europe. Microeconomic adjustment in the transformation to a market economy, however, presumes changing enterprise behaviour. In the remainder of this section on microeconomic restructuring, therefore, those institutional reforms which are intended to compel the behavioural change will be addressed. Recent literature on economic transformation in Central and Eastern Europe has indicated numerous examples of 'perverse' behaviour on the part of enterprises, indicating that it differed from the 'normal' response of autonomous profit-maximizing economic agents in a competitive market environment (see for example Belka, 1994; Stiglitz, 1992; Takla, 1994). The aspects which will be focused on here are the hardening of budget constraints, the establishment of fair competition, and the removal of impediments in factor markets.

The creation of a competitive environment was an integral part of the 'Balcerowicz Plan'. State subsidies were heavily cut and the percentage of financial transfers from the state treasury to enterprises declined from 7 per cent at the start of the transformation to roughly 2 per cent of Polish GDP in 1993 and despite political shifts to the left since then the percentage remained relatively stable (see World Bank, 1994(b); European Bank for Reconstruction and Development, 1996(a)). The reduction in enterprise subsidies contributed substantially to the hardening of budget constraints. Not really as an attempt to harden the budget constraint, but nevertheless making the constraint effective, anti-monopoly legislation was introduced in February 1990 by the Mazowiecki government and an Anti-Monopoly Office was operative from April the same year. This institution had broad powers to intervene (see Fornalczyk, 1993).

Though many problems have emerged in the process of privatization, there seems to be broad consensus with regard to the impact of these reforms on the restructuring of the economy (see Berg, 1994; World Bank, 1994(b); OECD, 1994(d)). Within five years of the introduction of the 'Balcerowicz Plan', five million jobs were eliminated in the state sector, while nearly 80 per cent of the jobless managed to enter the private sector, not just because of privatization but also and mainly from the establishment of newly emerging enterprises (see Angresano, 1996, p. 93). Furthermore, it has been pointed out that there was a substantial improvement in profit margins. This was the case in the private as well as in the state sector. Profits are generally perceived as a meaningful criterion for enterprise efficiency. Of course, this only makes sense under the assumption that profits are realized in the market and do not result from effective bargaining on subsidies, soft credits and so forth. If the latter prevails, budget constraints have not really hardened or were ineffective (see Kornai, 1986). The question is whether there were indeed impediments to ensuring that enterprises were completely dependent upon their performance in the market. If not, the imperfections were most likely to have occurred in factor markets, namely the financial and labour markets.

It has already been shown in the preceding two chapters that the design of a financial market has a profound impact on microeconomic adjustment. Financial institutions, especially banks, play a pivotal role in that respect. As was the case in Hungary, a two-tier banking system was developed shortly before the first post-communist government took office. It was the Banking Law in combination with the Act on the National Bank of Poland, both initiated and implemented by the Rakowski government in 1989, which started the creation of independent commercial banks (World Bank, 1994(a)). The increase in the number of private commercial banks licensed in 1991 and 1992 was enormous. Immediately after the introduction of the two-tier system, nine large commercial banks started business. In addition, the specialized state-owned banks were still operative, but were gradually developing into modern general banks. At the end of 1992, there were more than a hundred commercial banks in operation. However, since there were financial problems arising with newly created banks, the issuing of licences was restrained and consolidation of small and vulnerable banks was stimulated by the National Bank of Poland (OECD, 1994(d), pp. 117ff).

As is well known, one of the major issues impeding microeconomic adjustment is the problem of non-performing loans. As in the other transition countries examined in this study, the portfolio of the banking system deteriorated. Most of the customs were large state-owned enterprises which lost creditworthiness after the start of the transformation. The banks did not react immediately, or were not able to do so, and continued lending to insolvent firms. This attitude undermined the financial basis of the banks, already burdened with a bad legacy of non-performing loans from the past (Stiglitz, 1992). The emerging financial crisis impeded the development of the private sector, which was suffering above all from high interest rates as a result of the harsh monetary policy. There was a mechanism of 'crowding out'.

It was the Suchocka government which was able to turn the tide. In March 1993, the Sejm passed the coalition's 'Enterprise and Bank Restructuring Programme' (see World Bank, 1994(a), pp. 76ff). The idea the programme embodied was to lift the financial burdens from those state-owned enterprises which were able to present a convincing plan for viable restructuring by granting easier credits and debt-servicing terms. The treasury-owned commercial banks were delegated the tasks of selecting and monitoring the projects. The programme also arranged the legal basis for trade in badly performing loans and their conversion into equity of the indebted company.

The measures proved rather successful. A catastrophic financial crisis was averted and the general consensus is that Poland's financial system has moved away from the monopolistic structure in which specialized state-owned banks, in a subordinate position *vis-à-vis* the Central Bank, controlled most of the enterprise sector (OECD, 1994(d)). Despite this general feeling of approval, many problems remained and demanded further policy adjustment. The spread in lending between the prime rate and the one paid for short-term deposits remained fairly large, indicating still a lack of competition. Moreover, despite the legislation on enterprise and bank restructuring, new bad loans have been supplied, thereby further threatening the solvency of the banks involved. The basic policy response of the centre–left coalitions since the elections of 1993 has been to move forward in the consolidation of banks. To this end, several Acts have been passed by parliament (see World Economic Research Institute, 1995).

Besides further stimulating the development of a better-performing banking sector, the Polish authorities also tried to stimulate the establishment of other financial markets. For example, in April 1991, the Warsaw Stock Exchange was opened, and it has experienced a remarkable growth. The Warsaw Stock Exchange held only a few trading sessions per week with only nine quoted stocks at the end of 1991, but from October 1994, daily sessions were launched and the stock market is currently operating with more than fifty quoted stocks (*PlanEcon Report*, 1996, No. 37–38).

Similar to the effect of ill-functioning financial markets on micro-economic adjustment, distortions in labour markets may also impede the process of economic restructuring. Hence, the implementation of institutional reforms in this realm is consequential as well. As was illustrated in the section on macroeconomic stabilization, labour market policy as part of the 'Balcerowicz Plan' was basically aimed at the enforcement of wage restraints. An excess-wage tax ('popiwek') was effective from the start of the economic transformation and induced a substantial decline in real wages. In due course, the progressive tax rate for the upper boundaries regarding the nominal wage rise was reduced and, from January 1995, the 'popiwek' was abolished. The SLD–PSL coalition headed by Prime Minister Pawlak introduced a system of collective bargaining. This system very much resembled the Czech experience with tripartite negotiations between government, employers and trade unions.

The system of collective bargaining met enormous criticism on the part of liberally inspired economists. Their main problem was that the outcome of the tripartite negotiations on wages was a target for the entire corporate sector. All enterprises employing more than fifty employees, state-owned as well as private enterprises, were to meet these targets. On the other hand, very well-performing enterprises were bound to limit wage increases below the extent to which productivity gains under market conditions would allow for and hence would impede further improvement in productivity. On the other hand, and this was perceived as the most dangerous aspect of the collective-bargaining procedure, employees of badly performing firms would receive more than the appropriate rate (see World Economic Research Institute, 1995).

The impact of the new procedures is not entirely clear yet. Given the fact that they were implemented five years after the harsh monetary stabilization programme, they were unable to fulfil the function they had in the Czech Republic, where the tripartite consultation to a very large extent served to win the support of trade unions for temporary hardship.[10] Moreover, the political support of the Czech workers also stemmed from the fact that an active labour market policy was to be applied in order to keep unemployment within acceptable margins. As became clear from Table 5.1, despite a current modest decline, unemployment in Poland seems to have surpassed these reasonable margins and it is highly questionable whether the agreed 'matching' of demand and supply of labour will suffice to reach socially acceptable levels within a few years. In comparison to the policy applied in the Czech Republic, it is much cheaper and requires less engagement of the persons involved.

Considering the microeconomic adjustment in Poland, it has to be concluded that the term 'shock' certainly does not apply. Most striking is the cumbersome introduction of the mass privatization programme. The plans were presented in 1991. They were finally accepted in 1993, but the implementation began only in summer 1995. The alleviation of impediments in factor markets was not an example of shock-like treatment, but for quite a long time could better be characterized as a 'hands-off approach'. It was the price to be paid for the sequence of harsh macro-economic stabilization and subsequent microeconomic reforms. The stabilization was based upon the conviction of 'no return', but given the fact that other reforms were yet to follow, these were extremely difficult to design and to implement, and hard to monitor. The consequent political fragmentation of the former Solidarity opposition, which until the establishment of the Mazowiecki government was united by the common goal to reject communism, was the main impediment to reform. On top of that, relative to the other countries in Central Europe, Poland faced the legacy of farreaching managerial rights of the workforce, which hampered microeconomic adjustment as well. All in all, despite several claims of politicians and scientists, there seems to be no evidence that microeconomic restructuring was quicker and more thorough than in Hungary and the Czech and Slovak Republics.

EXTERNAL RELATIONS TRANSMITTING STABILIZATION AND LIBERALIZATION

As in other Central and Eastern European countries during the period of communism, Poland's organization of foreign trade was characterized by a state monopoly (see Matejka, 1986). The first attempts at genuine reform in foreign trade were made in 1982 under Prime Minister Jaruzelski. He faced Gierek's legacy of import-led growth and implemented organizational reform which to a large extent resembled that in Hungary. The basic idea was to terminate the principle of one specialized FTO being responsible for the import and export of one particular commodity, and to convert part of them into joint stock companies which could operate in all different kind of commodities. In addition to that, trade licences were issued to producing enterprises, implying that the FTOs lost their position as monopolist (see Biessen, 1996). There were reforms in the monetary realm as well. Most importantly, the exchange rate became unified (see Slay, 1994(b), p. 145) and limited retention rights on export earnings were given to enterprises involved in foreign trade. The hard currency earnings could either be used for import purposes or be sold at special foreign exchange auctions, which were set up in 1983.

These reforms were implemented to eliminate the state monopoly on foreign trade, but did not meet the target. The number of licences issued by the Ministry of Foreign Trade was rather moderate, while competition among FTOs remained negligible. Consequently, the state monopoly on foreign trade was not abolished. However, the abolition still took place before the political change-over. In December 1988, the Rakowski government decreed a law on entrepreneurship. It specified that all Polish enterprises, be they state or privately owned, were free to conduct foreign trade without a special foreign trade licence (see Rosati, 1991). An exception was made for those firms which traded strategic commodities. Despite the decentralization in decision making, the Act on Entrepreneurship did not fully liberalize foreign trade activities, since restrictions remained on obtaining hard currencies necessary to finance imports.

With the inauguration of the Mazowiecki government, the remnants of the practice of state monopoly power in foreign trade were abolished as part of the 'Balcerowicz Plan'. From January 1990, there was an almost complete liberalization of foreign trade, most tariff and non-tariff barriers were suspended or sharply reduced, and the convertibility of the złoty was introduced for current-account transactions (Lipton and Sachs, 1990). In the foregoing, it has already been shown that the start of the economic transformation in Poland was the simultaneous introduction of stabilization and liberalization. In the remainder of this section, both the foreign trade liberalization and the exchange rate regime will be addressed in order to illustrate that foreign trade reforms fitted in this joint treatment.

International experience of foreign trade liberalization shows that liberalization is immediately followed by or, preferably, coincides with the conversion of quantitative restrictions into tariffs which initially should ensure the same degree of domestic protection and prevent a too severe deterioration in the balance of payments (see McKinnon, 1991). In Poland, this was not the case. The abolition of quantitative restrictions through the establishment of a system which judicially guaranteed all companies the right to conduct foreign trade was replaced by temporary customs duties to the extent of securing the same level of domestic protection. On the contrary, the average level of tariff protection after the introduction of the 'Balcerowicz Plan' was only 10.9 per cent and declined to 5.5 per cent in mid-1991. High duties were only levied on luxury and durable consumption goods. In comparison to what happened in Czechoslovakia and especially Hungary in the period immediately following the start of the transformation, customs duties were rather low.

Despite a rather low level of average tariffs, the trade balance did not prove vulnerable to this, but improved instead. This was mainly due to the extraordinarily sharp devaluation of the national currency as part of the stabilization package. The currency was devalued from 6,500 złoty per US dollar at the end of 1989 to 9,500 złoty per US dollar at the start of 1990. As already indicated in the section on macroeconomic stabilization, the złoty subsequently became nominally anchored to the US dollar. However, because the initial devaluation was so harsh and probably far beyond the point of equilibrium, unexpectedly high Polish trade surpluses emerged. Imports were excessively expensive and the transition crisis impeded large investments and subsequent imports. In the first year and a half following the introduction of the 'Balcerowicz Plan', there was no need for further protection by means of higher customs duties.

Considering other elements of the exchange rate regime, the Polish authorities, more than those of the other countries under scrutiny, decided to make convertibility one of the main instruments of the stabilization package. Whereas in Western developed economies, currency convertibility was predominantly considered a positive side-effect of economic reform and development, the Mazowiecki government perceived it as an instrument to enforce the transformation to a market economy, necessary to augment the credibility of the reform programme, lower inflationary expectations and restore confidence in the national currency (Edwards, 1992; Rosati, 1991).[11] To support the convertibility of the złoty, the Western governments cooperating and consulting within the so-called 'Group of 24', established a special stabilization fund to ensure the required amount of international reserves during the first period of the transformation. The currency convertibility also implied the demise of the system of retention rights on export earnings established in 1982.

As already indicated, after the extraordinary devaluation of the złoty, the currency became nominally anchored to the US dollar. Due to unexpectedly high Polish trade surpluses – a partial result of 'overshooting' – the authorities were able to maintain the fix for one and a half years without having to rely upon the stabilization fund of the 'Group of 24' (World Economic Research Institute, 1995). However, in due course, real appreciation of the złoty endangered Poland's competitiveness on international markets as domestic inflation was much higher than in the countries with which Poland conducted most of its trade (see Oblath, 1994). Therefore, the Polish authorities reimposed tariffs at the end of 1991, returning the average customs duties to the pre-reform levels. Besides, similar to what happened in the Czech Republic, Hungary and Slovakia, special import surcharges were imposed. Poland introduced these in 1993 and removed them within a period of three years.

Besides relying on tariff protection, the Polish authorities were also forced to devalue the currency several times and to shift to another exchange rate regime. The first devaluation since the introduction of the 'Balcerowicz Plan' was in May 1991. The złoty was officially lowered by 17 per cent. Moreover, from that time, the currency was no longer solely fixed against the US dollar, but to a basket of foreign exchange, namely the US dollar (45 per cent), German Mark (35 per cent), pound sterling (10 per cent) and French and Swiss Franc (each 5 per cent). Fixing against this currency basket was perceived more stable and was to show Poland's intensifying trade relations with Western Europe.

In October 1991, the monetary authorities abandoned the nominal anchor and introduced a 'crawling peg' with a monthly 1.8 per cent devaluation against the currency basket mentioned above. The percentage monthly devaluation was reduced in August 1993, when the National Bank of Poland reduced it to 1.6 per cent. Since then, the policy has been further relaxed, although there were still a few discrete devaluations of the Polish currency (see Krzak, 1995; Stolze, 1996). The current foreign exchange system allows the złoty to fluctuate within a certain range against the above-mentioned currency basket and the centre of the range is daily adjusted to a level which induces a cumulative monthly devaluation of 1 per cent (European Bank for Reconstruction and Development, 1996(a)). Regarding full current account convertibility, implying free conversion for Polish as well as foreign economic agents, Poland accepted the IMF obligations in June 1995.

To conclude our discussion of Polish foreign trade reforms since the transformation, it should be remarked that Poland has become a very open economy. The country has fully aligned with the structures of eminent international organizations for trade and finance, such as the WTO and the IMF. The monopoly on foreign trade, which under central planning in practice operated as a system of implicit quantitative restrictions, was completely abolished within a very short time. The new foreign trade regime protects domestic producers only by tariffs, even in the field of agriculture, and allows all economic actors to conduct foreign trade. More than anywhere else in Central and Eastern Europe, foreign trade reforms have been used in Poland to link stabilization and liberalization.

CONCLUSION

In current literature on economic transformation in Central and Eastern Europe, Poland is always referred to as a textbook example of shock treatment. The economist Jeffrey Sachs, as a distinguished advocate of such a policy, personally advised the Polish authorities. The first post-communist government in Poland, presided over by Tadeusz Mazowiecki, inaugurated the shock therapy for a quick implementation of a fully-fledged market on January 1990 with the introduction of the 'Balcerowicz Plan'. The plan was named after the Minister of Finance, a Harvard economist and close collaborator of Jeffrey Sachs. As expected, the plan initiated a decline in economic activity. It was not anticipated, though, that the transition crisis would be so severe and that it would last for such a long time. Despite the fact that economic recovery in the region of Central Europe started in Poland and was displayed most strongly in that country, statistics reveal that, in 1997, the nation's welfare had not yet reached its 1989 level measured in GDP per capita.

Given Poland's recent economic history characterized by cyclical patterns of economic crisis followed by half-hearted and inadequate reform, a radical platform emerged at the start of the transformation. Unlike the Antall–Boross government in Hungary, the Mazowiecki government inherited a large degree of freedom regarding the transformation strategy. In that case, '*ex post*' political constraints apply and the task is to make use of the situation of extraordinary politics, that is, devising a plan which creates insuperable costs of return.

In passing the point of no return, Poland was successful. In terms of economic transformation policy, a radical and sustainable course is believed to have been established. Yet, in the political realm, developments have been far from stable. In the autumn of 1993, in fact, in the first entirely free parliamentary elections since the demise of communism, social democratic political forces – for the most part consisting of former communists – were victorious. Solidarity fell apart and the mass movement, whose legitimacy was based upon the single fact that communists had been forced to resign, became fragmented. Politics and economics being closely interrelated, the latter development had an undisputable impact on further economic reform. It influenced those reforms which inevitably took more time than macroeconomic stabilization.

When considering, for example, the transfer of ownership rights from the state to the public, an almost endless debate began. It took until 1995 before mass privatization commenced. It has to be added, though, that the constitutional rights of the President to veto parliamentary proposals further complicated the already difficult task of winning parliamentary approval for privatization. The choice of shock treatment in macroeconomic stabilization generated a sequence in transformation, and, given the fact that political instability followed stabilization, the desired solution of 'no return' coincided with the problem of how to proceed. This political void did not justify the description of genuine shock treatment, but rather suggested a 'hands-off approach' to be more appropriate in the field of privatization and restructuring.

This is not to say that nothing happened. On the contrary, partly based upon legislation implemented in the 1980s and partly as a result of private initiatives without official guidelines, the Polish economic restructuring proceeded. As far as the influence of the 1980s is concerned, the original strands of Solidarity can still be perceived. Concerning privatization, for example, in none of the countries in the region of Central Europe are the workers' interests so well preserved as in Poland. It is another question whether this is most desirable when considering the completion of the transformation to a fully-fledged market economy.

NOTES

1. The investment cycle was a systemic phenomenon in centrally planned economies. Taut planning persistently forced up the volume of investment at the start of a new Five Year Plan period and created the upward phase of the cycle. The tautness of planning, however, was attended by a deteriorating external position *vis-à-vis* the West, which after

a certain period automatically necessitated a deceleration of investment growth. Ultimately, new investment projects had to be cancelled and only the projects in progress were completed, if at all. In its turn, this downward phase was terminated by the launching of a new Five Year Plan, which formed the start of a new investment cycle (see Bauer, 1978).

2. In the 1970s, Western financiers appeared to be very willing to provide loans to Poland. Apart from the fact that a strong discipline was expected from a country with central economic and financial planning and a foreign trade monopoly of the state, bankers were convinced that if an Eastern European country were unable to meet its payments obligations, the Soviet Union would be expected to give financial support. This expectation rested upon the so-called 'umbrella theory'.

3. There were also elections for a newly installed senate with 100 seats. These seats were entirely freely contested and all but one were won by Solidarity (see Juchler, 1994).

4. Other tax reforms, such as the introduction of personal income tax and implementation of a value-added tax, followed in 1992 and 1993, respectively (European Bank for Reconstruction and Development, 1996(a)).

5. It may be useful to compare the crawling peg applied in Hungary and elaborated in Chapter 4.

6. Suchocka's minority coalition included the Democratic Union (UD), the Polish Peasant Party (PSL), two Christian parties, a party with its roots in Solidarity and closely affiliated with UD (Polish Convention), and a party supporting the interests of the German minority.

7. After being accused of collaboration with Russian intelligence units, Prime Minister Oleksy was forced to resign at the beginning of 1996. Włodzimierz Cimoszewicz, also a member of the SLD, was his successor.

8. In Poland, the ministry is referred to as the Ministry of Property Transformation.

9. An important difference with the initial proposals was the decline in the number of relevant enterprises. Of the initially 600 nominated enterprises, a mere 200 remained. For these enterprises, the aspect of voluntariness had been repealed. Another difference with regard to earlier proposals was that the number of investment funds declined from twenty to fifteen.

10. At the beginning of the transformation, Hungary held tripartite negotiations as well. It had even earlier implemented them. But as clarified in Chapter 4, these implied the start of substantial wage liberalization, whereas in the Czech Republic tripartite consultation did not. It was an instrument to restrain wage increases.

11. Experiences in Western Europe show, for example, that the establishment of current account convertibility took most countries ten to fifteen years after the end of the Second World War.

6. The External Economic Performance of Central Europe: Competitiveness on the EU Market

INTRODUCTION

The economic reforms of the formerly centrally planned economies in Central Europe, as outlined in the preceding chapters, all impinged on the idea of mutual interdependence of transformation and integration. Increasing participation in the international division of labour dominated the political agenda from 1990, and in Hungary and Poland it was even proclaimed official policy long before the demise of communism. The question is to what extent the countries under consideration have been able to increase their external economic performance and whether there emerge noticeable differences among the Czech Republic, Hungary, Poland and Slovakia which can be ascribed to the distinctive measures in speed and sequence of reforms.

This chapter scrutinizes the performance of the countries' exports to the EU. The aim is to indicate competitiveness and to link the changing performance to the organizational reforms. For several reasons, this is highly problematic. A one-to-one relationship is impossible to describe, let alone, to identify causality. For example, when considering the development of exports to the EU, the aspects of Central European countries' competitiveness and EU protectionism intertwine.

Despite numerous methodological problems, the development of the countries' market shares on the EU market will be observed by applying a decomposition analysis on export changes with regard to commodities and country of destination. Some of the methodological issues have been circumvented by the choice of the dataset. For the whole period 1985–95, market shares on the EU with its present fifteen members have been calculated. The entrance of Austria, Finland and Sweden in January 1995, should partly reveal the magnitude of EU protectionism. Furthermore, commodity groups have been specified in such a way as to enable us to view separately the development in the so-called 'sensitive sectors' in the Association Agreements.

The chapter's outline is as follows. The methodology, the data applied, and the results of the decomposition will be discussed in the following sections, after which an attempt will be made to link external economic performance and reform. The chapter starts with a brief survey of regional and commodity composition of the Czech Republic, Hungary, Poland and Slovakia. This will illustrate the enormous shift in trade from East to West and, regarding trade with the EU, from an emphasis on primary products to manufactures.

CENTRAL EUROPEAN COUNTRIES' FOREIGN TRADE STRUCTURE

The Shifts in Regional and Commodity Composition

Although structural change in production and trade is a continuous process in all countries, the transformation from a centrally planned to a market economy will induce far-reaching changes, correcting for the institutional bias, such as described in Chapter 2. This section will focus upon changes in the structure of foreign trade patterns of the Central European countries during the last decade, using 1985, 1990 and 1995 as benchmark years.[1]

In Table 6.1, the countries' general position in world trade is indicated by presenting both their share in total world exports and in exports to the fifteen EU countries. Regarding world exports in the second half of the 1980s, the table shows the shares to have been declining for all countries. Given the larger size of the Polish economy and the consequent higher shares of Polish exports, the trends for Hungary and Poland are more or less similar. The decline of Czechoslovakia's share in world exports is, however, remarkable. The differences are likely to be the result of Czechoslovakia's regional orientation before the demise of the communist system, although it could also be due to an overstatement of exports in the year 1985. Since the transformation, there has been a convalescent development in the share of the Central European countries in world exports. Nevertheless, the shares are not yet at the level they were during the mid-1980s. At the same time, the shares in exports to the EU have been increasing for all the countries under review.[2] Poland was the first and most profound in this respect. In the case of Czechoslovakia, market shares on the EU market in 1990 were still lower than in 1985, indicating that this country shifted trade from East to West after 1990, a process in which the country proved to be successful.

Table 6.1   *Percentage share of the Central European countries in world*
                exports and in exports to the EU, 1985–95

Exports to:	World				EU*		
	1985	1990	1995		1985	1990	1995
From:							
Czech Republic[†]	0.95	0.34	0.39		0.32	0.29	0.58
Hungary	0.40	0.28	0.31		0.29	0.31	0.48
Poland	0.54	0.39	0.47		0.50	0.54	0.88
Slovakia[†]	0.95	0.34	0.18		0.32	0.29	0.18

Notes: * For all years, EU refers to its current fifteen members.
            [†] For 1985 and 1990, figures refer to Czechoslovakia.
Sources: United Nations, *Commodity Trade Statistics*, various issues; OECD, *Trade by Commodities*, various issues; *PlanEcon Report*, various issues

Given the fact that mutual trade relations in Central and Eastern Europe have been declining dramatically in the early 1990s – and even before, as will be shown below – it can be concluded from Table 6.1 that these losses have not been completely compensated by the increase in exports to the EU. For none of the countries can a net gain in world market position over the period 1985–95 be observed. This also holds true for the Czech and Slovak Republics, whose combined market share in 1995 was far less than in 1985, before the split of the federation.

Regarding the regional foreign trade composition of the Central European countries, presented in Table 6.2, both the reorientation after 1989 and the possibility of a more gradual shift due to economic reforms in the preceding period have to be taken into account. Table 6.2 illustrates the relative importance of the CEFTA, the European Union and the Soviet Union as markets of destination for the Central European countries' exports. The CEFTA has been included for evaluating aspects of regional integration in Central Europe. Regarding the years 1985 and 1990, the CEFTA region and the Soviet Union absorbed the lion's share of the mutual trade relations of CMEA countries.

Table 6.2 clearly shows that the region of the former Soviet Union lost its dominant position as main trading partner, although it is important to realize that the abolition of the CMEA in 1991 was not decisive. In the period 1985–90, trade relations with the Soviet Union were already declining for both exports and imports of the countries under consideration. Taking the CEFTA and the Soviet Union as a proxy for CMEA trade, it is clear that the declining importance of this destination for the Central European countries' regional composition of foreign trade was part of a process under way at least since 1985.

Table 6.2   Regional foreign trade composition of the Central European countries, percentages in total exports and imports (in parentheses), 1985–95

	CEFTA		European Union*		Soviet Union†	
Czech Republic‡						
1985	12.4	(13.8)	9.1	(8.6)	43.7	(46.0)
1990	10.3	(12.0)	26.9	(24.0)	25.2	(21.6)
1995	22.8	(18.2)	45.9	(45.1)	5.7	(11.0)
Hungary						
1985	9.5	(9.7)	15.8	(21.2)	33.6	(30.0)
1990	5.8	(7.1)	32.2	(31.0)	20.2	(19.1)
1995	5.3	(6.2)	51.0	(45.4)	18.5	(22.5)
Poland						
1985	9.4	(9.0)	22.4	(20.1)	28.4	(34.4)
1990	4.8	(3.9)	47.2	(45.6)	14.5	(17.0)
1995	4.8	(4.2)	62.7	(67.7)	7.5	(7.9)
Slovakia‡						
1985	12.4	(13.8)	9.1	(8.6)	43.7	(46.0)
1990	10.3	(12.0)	26.9	(24.0)	25.2	(21.6)
1995	44.3	(33.6)	37.8	(34.4)	6.4	(19.4)

Notes: * Figures refer to the EU members in the respective years, that is EU-12 in 1985 and 1990, and EU-15 in 1995. Moreover, from 1991, the former GDR is included in the EU, and, therefore, affects data for 1995.

† The 1995 figure refers to the region of the former Soviet Union.

‡ For 1985 and 1990, figures refer to Czechoslovakia.

Sources: Handbook of Statistics; Countries in Transition 1995 (1995) and *PlanEcon*, various issues

Table 6.2 also reveals that the EU has become the most important partner. In percentages of total trade of all Central European countries, the share in trade with the EU is even higher than it was for the CMEA. This fact is not only an automatic result of declining importance of the CMEA – and in particular the Soviet Union – as trade partner, but to a very large extent reflects an absolute increase in trade relations with the EU.

Under the CMEA regime, trade among Czechoslovakia, Hungary and Poland had never been as extensive as their foreign trade relations with the Soviet Union. In the second half of the 1980s, it comprised approximately

10 per cent of each country's total exports and imports. But Table 6.2 also shows that after the collapse of CMEA, the share of mutual trade among the Central European countries nearly halved. Correcting for their mutual trade relations, this also holds true for the Czech Republic and Slovakia (see Fidrmuc *et al.*, 1994), but seems less severe than in the case of Poland and Hungary.

The declining importance of mutual trade relations in Central Europe raises the question of the desirability of restoring these trade flows. Recent literature shows that it is highly problematic to present an unambiguous answer, since it requires us to estimate 'normal' trade intensities under market conditions (see Richter and Tóth, 1993). Estimates based on gravity models mostly focused on potential East–West trade and tend to conclude that the intensity of intra-CMEA trade was far above what could have been expected under market conditions (see Brada, 1993 and Rosati, 1992). The basic argument applied to characterize declining trade relations in Central and Eastern Europe as a return to normalcy has been that large parts of intra-CMEA trade were politically motivated. Hence, there are no reasons for initiatives aiming at a restoration of these trade flows.

The conclusion of politically motivated mutual trade relations, and therefore integration, being pushed too far under communism only seems justified when taking trade relations with 'Moscow' into account. Taking the policy of forced industrialization under autarky as outlined in Chapter 2 into consideration, the conclusion of artificial and too intense integration is highly questionable when talking about mutual trade relations among the Central European countries. To the extent that there was specialization through the coordination of national plans, it was restricted to the level of agreements between sectors of production. Within sectors of production, specialization was merely non-existent. For example, within the context of CMEA cooperation, Czechoslovakia was responsible for the production of train units and locomotives, while production and assembly of coaches was a Hungarian responsibility. Deliveries of intermediates for the production of these capital goods by other CMEA members played an insignificant role. When comparing the process of economic integration of fully-fledged market economies, which makes it somewhat premature to speak, for example, of a 'German motor vehicle' – for many intermediates are not produced in Germany – integration in centrally planned economies cannot be qualified as refined. Subtlety was alien to economic cooperation among the people's republics in Central and Eastern Europe.

Economic integration being not particularly sophisticated among the Central European countries, it should not be concluded that structures of production are complementary to such an extent that there is no room left for further specialization within the CEFTA. On the contrary, it suggests that specialization is likely to occur within instead of between sectors of production. This would imply the development of 'intra-industry trade'. Of course, such a development would also depend on the comparative advantages of the various countries. A survey of the commodity composition of the countries' foreign trade should be able to give a first hint with respect to revealed comparative advantages of the nations under review.

Considering the commodity composition of the Central European countries' exports, the interdependence of regional shifts as described above has to be taken into account, since the commodity composition of exports to the former CMEA and EU countries is not the same, for reasons discussed in the previous paragraph. Although the commodity structure of the Czech, Hungarian, Polish and Slovak exports is expected to converge to a pattern which, given these countries' level of economic development and factor endowments, is compatible with market economies, the regional disparity in the commodity composition of exports will not necessarily be eliminated by the transformation into a fully-fledged market economy. Taking the same benchmark years used throughout this chapter, namely 1985, 1990 and 1995, Table 6.3, therefore, presents changing commodity structures in exports to both Eastern Europe and the EU.

Table 6.3 distinguishes primary products, basic manufactures, capital goods and light consumer goods. Primary products include food and beverages, inedible raw materials, mineral fuels, lubricants and related materials, and animal and vegetable oils. These products correspond to the single-digit groups 0–4 of the 'Standard International Trade Classification' (SITC). The specified basic manufactures are predominantly intermediate goods and comprise chemicals and those manufactures which are classified by material, that is SITC 5 and 6. Capital goods stand for the single-digit group SITC 7 of machinery and transport equipment, whereas light consumer goods include a large variety of miscellaneous manufactured goods and correspond to SITC 8.[3]

Table 6.3   Commodity structure of Central European countries' exports to the EU and Eastern Europe, 1985–95 (percentages)

	European Union[*]			Eastern Europe[†]		
	1985	1990	1995	1985	1990	1995
Czech Republic[‡]						
Primary products	38	27	25	4	6	19
Basic manufactures	38	39	32	16	17	42
Capital goods	11	14	24	63	63	28
Light consumer goods	13	20	19	17	14	11
Hungary						
Primary products	48	36	23	24	33	39
Basic manufactures	27	34	25	23	17	27
Capital goods	9	16	29	37	38	27
Light consumer goods	15	13	23	16	12	7
Poland						
Primary products	62	42	24	17	34	60
Basic manufactures	20	31	31	18	25	25
Capital goods	8	11	16	54	35	12
Light consumer goods	10	16	29	11	6	3
Slovakia[‡]						
Primary products	38	27	11	4	6	10
Basic manufactures	38	39	48	16	17	38
Capital goods	11	14	19	63	63	35
Light consumer goods	13	20	22	17	14	17

Notes: [*] For all years, EU refers to its present fifteen members. The GDR is included from 1991 and affects the percentages for 1995.

   [†] For 1985 and 1990, figures refer to the European member-states of the CMEA, whereas, for 1995, Eastern Europe is defined as CEFTA, CIS, and Bulgaria and Romania.

   [‡] For 1985 and 1990, figures refer to Czechoslovakia.

Sources: United Nations, *Commodity Trade Statistics*, various issues; OECD, *Trade by Commodities*, various issues; *PlanEcon Report*, various issues

Table 6.3 shows two important developments in commodity composition since 1985. Firstly, it clearly illustrates the convergence of commodity patterns with regard to exports to the EU and Eastern Europe. In the 1980s, primary products and basic manufactures dominated Central

European exports to the EU, whereas exports to Eastern Europe mainly consisted of capital goods. Exporting many agricultural products to the Soviet Union, Hungary's commodity composition appeared to be slightly deviating. Generally speaking, the division of labour under communism was such that in trade with the EU the Central European countries had many characteristics of less-developed countries, whereas in trade with the Soviet Union the commodity patterns revealed highly developed economies. After the start of the transformation, the relative importance of exports of light consumer goods to the EU increased, whereas it declined for the Eastern European region as a destination. Consequently, and according to the expectations based upon the transformation to a fully-fledged market economy, commodity patterns with EU and Eastern Europe do converge. For both the Czech and Slovak Republics, the speed of convergence in recent years is remarkably high, whereas it could be expected that, given the differences in structures of production in Czechoslovakia, as shown in Chapter 3, it would take longer in the case of Slovakia. Figures for 1995 certainly do not confirm this expectation.

Secondly, the table reveals that, despite similar processes of forced industrialization under central planning, there are marked differences in commodity structures among the Central European countries' exports. As already observed, Hungary's exports are more concentrated on agricultural products on both the EU and the Eastern European markets. But the table reveals that primary products are currently also important to Poland's exports to Eastern Europe. In this regard, not so much agricultural products but inedible raw materials are decisive.

This survey of recent developments in foreign trade structures of the Central European countries can be summarized as follows. The regional shift in the Central European countries' exports from East to West has not fully compensated the declining export markets in the CMEA region. For manufactured commodities, the regional shift coincided with a shift from capital goods to light consumer goods, above all because of the over-representation of capital goods in intra-CMEA trade. The share of primary goods has gained relative importance in the export structures of the respective countries. Although a recovery of Eastern markets cannot be excluded in the near future – in fact, various sources report this to be the case for Hungary – competitiveness on the market of the EU will be decisive for the export performance of all four countries under examination in this book. The next section will focus on this.

EXPORT PERFORMANCE ON THE EU MARKET

A Yardstick for Competitiveness

Centrally planned economies faced weak export performances due to effective constraints of supply. Throughout the period of communism, internal factors severely hindered these countries' competitiveness on the world market. Supply constraints under central planning manifested themselves first and foremost in a comparative disadvantage in those products characterized by a wide variety and for which after-sales services play an important role. This held true for reformist as well as for conservative communist governments. It has been shown in the preceding chapter that Hungary especially made serious efforts to intensify integration in world markets, but that country's export performance did not meet the expectations in the 1970s and the first half of the 1980s. Neither did it perform better than Czechoslovakia, which followed an outspoken conservative course during this period (see Hoen and Van Leeuwen, 1991). Therefore, it is interesting to study the extent to which competitiveness on Western markets during the first years of the transformation has improved for the Central European countries under examination.

Changing patterns of competitiveness will be explored by means of a 'constant market shares' analysis. The basic aim of this analysis is to identify factors of demand and supply. It is a decomposition technique which ascribes favourable or unfavourable export growth of a country to a selected area of destination either to its export structure, or to its competitiveness (see Leamer and Stern, 1970). The export structure is supposed to reveal demand factors on international markets. The assumption is that exports may increase relatively fast because international demand may be expanding on specific markets which are favourable to the exporting country. Competitiveness is supposed to come to the fore as a decisive supply factor. Exports may not have been expanding due to riding the waves of international trade, but may have been the result of domestic factors.[4]

In attempting retrospectively to quantify change in a country's exports under the assumption of constant market shares with respect to a certain reference group, which is export change in a situation of unaltered competitiveness ('structural effect'), the change in competitiveness ('competition effect') can be defined as the difference between the actual export change and the structural effect. In many applications, the structural effect is subdivided into a 'scale', a 'commodity' and a 'regional' effect, assuming a constant market share in total exports, in the exports of various commodities, and in specific regions, respectively. This subdivision takes into account that exports may be concentrated on commodities for which demand is growing relatively quickly (moderately), or on regions with relatively flourishing (stagnant) imports. In the literature, this decomposition of export growth is referred to as 'three-level' analysis (see Richardson, 1970) and is based upon the following identity:

$$\Delta q \equiv s_0 \Delta Q + \{\Sigma_i s_{0i} \Delta Q_i - s_0 \Delta Q\} +$$

$$\text{[i]} \qquad\qquad\qquad \text{[ii]}$$

$$\{\Sigma_i \Sigma_j s_{0ij} \Delta Q_{ij} - \Sigma_j s_{0ij} \Delta Q_i\} + \Sigma_i \Sigma_j \Delta s_{ij} Q_{1ij}$$

$$\text{[iii]} \qquad\qquad\qquad\qquad \text{[iv]}$$

In this equation, q and Q refer to the total value of exports of the country under scrutiny and of the reference group, while s is the market share of the investigated country in the exports of the reference group (q/Q). Subscripts i and j refer to specific commodities and regions, whereas the subscripts 0 and 1 indicate the beginning and the end of a discrete time interval. This three-level equation shows the scale [i], the commodity [ii], the regional [iii], and the competition effects [iv], respectively.

There are many methodological problems involved with decomposition of trade flows according to the identity specified above. One of these problems pinpoints the arbitrariness in the choice of the base year, that is the 'index number' problem. The 'index number' problem is a result of the fact that the analysis has to be applied to discrete time intervals, whereas one would have preferred to calculate time derivatives, such as dq/dt, dQ/dt, and ds/dt. As a consequence, a 'second order' effect appears, implying a change both in the market shares of the country under scrutiny and in the exports of the reference group ($\Delta s \Delta Q$). This 'second order' effect clearly disturbs interpretation possibilities, as the decomposition analysis, for reasons of its principal underlying assumption, tries to keep one of them constant. There is no satisfactory solution to the problem of incorporating this 'second order' effect into the decomposition identities (see Richardson, 1971(a)).[5]

Apart from unsolved 'index number' problems, the three-level analysis suffers from an asymmetric specification. This implies that the magnitudes of the commodity and the regional effect depend on the sequence in which these effects are specified in the identity, although the sum of the regional and commodity effects is identical in both specifications. In order to avoid this asymmetry, the method applied in this chapter follows the solution in which an 'interaction' effect is introduced. This effect shows the mutual influence of the commodity package and the regional dispersion of the exports of the countries under consideration (Jepma, 1986, p. 24). The inclusion of interaction leads to the following identity:

$$\Delta q \equiv s_0 \Delta Q + \{\Sigma_i \Sigma_j s_{0ij} \Delta Q_{ij} - \Sigma_i s_{0i} \Delta Q_i\} + \{\Sigma_i \Sigma_j s_{0ij} \Delta Q_{ij} - \Sigma_j s_{0ij} \Delta Q_j\} +$$

$$[1] \qquad\qquad [2] \qquad\qquad\qquad [3]$$

$$\{[\Sigma_i s_{0i} \Delta Q_i - s_0 \Delta Q] - [\Sigma_i \Sigma_j s_{0ij} \Delta Q_{ij} - \Sigma_j s_{0ij} \Delta Q_j]\} + \Sigma_i \Sigma_j \Delta s_{ij} Q_{1ij}$$

$$[4] \qquad\qquad\qquad\qquad [5]$$

The scale [1] and competition effects [5] are identical to those defined in the three-level identity. Due to the interaction term [4], the identity is symmetric with regard to the regional [2] and the commodity effect [3]. The commodity effect in this symmetric equation corresponds to the one defined after the regional effect in the asymmetric three-level identity, whereas the regional effect coincides with the one in which it is specified after the commodity effect in the asymmetric equation. The interpretation of these effects is quite straightforward. A positive commodity (regional) effect implies that the country's export composition is concentrated on commodities (or regions) for which import demand is growing relatively fast.[6] The only difference with regard to the 'three-level' analysis usually applied is that regional and commodity effects have been purified from interactions. These are separately brought into the equation in term [4]. In the case of negative interactions, it holds that:

$$[\Sigma_i \Sigma_j s_{0ij} \Delta Q_{ij} - \Sigma_j s_{0j} \Delta Q_j] > [\Sigma_i s_{0i} \Delta Q_i - s_0 \Delta Q]$$

The condition entails a relatively positive influence of regional dispersion on the commodity effect in comparison with the reference group. In this study, the symmetric equation with the refined structural effects is chosen for application.

Appealing as the analysis may be, several weaknesses still have to be taken into account. Leaving aside the 'index number' problem mentioned above, two problems need still to be emphasized. Firstly, the analysis is based upon an identity used to split export changes *ex post*, and therefore does not give causal interrelations.[7] The calculations do not suggest any explanation for slackening of or improvement in conditions of competitiveness. The analysis is a useful tool in the quantitative dissection of realized export change into different components, but it is not able to clarify why exports changed in a certain manner. Secondly, the competition effect is a residue in a mathematical identity, implying that it not only includes aspects such as quality, prices, time of delivery, and other services *vis-à-vis* competitors, but it also comprises matters which are not related to supply factors of the country under investigation, such as protective non-tariff barriers. In order to disentangle aspects of protectionism, it is extremely important to choose appropriate data and to further split effects into separate markets.

Data

The problems of decomposition analysis of trade flows necessitate a well-considered choice of the data set, since the complications concern the fact that the outcomes are very sensitive to the specific choice of years, reference group, commodity composition and regional destination. This sensitivity impedes meaningful interpretations (see Richardson, 1971(b)).

In the literature, one can find several solutions to the sensitivity of decomposition analysis, for example, by using moving averages of export data (see Jepma, 1986, pp. 158–60). The calculations in this chapter are based on the traditional discrete approach without modifying the trade statistics. In order to reduce the magnitude of disturbing 'second order' effects, discrete periods should be as short as possible. At the same time, however, one is interested in structural developments of export changes over the medium term of several years. In the following decomposition calculations, these restraints are taken care of by decomposing export changes on a yearly basis, that is, minimizing 'second order' effects by choosing the base year as near as possible to the period under consideration and by subsequently cumulating the results for various years.

This procedure has been applied for the following discrete periods of time: 1985–90, 1990–93 and 1993–95 and therefore it closely follows the benchmark years defined at the beginning of this chapter. The year 1993 has been included as a new benchmark because of the break-up of Czechoslovakia. For the sake of comparability, the method outlined above requires us not only to start the decomposition of export growth again after the independence of the Czech and Slovak Republics, but for

Hungary and Poland as well. Consequently, three discrete periods of time have been used to decompose changes in the Central European countries' exports to the EU.

The aim of the following decomposition analysis is to quantify relative export performance of the Central European countries and to identify the success or failure of different transformation strategies. Theoretically, arguments for taking the other countries as a reference group (Q_{ij}), while investigating the remaining country (q_{ij}), are very well founded (see Leamer and Stern, 1970, pp. 176-7).[8] However, due to sensitivity problems, the choice of the reference group is not obvious. The Western market shares of the Central European countries are too small and lead to unstable results of the decomposition. Unfortunately, a reference group consisting of all other transition economies in the region turned out not to ease the problem of instability and consequent problematic interpretation of the results. In order to circumvent this inconvenience, total world exports have been taken as the standard of reference and the analysis is repeated for each country.

Regarding the specification of commodities (i) and regions of destination (j), it is important to notice once again that small export groups may cause large fluctuations in the calculated components. It enhances the robustness of analysis to restrict the number of specified commodities and regions. At the same time, the classification on which Table 6.3 relies does not seem appropriate to the purpose of decomposition analysis. Based upon the SITC, the following commodity groups are specified: meat and meat preparations (SITC 01), food, beverages, and animal and vegetable oils, excluding meat and meat preparations (SITC 0/01 + 1 + 4), inedible raw materials, except fuels (SITC 2), mineral fuels, lubricants and related materials (SITC 3), chemicals (SITC 5), manufactured goods, classified mainly by material (SITC 6), machines and transport equipment (SITC 7), miscellaneous manufactured goods, excluding clothing (SITC 8/84), clothing (SITC 84). The underlying consideration for the selection of commodities is that these groups cover at least 5 per cent of total exports of the Czech Republic, Hungary, Poland and Slovakia in one of the benchmark years, and therefore contribute to fairly stable results of the decomposition. Moreover, the classification separately includes so-called 'sensitive' products of the Association Agreements between the EU and the respective Central European countries, of which clothing is the most important in this respect. As outlined in Chapter 2, for reasons of irreconcilable bargaining positions, agricultural products are not included in the Association Agreements. It is interesting to explore the extent to which the trade flows of these products are influenced by protectionist measures, since it should not be overlooked, for example, that during the past decade, meat products alone counted for more than 10 per cent of Hungary's exports to the EU.

As emphasized in Chapter 2, the EU and the Central European countries do have common borders, have agreed upon the Association Agreements, and official requests for EU membership have been made. Consequently, the EU as market of destination for Central European exports is of enormous importance. It has already been shown in Table 6.3 that the EU is the number one trading partner of all four countries under investigation. To this can be added the fact that the EU is currently absorbing approximately 90 per cent of these countries' joint exports to the entire OECD region. Considering the investigated market of destination, the countries included in the decomposition analysis of Central European countries' export growth are those which in 1995 belonged to the EU, namely Austria, Belgium, Denmark, Finland, France, Germany, Greece, Ireland, Italy, Luxembourg, the Netherlands, Portugal, Spain, Sweden and the United Kingdom. In order to obtain viable results, Finland and Sweden are taken as one group. The same has been done with regard to the Mediterranean countries, Greece, Portugal and Spain, to Belgium and Luxembourg, for which trade flows in statistics are not separated anyway, and to Ireland and United Kingdom. The reason for including the present fifteen EU members for all subsequent periods is that this may possibly reveal protectionist strands in the EU if competitiveness appears to be significantly different on the markets of Austria, Finland and Sweden at the time these countries were not yet members of the EU. Protectionism should be separated out by cross-section analysis. Because the former EFTA countries became EU members from January 1995, it is unlikely, however, that the decomposition would illustrate differences for these countries over time.

Results

The decomposition of export changes of the Czech and Slovak Republics, Hungary and Poland is presented in Table 6.4. It shows the yearly cumulated effects and does not present the results of the decomposition for each year. The results are generally rather smooth for all countries. The absence of extreme jumps can be interpreted as a justification for the chosen classification and avoids the problem of difficult-to-interpret calculations. Moreover, the table reveals that with the exception of decomposition of Polish export change in the second period, the interaction effects are relatively small. These findings also enhance the plausibility of the results.

Table 6.4   Decomposition of Central European countries' change in exports to the EU, 1985–95 (million dollars and percentages)*

	1985–90		1990–93		1993–95	
Czech Republic†						
Export change	2211	100%	3722	100%	2048	100%
scale effect	2491	113%	330	9%	652	32%
regional effect	72	3%	258	7%	118	6%
commodity effect	-129	-6%	93	3%	148	7%
interaction effect	44	2%	-115	-3%	-112	-5%
competition effect	-266	-12%	3158	85%	1243	61%
Hungary						
Export change	2658	100%	1131	100%	1337	100%
scale effect	2269	85%	-355	-31%	580	43%
regional effect	94	4%	-6	-1%	29	2%
commodity effect	-56	-2%	56	5%	-13	-1%
interaction effect	10	0%	-30	-3%	-31	-2%
competition effect	340	13%	1465	130%	771	58%
Poland						
Export change	4373	100%	2346	100%	2705	100%
scale effect	3667	84%	-580	-25%	996	37%
regional effect	-42	-1%	199	9%	46	2%
commodity effect	-1119	-26%	340	15%	-98	-4%
interaction effect	39	1%	-300	-14%	-34	-1%
competition effect	1828	42%	2688	115%	1795	66%
Slovakia†						
Export change	2211	100%	3722	100%	921	100%
scale effect	2491	113%	330	9%	171	19%
regional effect	72	3%	258	7%	31	3%
commodity effect	-129	-6%	93	3%	31	3%
interaction effect	44	2%	-115	-3%	-28	-3%
competition effect	-266	-12%	3158	85%	715	78%

Notes: * Due to rounding, totals do not necessarily correspond to the sum of the parts.
† The results for 1985–90 and 1990–93 refer to Czechoslovakia. Regarding the second period, therefore, decomposition relied on statistics for 1990–92.

Table 6.4 indicates a clear development during the past decade. Three conclusions can be drawn from the table. Firstly, the export change of the Central European countries between 1985 and 1990 can mainly be ascribed to the scale effect, indicating that Czechoslovakia, Hungary and Poland rode the waves of the EU's import demand in this time interval. The countries' export development was slightly hampered, however, by an unfavourable commodity composition, especially in the case of Poland. None the less, considering all discrete periods, both commodity and regional effects appear to be quite small in comparison with either the scale effect, the competition effect, or both.[9]

Secondly, the competition effects for Hungary and Poland positively contributed to their exports during the period 1985–90. These calculations indicate that the economic reforms during the 1980s had a beneficial impact on these countries' external performance. In the five years preceding the collapse of the system, Czechoslovakia still faced the problem of declining market shares in the EU. It is plausible to interpret these results in terms of conservative policy, in which the EU was deliberately neglected, and lack of genuine economic reforms. At the same time, however, the improvement in Hungary's competitiveness did not lead to an advantageous export performance in comparison with Poland.

Thirdly, the transformation to a fully-fledged market economy since 1990 is clearly coming to the fore with an increase in competitiveness for all countries. All Central European countries have been able to increase exports to the EU more than could be expected on the assumption of constant market shares. Moreover, there are no significant differences among the four countries. There is neither a sign of a better performing Hungary due to past reforms, nor is there an indication that Slovakia is really surpassed by the Czech Republic.

Since the competition effects are the principal contributors to the countries' export change since the start of the transformation, it seems useful to decompose these effects further, either with respect to regions, or with respect to commodities. This would enable us to pinpoint those sectors or regions of destination within the EU which contributed the most to the improvement in overall competitiveness. The decomposition formulae and the complete results of the decomposition of the competition effects can be found in this chapter's appendix, but the main findings can be summarized as follows. The decomposition of the competition effects into commodities shows some interesting results. Regarding the whole period 1985–95, it reveals clear shifts in commodities which positively contribute to the export growth above what could be expected on the basis of constant market shares. A fairly stable pattern emerges, with intermediates and light consumer goods contributing to the positive competition effects of the respective countries' export growth since the start of the transformation. In the period 1993–95, Polish exports of light consumer goods manifest better performance than exports of capital goods, whereas for the Czech Republic, Hungary and Slovakia, it rather seems the other way around. The pattern for Poland is deviant in other aspects as well. Contrary to the other countries' performance since the start of the transformation, Poland also faces weakly performing commodity groups, such as in food, beverages, and animal and vegetable oils, excluding meat and meat preparations (SITC 0/01 + 1 + 4). The deviation certainly does not support the conclusion of a protectionist stance on the part of the EU. At the same time, Poland appeared to be the only country able to perform relatively well in mineral fuels, lubricants and related material. Besides small deviating patterns, there are also striking similarities to be observed. These concern the similarity in the classified commodity groups contributing to the respective competition effects of the Czech and Slovak Republics in the third period, which does not confirm the generally assumed impact of differences in production structures between the newly independent countries.

Considering the regional decomposition of the competition effects, it appears that Germany is the most important market on which gains in market shares have been realized, although they were much larger in the second than in the third period, indicating that Germany may no longer remain the sole dominant market contributing to the Central European countries' increasing market shares in the EU. Besides, considering the whole period 1985–95, it appears that in the case of Hungary, German dominance is less severe, since the country's competitiveness is also very much due to its performance on the Austrian and Italian markets. Regarding Polish exports to the EU, the results do indeed reveal a slight difference in performance on Scandinavian markets relative to the other countries, although it cannot be concluded that the Nordic countries are as important as Austria and Italy are for Hungary. These markets of destination, contrary to what might be expected on the basis of geographical considerations, did not contribute to the Czech Republic's recent positive export performance. Considering possible protectionism on the part of the EU, it is interesting to observe that the patterns for Austria and the two Scandinavian countries which have recently become EU members do not significantly deviate from other specified regions of destination.

REFORM AND COMPETITIVENESS

The empirical results obtained from the decomposition of export change do not suggest any explanation for slackening or improving competitiveness and it is beyond the scope of this study comprehensively to analyse the causes of weak and strong competitiveness of the Central European countries during the period 1985–95. The comparison of the export performance of the four countries, however, raises questions regarding both the impact of market-oriented reforms on competitiveness in the framework of centrally planned economies and the impact of differences in strategies of transformation to a fully-fledged market economy on the countries' relative export performance.

The empirical evidence obtained from decomposition of the Central European countries' export change yielded ambiguous results. On the one hand, when analysing the period before the collapse of communism, it indeed confirmed the expectation that Hungary, which was placed in the vanguard of communist reform attempts with the introduction of the ÚGM, would outperform Czechoslovakia on the EU market, since the latter country neither took any significant decentralizing measures with respect to its foreign trade organization, nor stated any political intention to shift trade from East to West. On the other hand, regarding the same period, the results from decomposition of export change did not identify noticeable differences between competitiveness of Hungary and Poland. This could either indicate the relative success of the Polish economic reforms initiated after the declaration of martial law in December 1981 and reinforced by Jaruzelski in 1987, or reveal the limits of market-oriented reforms during the Kádár era.

The latter explanation seems the more plausible. It has to be emphasized that Hungarian foreign trade reforms during the ÚGM were restricted to the hard currency area. CMEA trade continued to be conducted on a strictly bilateral basis. The Hungarian authorities had strong interests in the non-violation of CMEA relations, since this enabled them to continue experiments with market-oriented reforms. As a consequence, a large part of the foreign trade organization was excluded from these reforms. With CMEA trade remaining an important rent-seeking opportunity for Hungarian exporting enterprises, the ÚGM was rendered inconsistent on the whole, unable to effect larger gains in market shares relative to Poland. In the light of these considerations, only the last years of the ÚGM yielded positive results. As indicated in Chapter 4, the reforms implemented by the Németh government clearly had to be distinguished from those in the 1970s and 1980s. However, in the late 1980s, Poland accelerated economic reforms as well.

To a certain extent, the findings for the period after 1990 also thwart expectations with respect to the advantage Hungary could take from its pro-reformist communist past. Was the country able to reap the fruits of the ÚGM? The argument to be put forward in this regard is that decentralization of economic decision making had already been achieved. What remained to be done after 1990 was to constitute an economic order in which enterprises were forced to base decisions on conditions set by the market. For genuine market conditions to prevail, decentralization and commercialization should coincide. The first step was realized under the ÚGM; the second, making the reforms consistent as a whole, had to follow. The assumption underlying expectations regarding Hungary's head start was that the reforms during the 1970s and 1980s had taught Hungarian managers to behave as profit-maximizing entrepreneurs. What had been lacking were the commercial relations which forced them to generate profits in the market.

However, instead of confirming the expectation of favourable starting conditions for the transformation to a market economy, stimulating a rapid improvement in Hungary's relative competitiveness on the EU market, the decomposition of the Central European countries' export change rather suggests a neutral impact. In a more dynamic perspective, indeed, the results even suggest that the legacy of the past was negative. After all, Czechoslovakia and – after the splitting of the federation – the Czech Republic and Slovakia have also shown an ability rapidly to gain market shares in the EU for a wide range of commodities.

In linking competitiveness and reform, it might be useful to include interest group behaviour, as suggested by Olson, as an important explanatory variable (see Olson, 1965; 1982). An application of the theory of collective interests as a plausible explanation for relatively slackening or improving competitiveness in exports necessitates scrutinizing the persistence or termination of autarkic behaviour (see Krueger, 1974). In fact, trade protection is almost a classic example of an economic event in which social costs are spread out over a large number of consumers and, consequently, will be rather moderate when considered individually and therefore will not induce organized protests against the loss in comprehensive welfare, whereas the redistribution of welfare will significantly benefit a relative small number of enterprises which try to gain a larger share of the pie.

It has to be admitted that it is extremely difficult to pinpoint interest groups, as they change over time. When scrutinizing them for the period of central planning, though, two convincing arguments for strong bargaining positions of import-substituting producers come to the fore (see Brada, 1991; Wass von Czege, 1987). Firstly, from the traditional environment of the centralized bureaucratic system of administrative allocation and control, they had long enduring relations with the Ministries of Foreign Trade. As shown in Chapter 2, foreign trade merely served as a stand-by instrument for the achievement of domestic production targets. The function of exports was basically to finance necessary imports. In fact, under mandatory planning, exports had a pure residual status which did not stimulate durable bargaining power at the higher levels of the hierarchy. Secondly, with the introduction of a strategy of diversifying exports, as was the case in Hungary during the 1980s, the homogeneity of the exporters interested in free trade was to a certain extent a distortion. Within the export sector, lobbies were dominated by producers relatively less dependent on imports, which in most instances were diversified. The exports mostly entailed homogeneous commodities, such as agricultural products, chemicals and steel. Enterprises interested in genuine liberalization existed in a very large but dispersed group. In short, despite evolving attempts at economic reform, of which import liberalization was supposed to be an important part, autarkic situations tended to prevail for quite a long time.

The start of the transformation may in itself be conceived as a break with vested interests along the lines Olson described in his *Rise and Decline of Nations* (1982). First of all, the monopolistic power of the foreign trade organization collapsed. So did the old boys' network of political patronage. Interesting here is that partial decentralization of economic decision making preceding the start of the transformation may have hindered far-reaching liberalization of foreign trade after the demise of communism. Whereas, for example, Czechoslovakia and Poland decided to introduce *de jure* currency convertibility overnight, it took longer in the case of Hungary. Given the fact that the foreign trade organization had already been partially liberalized, it was more difficult to do so in the Hungarian case. The authorities responsible for initiating and monitoring such reforms had already lost part of their dominant position.

CONCLUSION

To conclude, for all the Central European countries, competitiveness on the EU market improved dramatically following the fall of communism, and in the case of Hungary and Poland, progress had already started in the second half of the 1980s. These results can mainly be ascribed to a capacity to adapt to situations of changing market conditions, in the context of this study referred to as positive competition effects. Although market accessibility is under any circumstances to be preferred, the regional and commodity decomposition does not confirm systemic differences between relative performance in EU and former EFTA countries and in 'sensitive' and 'non-sensitive' products. So, despite the fact that intra-EU trade played a large role in the exports of the reference group, the decomposition of export change does not indicate protectionism to be decisive in the countries' export performance *vis-à-vis* the reference group, leaving competitiveness to be explained in terms of domestic factors in Central Europe.

A possible explanation is sought in the theory of collective interests. The application of the theory to foreign trade performance helps to clarify the persistence of autarkic behaviour during the era of central planning, and illustrates why Hungary as a reformist country did not really perform better than Poland, whose export performance was not so much due to system reforms, but was at least partly the result of policy. At the same time, it illustrates the fact that reformist countries did not necessarily have more favourable conditions at the start of the transformation. The final chapter examines the extent to which this hypothesis seems relevant in other fields of economic transformation from a centrally planned to a market economy in Central Europe.

NOTES

1. When analysing trade structures of centrally planned economies, the problem of compatibility of trade data arises. This holds true for both intra-CMEA and East–West trade and is related to diverging pricing principles and to the applied exchange rate. Changes since 1989, among them the introduction of currency convertibility in various countries, will have adjusted for the problem, although not to the same extent in all countries and not in retrospect for each year. Differences in export and import registration are another problem with regard to data consistency. When analysing changes in, for example, Hungary's export structure, Hungarian export data are indispensable, but when analysing a country's relative export performance on Western markets, import data of the region of destination have to be used. However, discrepancies between export and import registration regarding the same bilateral flows can be substantial (see Hoen and Van Leeuwen, 1996). Unless otherwise indicated, data are taken from various issues of United Nations, *Commodity Trade Statistics*; OECD, *Trade by Commodities*, and *PlanEcon Report*.

2. In an attempt to circumvent the problem of different export registrations of the Central European countries, the market shares in exports to the EU have been calculated by using import registration of EU members. Undoubtedly, these suffer from inaccuracy as well, but at least adhere to what is sometimes referred to as the 'law of equal cheating'. Regarding data registration, the same procedures have been applied to all the respective countries. This enlarges mutual comparisons.

3. For reasons of data comparability, the small and heterogeneous group of residual manufactures (SITC 9) has not been included.

4. For an extensive treatment of decomposition analysis, the reader is referred to Brakman (1991), Merkies and Van Der Meer (1988), Jepma (1986), and Richardson (1970).

5. When calculating time derivatives, the basic identity is:

$$dq/dt \equiv s\{dQ/dt\} + \{ds/dt\}Q$$

In discrete-time analysis, a 'second order' effect appears, implying a change in the exports of the reference group Q and in the market shares s of the country under scrutiny. The appearance of this 'second order' effect converts the equation based on time derivatives into the following identity:

$$\Delta q \equiv s_0 \Delta Q + \Delta s Q_0 + \Delta s \Delta Q$$

The 'second order' term $\Delta s \Delta Q$ has to be allocated to the first $(s_0 \Delta Q)$ or second term $(\Delta s Q_0)$, which leads to the following possibilities:

$$\Delta q \equiv s_1 \Delta Q + \Delta s Q_0 \quad \wedge \quad \Delta q \equiv s_0 \Delta Q + \Delta s Q_1$$

There is no theoretical foundation to prefer one over the other, but, of course, the choice of the base year influences the magnitude of the effects (see Richardson, 1971(a), pp. 234–6; Jepma, 1986, pp. 25–32). In the underlying analysis, the second option has been taken.

6. A positive commodity effect implies that both $s_i > s$ and $\Delta Q_i > 0$.

7. This critical argument also entails a more general point, namely the rather artificial distinction between structural and competition effect. The fact that countries concentrate exports on certain regional and/or commodity markets indirectly reveals aspects of a nation's competitiveness.

8. In this case, the decomposition identity has to be reformulated in growth rates, since it is impossible to calculate, for example, market shares of the Czech Republic in joint exports of Hungary, Poland and Slovakia.

9. The negative scale effects for Hungary and Poland in the second are due to a decline in nominal export values of EU imports in 1993. Since for Czechoslovakia the second period refers to 1990–92, negative scale effects do not apply here.

Appendix

This appendix shows the complete results of a decomposition of the competition effects. The competition effects as presented in Table 6.4 can be split into the contribution of specific regions and commodities. For each market, the further decomposition of the competition effect into regions and commodities is given by the following formulae:

$$\Sigma_j \{ q_{1ij} - q_{0ij} * [Q_{1ij}/Q_{0ij}] \} \qquad [1]$$

$$\Sigma_i \{ q_{1ij} - q_{0ij} * [Q_{1ij}/Q_{0ij}] \} \qquad [2]$$

Considering these terms, [1] refers to the competition effect of a particular commodity i, as it is cumulated over regions of destination j, whereas [2] refers to the competition effect of a specified region j (see Leamer and Stern, 1970).

This method of decomposing the competition effect has been criticized by Jepma (1986, pp. 47–9). According to Jepma, it cannot be concluded that the calculations represent the size of the competition effect which can be solely attributed to the region of destination or to the commodity market, since the two are interrelated. The magnitude of the effects on a certain regional market is also influenced by the competitiveness of the commodities actually sold on those markets and *vice versa*. A solution is proposed by normalizing the elements. In this study, however, the suggestion had not been followed, as the solution only allows cross-section analysis, while inter-temporally the analysis becomes meaningless. Of course, when interpreting the calculations it is important to acknowledge the problem of interrelated regional and commodity markets.

Table A.1 and A.2 present the results of the decomposition with respect to commodities and regions, respectively. As with Table 6.4, due to rounding, totals do not always correspond to the sum of the parts.

Table A.1   Commodity decomposition of competition effects of the Central European countries' change in exports to the EU, 1985–95 (million dollars and percentages)

	1985–90		1990–93		1993–95	
Czech Republic*						
Competition effect (total)	-266	-100%	3158	100%	1243	100%
SITC 01	-31	-12%	-85	-3%	-3	-0%
SITC 0/01 + 1 + 4	47	18%	64	2%	4	0%
SITC 2	-1	-0%	22	1%	94	8%
SITC 3	-20	-7%	46	1%	49	4%
SITC 5	-59	-22%	189	6%	65	5%
SITC 6	-154	-58%	1382	44%	393	32%
SITC 7	-117	-44%	1020	32%	365	29%
SITC 8/84	138	52%	170	5%	190	15%
SITC 84	-18	-26%	350	11%	84	7%
Hungary						
Competition effect (total)	340	100%	1465	100%	771	100%
SITC 01	-38	-11%	-88	-6%	10	1%
SITC 0/01 + 1 + 4	112	33%	-134	-9%	8	1%
SITC 2	-23	-7%	77	5%	-7	-1%
SITC 3	1	0%	29	2%	6	1%
SITC 5	-20	-6%	106	7%	-33	-4%
SITC 6	344	101%	-24	-2%	177	23%
SITC 7	185	54%	647	44%	547	71%
SITC 8/84	12	3%	266	18%	42	6%
SITC 84	-232	-68%	585	40%	21	3%
Poland						
Competition effect (total)	1828	100	2688	100	1795	100%
SITC 01	-63	-3%	-85	-3%	-2	-0%
SITC 0/01 + 1 + 4	477	26%	-341	-13%	-9	-1%
SITC 2	83	5%	-255	-10%	-99	-6%
SITC 3	120	7%	96	4%	277	15%
SITC 5	357	20%	14	1%	-66	-4%
SITC 6	467	26%	957	36%	597	33%
SITC 7	31	2%	979	36%	39	2%
SITC 8/84	136	8%	481	18%	826	46%
SITC 84	222	12%	841	31%	233	13%

Table A.1 continued

	1985–90		1990–93		1993–95	
*Slovakia**						
Competition effect (total)	-266	-100%	3158	100%	715	100%
SITC 01	-31	-12%	-85	-3%	-1	-0%
SITC 0/01 + 1 + 4	47	18%	64	2%	-0	-0%
SITC 2	-1	-0%	22	1%	-4	-1%
SITC 3	-20	-7%	46	1%	-0	-0%
SITC 5	-59	-22%	189	6%	47	7%
SITC 6	-154	-58%	1382	44%	330	46%
SITC 7	-117	-44%	1020	32%	242	34%
SITC 8/84	138	52%	170	5%	15	2%
SITC 84	-68	-26%	350	11%	87	12%

Note: * The results for 1985–90 and 1990–93 refer to Czechoslovakia. Regarding the second period, therefore, decomposition relied on statistics for 1990–92.

Table A.2 Regional decomposition of competition effects of the Central European countries' change in exports to the EU, 1985–95 (million dollars and percentages)

	1985–90		1990–93		1993–95	
*Czech Republic**						
Competition effect (total)	-266	-100%	3158	100%	1243	100%
Austria	-86	-32%	428	14%	102	8%
Belgium/Luxembourg	-4	-2%	51	2%	78	6%
Denmark	-38	-15%	5	0%	24	2%
Finland/Sweden	-34	-13%	-7	-0%	26	2%
France	-34	-13%	104	3%	72	6%
Germany	254	96%	2275	72%	847	68%
Italy	-50	-19%	262	8%	52	4%
Netherlands	-85	-32%	81	3%	30	2%
Spain/Portugal/Greece	-138	-52%	96	3%	9	1%
United Kingdom/Ireland	-49	-19%	-139	-4%	4	0%

Table A.2 continued

	1985–90		1990–93		1993–95	
Hungary						
Competition effect (total)	340	100%	1465	100%	771	100%
Austria	112	35%	150	10%	88	12%
Belgium/Luxembourg	68	20%	48	3%	48	6%
Denmark	-25	-8%	-10	-1%	-1	-0%
Finland/Sweden	10	3%	-46	-3%	24	3%
France	-48	-14%	77	5%	-0	-0%
Germany	125	37%	1016	69%	334	43%
Italy	119	35%	191	13%	81	11%
Netherlands	28	8%	47	3%	8	1%
Spain/Portugal/Greece	-63	-19%	8	1%	83	11%
United Kingdom/Ireland	11	3%	-16	-1%	105	14%
Poland						
Competition effect (total)	1828	100%	2688	100%	1795	100%
Austria	119	7%	8	0%	694	39%
Belgium/Luxembourg	71	4%	5	0%	102	6%
Denmark	189	10%	65	2%	167	9%
Finland/Sweden	25	1%	50	2%	105	6%
France	14	1%	116	4%	69	4%
Germany	1007	55%	2268	84%	489	27%
Italy	143	8%	283	11%	-29	-2%
Netherlands	202	11%	125	5%	42	2%
Spain/Portugal/Greece	-16	-1%	-34	-1%	52	3%
United Kingdom/Ireland	74	4%	-197	-7%	103	6%
*Slovakia**						
Competition effect (total)	-266	-100%	3158	100%	715	100%
Austria	-86	-32%	428	14%	57	8%
Belgium/Luxembourg	-4	-2%	51	2%	-9	-1%
Denmark	-38	-15%	5	0%	8	1%
Finland/Sweden	-34	-13%	-7	-0%	32	5%
France	-34	-13%	104	3%	35	5%
Germany	254	96%	2275	72%	331	46%
Italy	-50	-19%	262	8%	128	18%
Netherlands	-85	-32%	81	3%	13	2%
Spain/Portugal/Greece	-138	-52%	96	3%	17	2%
United Kingdom/Ireland	-49	-19%	-139	-4%	103	14%

Note: *   see Table A.1.

7. The Strategies Reconsidered: A Political Economy of Transformation

INTRODUCTION

The preceding chapters illustrated that the dichotomous 'shock versus gradualism' dispute blurs key elements of the transformation from a centrally planned to a market economy. This chapter attempts to question further the merits of the theoretical debate by reconsidering and more explicitly comparing the Central European countries' strategies. It maintains that the labels attached to the policies applied are inappropriate and raises some theoretical reflections on the transformation.

After several years of contraction in economic activity, the economies in the region of Central and Eastern Europe seem to be recovering. It has been suggested several times that well-founded theoretical reflections were the basis for this recuperation (see for example World Bank, 1996). The question remains, 'which theoretical strands may those have been?'. Time and again, scholars in general and economists in particular have been embarrassed over issues concerning Central and Eastern Europe. In retrospect, of course, everybody tends to present the facts so as to prove their own correctness, but two aspects of the contemporary economic history of Central Europe should not be overlooked. Firstly, there is no well-attested evidence of any forecast regarding the collapse of the communist system. On the contrary, discussions of the existence and feasibility of a socialist economic order were closed several decades ago (see Van Ees and Garretsen, 1994; Wagener, 1979; Lavigne, 1995). No matter precisely how and in what form, economic coordination by means of central planning simply existed. This was referred to as 'really existing socialism'. The system had its advantages and disadvantages and the prevailing view was that it needed to be reformed rather than transformed. After all, communism and its concomitant organization of central planning had an outstanding reputation in terms of stability.

Secondly, once the curtain fell, nobody really knew how to cope with the transformation from a centrally planned to a market economy. To quote Van Brabant, 'they [economists] know next to nothing about undoing the planning environment and coming to grips with the wide-ranging legacies of the earlier communist dominance in societal affairs' (Van Brabant, 1993, pp. 80–81). There was no possibility of relying upon historical precedents on which to formulate general guidelines for the policy to be applied. Neither was there a theoretical framework available, since accepted economic analyses were predominantly based upon the assumption of well-functioning markets. Consequently, on the basis of these analyses, it is extremely difficult to underpin the creation of markets theoretically.

All in all, attributing recent economic growth in the region of formerly centrally planned economies to well-founded theoretical presumptions is at least premature. What can be done on the basis of current economic thinking is to define the necessary elements of the desired economic order, in Chapter 1 summarized as a stable macroeconomic environment, liberalization of trade, production and prices, decentralization of property rights, and the establishment of institutions which basically guarantee a consistent incentive system.

Despite being able to identify necessary ingredients of the desired economic order, the question regarding what kind of economic order will emerge from the transformation remains unanswered. The basic statistics on economic performance of the Central European countries reveal that recovery in economic activity as an indicator for sound theoretical conceptions should at least be measured against the fact that, so far, none of the countries in Central and Eastern Europe have been able to generate the per capita GDP level of 1989. Forecasts regarding this 'magic marker' indicate that for a very restricted number of countries, this level of welfare will be reached in 1998 (European Bank for Reconstruction and Development, 1997).[1] Furthermore, it is questionable whether the countries under scrutiny can already be characterized as fully-fledged market economies, since they are still in transition. So, what is needed is a theory which gives a possible explanation for, or at least underpins the plausibility of, the observed difference between the desired economic order and the factual economic order, that is, following economic reforms.

This final chapter seeks to distil similarities and differences in the Central European countries' performance in transformation and, again, tries to put the dynamics of changing economic orders into a more theoretical perspective. On the basis of insights from political economy, it attempts to clarify deviating paths of transformation. It should be stressed in advance, though, that an appeal to political economy is essentially an aspiration. Yet, it is believed indispensable to endeavour to specify the different actors in the process of transformation, their interests, and, most importantly, their relative bargaining position. Rather than explaining differences in relative economic performance, which is the domain of neo-classical economics, a political economy approach is more suitable to illustrate different paths of change in an economic order. Not just the question 'why does a country perform better or worse than its neighbour?', but rather 'why did neighbouring countries make different choices with regard to the strategy of transformation?' is what matters in a political economy of transformation. In other words, this is an attempt to place reform decisions in that context.

The outline of this chapter is as follows. The next section will examine the applicability of theories of political economy to transformation from a centrally planned to a market economy. It will pay special attention to interest-group behaviour, since this theory explicitly acknowledges the fact that, as in commodity markets, political decision making is vulnerable to an uneven distribution of bargaining actors. Subsequently, the transformation strategies applied in the Central European countries under scrutiny, as described in the foregoing chapters, will be reconsidered from this theoretical perspective. The chapter concludes with a summary of the most significant findings of the book.

A POLITICAL ECONOMY OF TRANSFORMATION

Regulation and the Regulated

It has been raised several times in the foregoing and, of course, elsewhere in the literature on Central and Eastern Europe, that economists face enormous difficulties when theoretically underpinning the transformation. However, the qualification 'economists know very little about transformation' should not be confused with 'economists know nothing at all'. This section describes the extent to which economics may be fruitful and intends to lay bare the necessity of a political-economy approach.

A theory on economic transformation, which is also referred to as 'reform economics' (see Grosfeld, 1990), has a twofold objective. On the one hand, it focuses on the formulation of an economic system with an optimal combination of centralization and decentralization, of hierarchy and market, of control and autonomy, and of public and private ownership. It is undeniable that an economic perspective prevails here. Theoretical considerations and methodological principles which find their roots in economics should lead to a comparison of the relative costs and benefits of alternative institutions. To put it differently, economics offers the possibility to contrast the fallibility of administrative and market coordination. The motives for regulating markets are very well documented in economic literature (see Posner, 1974). These focus on market failures due to negative external effects, inefficiency with increasing returns and diminishing marginal costs, and market imperfections as a result of slow adjustments and uneven income distribution.[2] In an identical way, it is possible to pinpoint drawbacks of administrative coordination, that is, 'non-market failures'. These can be explored in terms of negative internal effects as a result of remuneration not related to external price regulation, allocative inefficient production, undesired side effects of government regulation, and uneven income distribution through concentration of power (Wolf, 1979).

On the other hand, theory has to be focused on the question of how to accomplish this optimal economic order – leaving aside the problem that the desired order is not always clear to those responsible for reform – from a given situation. This is the transformation problem perceived from a policy perspective, which since the pioneering work of the Nobel laureate Tinbergen (1959) is not an untrodden field for economists, even though the purpose has always been to conceive policy targets and instruments within a given economic order, rather than contriving transformation targets and instruments, that is, the conversion of one economic order into another. Regarding economic reforms in the 1970s and 1980s, it is legitimate to wonder why, for example in Hungary, during the stage of a one-party state in which relations between the party and other institutions were so unambiguously set, final results of economic reform deviated to such a large extent from the targets set by the communist party. Which instruments are at the disposal of reformers for the implementation of reform?

In order to be in a position to answer these kinds of questions, historical and political analyses are indispensable. These are required to generate insights into the relevant actors, their interests, and their relative bargaining positions. The study of transformation requires us to depict the forces responsible for change and, probably even more important, for relative immobility, despite the objectives and intentions of policy makers. Moreover, when referring to the terminology introduced in Chapter 1, the question is related to both organic–evolutionary change, that is, evolution, and pragmatic–constructivist change, that is, the transformation. At this point, the problem seems to be beyond the scope of pure economics. The extent to which reforms that are deemed necessary are accepted at all levels in society is rather a matter of politics. Starting from the assumption of the importance of the economic impact of political decisions and the interrelationship among several interest groups in a hierarchical system consisting of the state and other governmental institutions, it is plausible to examine theories of political economy. Elaborating on the hypothesis formulated in the preceding chapter on the Central European countries' external economic performance, the remainder of this chapter explores theories of interest-group behaviour.

In the theories of political economy focusing on interest groups, economic regulation plays a pivotal role (see Posner, 1974). Economic regulation implies government intervention in markets. It refers not only to fiscal aspects of taxing and subsidizing, but also to legislation and administrative control over economic activity. The basic principle of interest-group theories is that government responds and initiates regulatory reform at the request of interest groups which try to maximize the income of their members. Regulations are nearly always beneficial to the regulated actor. Consequently, the theories' basic tenor is that regulation does not serve the public interest, but rather that of specific interest groups.

This notion has been put forward by political scientists in so-called 'capture theory'. The phrase 'capture' points the fact that, over time, regulating institutions are vulnerable to being hedged in by regulated enterprises. The exclusive right to initiate and establish economic regulation is taken advantage of by regulated institutes which try to increase profits by other means than performing in the market. Following the idea of economic regulation being in the interest of politically the most powerful groups, that is the regulated, capture theory has been worked out in a framework of demand and supply (Stigler, 1971). Four issues are specified which the government as regulator is able to supply and which can be beneficial to the regulated enterprises. Firstly, thé government may subsidize firms. It is clear that, in all circumstances, this is beneficial to any enterprise. Secondly, the government is able to regulate and control entry into the market. In this respect, Stigler's opinion is that 'every industry of occupation that has enough political power to utilize the state will seek to control entry' (Stigler, 1971, p. 14). Thirdly, for certain industries, government regulation may stimulate spending on complementary products, or may discourage the utilization of substitutes. Fourthly, the government may regulate prices. The larger the number of enterprises within the regulated industries, the fewer are the possibilities for successful continuation of price discrimination. Stigler's conclusion is that economic regulation is mostly applied at the request of industries and that it always works in their interests.

Interest-Group Behaviour and Change Within Economic Orders

Since capture theory only defines regulated enterprises as the relevant interest group, the theory is more specific than general interest-group theories (see Eggertsson, 1990, pp. 271ff). The implicit notion of these concepts is also that not all kinds of groups are able to look after their interests. In the field of unbalanced structures of interests, Olson in particular played a pioneering role. In *The Logic of Collective Action* Olson concludes that the size of a group is decisive for its ability to organize itself effectively (Olson, 1965). Whereas in small groups individual effort is perceived as necessary for the realization of the common interest, large groups suffer from shirking by individual members: this is the problem of the 'free rider'. The decision whether or not to join a group is supposed to be rational and according to one's own interests.

In 1982, Olson's *The Rise and Decline of Nations* was published. This book was an application of interest-group theory to problems of economic growth and stagnation. An important constraint in the generation of economic growth is deployed by distributional coalitions. These are interest groups which try to change the income distribution to their members' benefit (Olson, 1982, 43–7). Instead of contributing to an increase in total income, distributional coalitions attempt to have a larger share of a given quantity of welfare. In the literature, this behaviour is also known as 'rent-seeking'.

Besides distributional coalitions, encompassing organizations are identified (Olson, 1982, pp. 47–53). When looking after their interests, encompassing interest groups do take notice of the impact of their activities on national welfare. Not only the division but also growth of income is considered important to these groups. This is the problem of the size and the share of the pie. Olson's message is that economic growth in those countries which experienced an important break in history, for example with the occurrence of a revolution, the establishment of a military regime or a foreign occupation, was greater and more sustainable than in other countries, since, because of these events, interest groups lost their influence. After the situation is stabilized, distributional coalitions regain position, retard productivity, and induce an increase in government regulation. More regulation increases complexity and complexity ensures that only the well organized are in a position to look after their interests.

Theories of interest-group behaviour have predominantly been applied to developments in market economies (see Mueller, 1983; Murrell, 1982). Since perceived undesirable regulation assumes market intervention, it is obvious that attention has been restricted to this. Application of interest-group theory to centrally planned economies appeared only after the collapse of communism in Central and Eastern Europe. In an attempt to explain alternating periods of post-war economic growth and decline in Eastern Europe, interest-group theory has been used (see Murrell and Olson, 1991). The successful period of 1950–65, which was characterized by vast economic growth, is explained in terms of leadership, regarding the whole society as being within the competence of just one party secretary or, at the most, of a very few persons in the Politburo. Their political fate was largely dependent upon the well-being of the community.[3] Interestingly enough, the analysis does not refer to the fact that, after the Second World War, the Central and Eastern European countries had to be rebuilt from scratch, while well-established interests were dismantled by totalitarian regimes or foreign occupation and, therefore, did not hamper economic recovery. In Olson's *Rise and Decline of Nations*, this was the pivotal argument in explaining Japan's and West Germany's post-war success and the relative stagnation in Britain (Olson, 1982, 75–9).

The period of economic stagnation in Central and Eastern Europe, broadly defined as the interval 1965–80, is made plausible with the gradual emergence of an unbalanced structure of interests resulting from ministerial and enterprise activities. Ministries and enterprises became indispensable agents in supplying information to the planner. Consequently, they organized as distributional coalitions and 'institutional sclerosis' crept in.

The analysis of rise and decline of Central and Eastern Europe's post-war history was, however, restricted to classic mandatory planning and did not, for example, take Hungary's experience in the 1970s and 1980s into account. None the less, an oscillating course in economic growth and stagnation as a result of emerging distributional coalitions could have been depicted as well. As described in Chapter 4, reforms within the ÚGM mainly comprised the substitution of economic regulators for directive plans. In the course of this path of reform, negotiations on what, how, how much, and for whom to produce, that is, plan bargaining, changed into a situation in which regulators were at stake, in other words 'regulator bargaining' (see Bauer, 1976). In addition it made negotiations more complex, which in itself was beneficial to the well-organized groups, given their advantage of better access to information. Hungary's reforms during the 1970s and 1980s were an example of regulations being beneficial to the regulated (see for example Kornai, 1983, 1986).

Having shown interest-group theory to be relevant to circumstances of mandatory planning and also a plausible explanation for the course of economic reform under communism, the question still remains whether it is relevant and applicable to transformation from a centrally planned to a market economy. In the remainder of this chapter, on reconsidering the strategies applied in Central Europe, an attempt will be made to investigate this.

Interest-Group Behaviour and Transformation

The foregoing made clear that interest-group theory has been applied to the development of reforms within a given economic order. Application of interest-group theories to the transformation of economic systems has been rather moderate (see Krug, 1991). Given the fact that transformation is politically dominated, and that decision making with regard to economic reforms is so interwoven with the configuration of political actors, this might be perceived as rather strange. One important reason for the relative neglect is that interest-group theories are not very well formalized mathematically. Political processes seem to be too complicated for that. But there are other factors involved as well. These centre on the major flaws in the theory.

Despite the intuitive appeal of the notion that a configuration of interest groups explains why countries remain successful economically or not, many critical points have been raised (see Mackintosh *et al.*, 1996). Suffice it to mention three points here. Firstly, the theory suffers from mono-causality. It is problematic to ascribe all processes of economic growth and stagnation in terms of the configuration of interest groups. It goes without saying that many other factors play a pivotal role as well. But there is no problem in defining these in terms of necessary preconditions which have to be fulfilled. Within the context of this study, it is maintained that mono-causality in relations between variables is to be rejected rather than the possible insights of the theory itself.

Secondly, the basic idea of interest-group theory is that, in principle, all groups can be conceived as seeking their own particular interest. Therefore, they need to be ignored, dismantled or suppressed in order to restore a society's capacity to adapt to change. There are, however, many organizations which have a broader interest. In other words, not all group behaviour is economically motivated. Classic examples are the existence of solidarity movements, such as anti-racism organizations, where members do not have a direct interest in the achievement of the organization's goals, neither are they victims of the attitudes against which the organization protests. Considering the subject of transformation, the theory is highly problematic as an explanation for the emergence of Solidarity and Civic Forum. Even under normal circumstances, it is problematic for clarifying people's incentives to vote, but it is even more difficult to explain why people would join organizations which try to initiate revolution. The costs in terms of failure are enormous, whereas the benefits are non-exclusive. What is lacking is the possibility to estimate the extent to which the factor of an individual joining an interest group is decisive. That makes the theory unlikely to be applicable to explaining revolutions, such as the one in Eastern and Central Europe in the late 1980s. The analysis rather takes a revolution as an exogenous factor.

Thirdly, the theory suffers from the fact that the emergence of groups is not explained. What is explained is what happens after groups have been able to organize or not: in other words, the evolutionary path of coalitions of economic agents whose struggle over distributional issues establishes a set of institutional rigidities, which then inhibit anything other than a narrow defensive response to unexpected exogenous shock (Mackintosh *et al.*, 1996, p. 499). Here, the criticism focuses on the point that Olson's theory is in fact suffering from the same disease as neo-classical economic theory, namely an inability to clarify the role of the entrepreneur. Just as in markets enterprises do not come into existence out of the blue, but are the result of entrepreneurial efforts, so interest groups are also the result of political leadership by certain members. These members make more efforts to mobilize the group, take higher risks and pay far higher costs than those who join an already existing group (see Barry and Hardin, 1982). This criticism is not fully subscribed to in this study. Entrepreneurial behaviour is very well explained when taking into account that there are not only group interests, but once these have materialized, individual advantages can emerge as well. In other words, if nobody is willing or able to organize people with a common interest, a group will not emerge, whatever the size of the interests. Here, selective incentives motivate. It is possible to perceive this point as an extension and a refinement of the theory. Considering again the example of solidarity movements, the individual gains for the successful revolutionary may be a presidency, such as was the case with Havel and Wałęsa. It is not inconsistent with the theory to indicate that these revolutionaries identified specific interests with the organization of groups.

What then makes the theory attractive for analysing the transformation from a centrally planned to a market economy? Despite neo-classical strands of rational behaviour and its concomitant deficiency in deciphering the emergence of groups, it seems a suitable framework for analysing long-term evolutionary developments in processes of institutional change. Considering the emergence of interest groups, it may be comparatively static in nature, but regarding evolution in the configuration of interest groups, the theory may be illuminating. Two aspects come to the fore in this regard and will be examined in the remainder of this chapter. Firstly, it is a disequilibrium approach. The criticism raised by Eggertsson that the theory does not make clear whose exclusive right it is to reform, 'except presumably an aggregate of competing interest groups who somehow reach an equilibrium' (Eggertsson, 1990, p. 279), is not certainly confirmed. On the contrary, the fact of the matter is that interest-group theory dispenses with any equilibrium concept. Political decision making is not equivalent to some kind of 'invisible hand' arranging equilibrium in exchange. Consequently, the theory is considered suitable for this study. Secondly, different legacies of transformation with respect to interest groups seem an appropriate starting-point for testing differences in initial situations. In other words, it seems useful to study the extent to which different configurations of interests had an impact on the process of stabilization, liberalization, privatization and restructuring, as well as institution building. This will be looked at in the next section.[4]

TRANSFORMATION STRATEGIES COMPARED

Stabilization

Regarding stabilization, the strategies applied can, by and large, be characterized by the commonly attached labels of 'shock' and 'gradual'. Therefore, stabilization issues will be rather briefly illustrated. The shock approach towards stabilization is most clearly embodied in the Polish reform programme, which the Mazowiecki government implemented in January 1990. A restrictive monetary policy, tight wage control, severe cuts in subsidies, in combination with liberalization of the vast majority of prices and external trade relations, were the main ingredients of this IMF-approved policy. A huge decline in economic activity as a negative consequence of this shock treatment was expected to last for a quite short time, and, moreover, had to be interpreted as a necessary reduction of inefficient production.

In many ways, the Polish policy served as a yardstick for the transformation throughout Central and Eastern Europe. But it did not serve as an example for all of these countries. Hungary followed a rather deviant path. The Antall–Boross government speeded up the reforms initiated by the Hungarian communists in the 1970s and 1980s, instead of disposing of this legacy as soon as possible. With respect to stabilization, certain Keynesian-inspired elements supporting a more gradual approach are clearly visible. The government tried to maintain the purchasing power of the population in order to avoid a dramatic decline in aggregate demand. For example, contrary to the Polish macroeconomic stabilization scheme, there were no serious attempts to tax away wage increases that exceeded inflation. As a result of the liberal wage policy, real-wage falls were quite moderate in comparison with the surrounding countries and now Hungarian employees are among the best-paid in Central and Eastern Europe.

The fact that Hungarian stabilization policy reveals some gradualist strands does not necessarily imply that the Hungarian authorities were inspired solely by the arguments put forward by adherents of a gradual approach towards the transformation. In fact, it may very well have been the case that policy contingency was less than in Poland. Because of relatively smooth political changes, to some extent initiated from within the socialist party, the former communists could not solely be blamed for the decline in output as being necessary for the creation of the market economy. As opposed to this, the post-communist leaders in Poland could initially argue that the negative social impact of the shock therapy was simply the result of the communist legacy. Hence, policy responsibility at the start of the transformation was more intricate in Hungary. Even if they wanted to implement a shock therapy, they were not able to do so because of public resistance at the start of transformation. Here, it seems that the nature of the political restrictions shaped the policy. It has to be added, though, that in order to restore macroeconomic equilibrium, the current socialist government headed by Prime Minister Horn was forced to apply real shock treatment in the end. The Hungarian situation suggests that, taking into account the necessity of a quick restoration of macroeconomic stability, the 'reformist' legacy of the past did not automatically imply a relatively favourable position.

After the political turmoil of 1989, stabilization policy in Czechoslovakia resembled that of Poland, although the implications were totally different. The Czechoslovak government implemented a monetary and fiscal policy that was restrictive in nature, but since macroeconomic disequilibria in terms of the size of monetary overhang and hard currency debts were rather modest, 'Polish' inflationary outbursts did not emerge. None the less, the restrictive monetary policy entailed high interest rates, the prescription of minimal reserves for commercial banks, and the implementation of administrative burdens with regard to credit accommodation. Since the Slovaks were in a relatively backward position, they claimed to be harder hit by the stabilization policy of the Czechoslovak federal authorities, and therefore expressed the desire to delay or postpone part of these painful reforms. In order to do so, they needed greater political independence. Therefore, after the break-up of the federation in 1993, it was expected that the stabilization policies of the Czech Republic and Slovakia would start to deviate. Indeed, the Czech authorities initially maintained a restrictive monetary and fiscal policy, whereas Slovakia took measures to ease the pain. However, only half a year after the split, stabilization policies converged again. Owing to international pressure, especially from the International Monetary Fund and the European Union, Slovakia was forced to tighten its belt once more, whereas the outstanding Czech stabilization performance gave the authorities some leeway to adjust their stabilization policy and make it less restrictive. This was a move towards a more gradual approach.

In terms of interest groups, the differences among the countries in transition were clear and certainly not to the advantage of the most reformed at the start of the transformation. Whereas Czechoslovakia and Poland were in a position to severely restrain effective demand, Hungary was far less able to do so. Well-organized pressure groups were able to prevent too restrictive reforms until external pressure from the IMF eventually forced the Hungarian authorities to do so. This role of the Fund was also manifested in Slovakia.

Liberalization

Liberalization is closely related to stabilization. It was perceived as an important item in all the Central European countries, and, with the notable exception of labour markets, more or less the same differences can be observed between, on the one hand, Poland and Czechoslovakia, and Hungary on the other. Poland and Czechoslovakia opted for a quick liberalization of nearly 90 per cent of all prices within a period of approximately half a year. The only difference between the two countries was that Poland started price liberalization in January 1990, whereas Czechoslovak prices were liberalized from the start of 1991. The emphasis on full liberalization of prices, which implies a focus on allocative efficiency, reveals pure neo-classical influence. Furthermore, the efforts to implement a market economy almost overnight witnessed a strong belief in the possibility of pragmatically constructing a market economy. Because of the rational behaviour of agents, the legacy of the past was not believed seriously to thwart the purposes of the transformation strategy.

Although 90 per cent of prices in Hungary were liberalized at the end of 1991, the process took longer. During the period of reforms in the 1970s and 1980s most attempts to free prices failed, but genuine liberalization had already been introduced in 1989 – before the system collapsed. The same holds true with respect to the liberalization of foreign markets. In Hungary, import liberalization as an important step towards currency convertibility was partly introduced before the political change-over and started from January 1989. It entailed a liberalization of 80 per cent of all imports within three years. After the communists were obliged to resign, the timetable was shortened, but compared to Czechoslovakia and Poland, which introduced internal convertibility more or less overnight and relied upon the idea that devaluation of the currency was the only mechanism to protect domestic industries, import liberalization proceeded more gradually. It implied that not all industrial sectors were exposed to world market conditions at once, whereas in Czechoslovakia and in Poland, foreign trade was liberalized almost overnight. This has to be added, though, that the observed differences should not be exaggerated. All the Central European countries under consideration effected genuine liberalization of imports within an astonishing and unprecedentedly short period of time, and even though the Hungarian currency was legally not fully convertible, in practice it was so from approximately half a year after the first post-communist government took office in May 1990.

The liberalization of labour markets in the Central European countries under investigation largely differed from the process of price and foreign trade liberalization in these countries and this seems to be an aspect which opposes common perceptions of the nature of the transformation in the countries under consideration. Due to the legacy of the reforms in the 1980s, the Hungarian labour market was the most liberal and the authorities were not in a position to reimpose effective wage controls. At the other extreme, the Czechoslovak authorities to a large extent directly intervened in this respect and at first even continued to use central planning's powers of decree in order to implement a tough wages policy administratively. The Czechoslovak reformers were in a position to manoeuvre without seriously being counteracted by distributional interest groups. In fact, according to interest-group theory, the starting condition of centralized decision making was ideal, given that responsible authority made decisions according to the interests of society at large.

The Czech authorities were able to capture trade unions, instead of the other way around, by making them responsible for the economic performance of the country. Therefore, it was in unions' interest to collaborate. As shown earlier, since 1991 wage restraints have been negotiated in the context of a tripartite council consisting of representatives of the government, the employers and the employees, after which the government has the power to fix the negotiated results by decree. Therefore, the Czech Republic is unique not in the achievement of restricting wages, but in how wage restrictions are accepted without major upheavals. Despite the liberal rhetoric of Prime Minister Klaus of the Czech Republic, corporatist labour relations seem to enhance the population's willingness to accept the cost of transformation. Moreover, as part of the implicit 'social contract' the Czech authorities apply a very active labour market policy. In order to attune demand and supply of labour in an as yet poorly functioning market, the government mandates district labour offices to create socially useful jobs and introduces extensive retraining programmes for the unemployed. This labour market policy fits very well into an approach which links a transformation strategy with the nature of political constraints. In the Czech Republic, the present government still seems to have the support of a large part of the population, whereas high unemployment rates may have contributed to major political shifts that (partly) led to the return of socialist powers in Poland and Hungary. But whatever the underlying motives may have been, the fact of the matter is that the Czech liberalization of labour markets has been of a gradual type, rather than an example of a shock approach, an immediate opening of the market. At the same time, developments show that the monitoring of liberalization within initially strictly centralized hierarchical structures is easier to pursue than in circumstances characterized by more intricate configurations of bargaining groups due to decentralization in the past, that is, before the start of real transformation.

Privatization and Restructuring

Privatization dominates the agenda of transformation in the formerly centrally planned economies, and this also holds true for the Central European countries (see for example Bolton and Rolánd, 1992). Whereas price liberalization in combination with a restrictive monetary and fiscal policy is supposed to support macroeconomic stability, the importance of privatization lies in microeconomic restructuring. Privatization ultimately has to improve enterprise efficiency, since the budget constraints of private enterprises are ultimately tougher than those of state enterprises. Large-scale transfers of property rights from the state to the public, however, have far-reaching consequences for the division of capital and income. So, while there may be broad consensus with respect to the importance of privatization, because of the massive welfare effects, it remains to be seen how to transfer state property. Should privatization precede restructuring, or should both take place simultaneously, and, if there are firm reasons to sequence privatization, which criteria guide the decision? The transfer of property rights in the Central European countries perfectly illustrates the different views and the scope for policy making.

Whereas Poland set the stage for stabilization, Czechoslovakia did so for privatization with the introduction of the so-called 'voucher schemes'. Voucher schemes can be perceived as the most decentralized way of privatization, but, in fact, they were not. By distributing vouchers to the population almost free of charge, and subsequently organizing several auctions at which these vouchers could be exchanged for enterprise shares, the Czechoslovak authorities tried to create a capital market at once and provoke entrepreneurial behaviour. The danger of an extreme dispersal of ownership rights, which would lead to ineffective control over the management, more or less disappeared thanks to an unexpected spontaneous development of investment funds, which fulfilled an intermediation function. There is no active role left for the state to intervene as far as restructuring is concerned. Privatization is an instrument for restructuring, not the other way round. It has to be added, though, that before the actual issuing of vouchers, the Czechoslovak authorities made every effort to prevent enterprises themselves from starting negotiations with possibly interested foreign partners. At the very start of the process, the Czechoslovak authorities set up a Ministry of Privatization and all interested in buying state property were asked to contact the ministry. So, initially, there was complete centralization in the process of transferring ownership rights from the state to the public. This was a deliberate attempt to keep tight control of the privatization process, as was also the case in the labour market.

Poland to some extent followed the Czechoslovak example after initial failures of so-called 'nomenklatura' privatization. But with respect to the implementation of voucher schemes as part of mass privatization programmes, the Polish authorities did not intend to rely completely upon the Czechoslovak *laissez-faire* approach. In order to avoid too much dispersion of enterprise shares, they deliberately created holdings, each of which consisted of a number of state-owned enterprises operating in a common sector. These holdings serve as financial intermediaries between the population and the state. The population cannot exchange vouchers for enterprise shares, but is only allowed to change them for shares of the holding. This might be called an 'interventionist' voucher scheme which is designed to let privatization and restructuring proceed simultaneously. Since it took so much time to win parliamentary and presidential approval for privatization, liquidation of state-owned enterprises – not necessarily implying bankruptcy – dominated the Polish privatization, in other words the direct selling of state assets without transforming the enterprise into a share partnership. Here, legislation of the 1980s was decisive.

With the exception of restitution of land, the Antall–Boross government in Hungary did not make use of vouchers, although the option of voucher schemes had been discussed repeatedly in parliament. The Hungarian authorities decided to sell state property after spontaneous privatization led to enormous distrust on the part of the population with respect to the general reforms. A special state property agency is required to select enterprises for privatization. In choosing this approach, the state interfered actively, since it implicitly made decisions about which sectors were believed to be vital and not to be left solely to the market. On top of that, the Hungarian parliament decided in the summer of 1992 to create a state organ responsible for the exploitation of state property that was deemed to be ineligible for privatization. Although the establishment of this state body was meant to support the state property agency by more clearly distinguishing privatization from exploitation of state enterprises, two functions which until then had been unified within the state property agency, it implicitly set a maximum to the number of enterprises to be selected for privatization.

Although it is extremely risky to generalize about privatization experiences, it can be asserted that arguments related to a more gradual sequencing to a larger extent led decision making in Hungary compared with what happened in Czechoslovakia and Poland. Hungarian privatization seems to accompany some kind of industrial policy, which has to be interpreted as guiding the market. Furthermore, the fact that the Hungarian policy refrained from the idea that privatization should in principle include all companies amplifies this line of thought. Czechoslovakian and Polish privatization experiences were somewhat different. The voucher privatization in Czechoslovakia was introduced in order to privatize the whole industrial sector at maximum speed. It can even be maintained that giving away state property to the population at large, without taking welfare considerations into account, is fairly close to the Coase theorem, which states that, under the assumptions of zero transaction costs and free exchange, no matter how the property rights are initially divided among the population, they will eventually always be distributed in the most efficient way. In other words, transaction costs related to the redistribution of ownership rights, after privatization was completed, are assumed to be free of charge. In this respect, the Czechoslovak experience presents a neo-classical-inspired shock approach. But there certainly are gradual elements as well. These are to be found in subsequent restructuring. The enormous dispersion of property rights among the population stresses confidence in individual entrepreneurship as the driving force that must accomplish economic change. Furthermore, the distribution of property rights implies that the state is not inclined to restructure state properties. This is envisaged as the essential task of the new private owners. Restructuring is assumed to be a waste of time and money. On top of that, the Czechoslovak authorities refrained from intervention aimed at the prevention of dispersed ownership rights. The emergence of investment funds was a process of spontaneous evolution. It might be suggested that the Czech path of privatization as part of the transformation to a market economy reveals important strands of Austrian economics.

The Polish option is extremely hard to categorize, but seems to a large extent to resemble aspects of both the Czech and the Hungarian experiences. Regarding the Czech resemblance, it should be noted that the installation of privatization intermediaries in mass privatization, as opposed to *laissez-faire* voucher privatization, may be interpreted as a deliberate attempt to preserve interest in certain pivotal sectors. However, there was also one aspect which was quite similar to what happened in Hungary and which indicates that partially decentralized economic decision making as a legacy of the communist past made it more difficult to monitor the transfer of ownership rights. One could argue that a decentralization of economic decision making in the late 1980s led to a system of diffuse property rights. Managers were in a position to delay privatization or, conversely, initiate it when they believed it to be beneficial to themselves. The foundation of state property agencies was an attempt to monitor this 'nomenklatura' privatization in Poland and 'spontaneous' privatization in Hungary. The authorities were unable to regain control to the extent possible in Czechoslovakia. The relatively 'liberal' legacy turned out to be a burden rather than an advantageous head start.

The ultimate proof of successful privatization is in changing the economic behaviour of privatized firms. Privatization in itself may be quite quick, but at the same time will not necessarily improve enterprise efficiency, since the enforcement of market-conforming behaviour needs more than privatization alone. Hence, the speed of privatization is a meaningless criterion for shock treatment or gradualism, without taking limiting conditions in the institutional sphere of market building into account.

Institution Building

Institution building refers to providing a framework for the well-functioning of markets and most specifically refers to those reform attempts that will have an impact on incentive structures. Most fundamentally it aims at a hardening of the budget constraints, to ensure that enterprises can no longer adjust the budget to the costs *ex post*. It is difficult to sum up all the relevant measures, but one might suggest that most of the reform attempts that try to impose financial discipline on enterprises are closely linked to the implementation of a new financial system.

Since financial markets were completely absent in the formerly centrally planned economies, or at most functioned at an embryonic stage, investment capital needed for restructuring the economy is mainly to be supplied by banks. The banking sector, however, is seriously constrained in supplying credits. The state banks inherited bad portfolios, as under central planning credits resulted from retrospective adjustment for changes in the real sphere of the economy. Therefore, once a market economy was required to replace this passive financial system, the banks started with the burden of several decades of badly performing loans and were not in a favourable position to generate new investment capital.

Surveying the creation of investment capital, one can observe delays which are common to all Central European countries. Although Hungary implemented a two-tier banking system as early as 1987, an efficient mechanism of capital allocation failed to emerge. Since the enforcement of financial discipline was ineffective, the large state-owned enterprises received the bulk of the credits, whereas tight credit controls squeezed out investment opportunities for new private enterprises. But after being in power for nearly one and a half years, in December 1991 the Antall–Boross government introduced a whole package of institutional measures which should at once have terminated perpetuating superfluous lending to state-owned enterprises. A pivotal part of the institutional package was the enforcement of a bankruptcy law. Furthermore, in order to tackle the problems due to the inherited badly performing loans, the banks were forced to arrange special provisions. As a consequence, a rocketing number of state-owned as well as private enterprises went bankrupt. This policy certainly does not fit into the perception of a strategy of gradual transformation: it was a pure shock treatment.

Notwithstanding a commonly accepted shock approach, the Czechoslovak authorities intervened directly and complemented tight monitoring of banks with financial support for distressed enterprises. To a greater extent than in Hungary, banks were able to write off non-performing loans, whereas new provisions were more relaxed. In addition, the Czechoslovak government founded a special 'Consolidation Bank' in an attempt to reduce the financial burden on enterprises in the process of privatization. Czechoslovak policy was explicitly aimed at preventing the above-mentioned credit crunch, since the spread on interests could remain within reasonable margins. This had a positive impact on lending possibilities for private investment projects. In the meantime, however, the Consolidation Bank evolved from being one of the largest creditors into an important institution in the field of restructuring large enterprises. This hampered the process of restructuring. Furthermore, a bankruptcy Act did not come into effect until April 1993, and even now only a few liquidations have materialized. Moreover, the bankruptcy Act explicitly disallows the closing of state-owned enterprises during the process of privatization. For political reasons, the Czech government is tolerating the survival of a large number of loss-making enterprises, while it is not in the interest of large commercial banks to initiate bankruptcy proceedings.

The Polish policy is less easy to interpret. A main characteristic seems to be slowness, since arrangements with respect to badly performing debts became effective only in March 1993. But it is unclear whether this can be perceived as gradual, or has to be seen as a muddling through as a result of a continuous political struggle.

In sum, with respect to creating market institutions, the identification of Hungarian gradualism versus Czech and Polish shock treatment is completely misleading. Taking into consideration the reforms aimed at hardening the budget constraints into consideration, it rather seems the other way around. In the absence of well-functioning markets, the Czech authorities in particular decided to intervene, and, most importantly in this respect, were able to do so.

DIFFERENT STRATEGIES AND COMMON ECONOMIC CRISIS?

The Central European countries applied different policies during the first years of transformation. Although diverging courses were partly due to different ideas the policy makers had when starting the transformation, it is maintained that they were mainly the result of differences in scope for policy manoeuvring. This section briefly outlines economic performance since 1990 and, on the basis of these factual developments, will present hypotheses concerning the differences in reform policies.

As could be observed from Tables 3.3, 3.4, 4.1 and 5.1 in the preceding chapters, all four Central European countries experienced severe falls in GDP. Poland was the first country that suffered from heavy production declines, but also appeared to be the first country with positive GDP growth. Approximately one year later, Czechoslovakia and Hungary suffered from the transition crisis. In the tables regarding the Czech and Slovak Republics (3.3 and 3.4), economic performances have been calculated in retrospect, but it goes without saying that during the last two years of the federation both the Czechs and the Slovaks were heavily hit by the recession. Whereas for the Czech Republic the fall in economic activity stopped in 1993 and became slightly positive in 1994, Slovakia still experienced negative growth in 1993, although at a decreasing rate, but achieved remarkable growth in 1994. Hungary is generally believed to have followed a more gradual path of transformation, but the decline in economic activity was no less than in the other countries. Other calculations also reveal that during the first five years following the collapse of communism, all the countries under consideration were confronted with a cumulative contraction of GDP within a range of 18 to 22 per cent (see European Bank for Reconstruction and Development, 1996(a); Zloch-Christy, 1994, p. 124).

With economic activity declining in subsequent years, unemployment started to rise to a current level of approximately 15 per cent in all the Central European countries, whereas the budget deficits crept up to the critical IMF level of 5 per cent – the Czech Republic taking a different stand in these respects. The initial price shock, resulting from price liberalization, was certainly larger than expected, but what is more noteworthy, in none of the countries did the stabilization schemes succeed in returning inflation rates to single-digit levels on an annual basis, Poland in this respect remaining a notorious negatively performing outlier.

The results fit into the general J-curves framework (see Brada and King, 1992), which assumes the inevitability of a transition crisis and suggests that a drop in economic activity is unavoidable before there can be an improvement of economic performance. In fact, adherents of both a shock and a gradual approach towards the transformation confirm the inevitability of such a contraction in economic activity. It applies to all the Central European countries under consideration and mainly stems from three factors. Firstly, the transformation towards a market economy implies a reallocation of means of production from loss-making to profitable industries and services. This shift will not proceed without frictions and necessarily coincides with a short-term decline in output. Secondly, a price has to be paid for the attainment of macroeconomic equilibrium. Thirdly, contrary to a supply-constrained centrally planned system, a demand-constrained market economy has to remain flexible by not producing part of the potential output (Ellman, 1993). During the adjustment processes, production will decline, as apparently was the case in Czechoslovakia, Hungary and Poland. Of course, the question remains whether the transition crises in these countries were too severe or not, and whether part of the pain could have been eased by applying other policies.

The indicators support the inevitability of the transition crisis, but they also suggest either that the frequently attached labels of shock versus gradual over-emphasized differences in the strategies applied, or that the common decline in output has to be explained by external shocks. Although the latter view cannot be completely ruled out (see Brada and King, 1992), this study has indeed illustrated that there are firm reasons to challenge the appropriateness of the frequently suggested labels.

CONCLUDING REMARKS

This chapter has not presented interest-group theory as a panacea for illustrating diverging transformation strategies. It certainly was not. The fact that economic crises were common to all countries, irrespective of the chosen strategy of transformation, more or less refuted the basic assumption. Nevertheless, in certain areas of the transformation, the theory underlines the following main conclusions of this study.

Firstly, due to its comparatively static nature, mainstream economic theory faces enormous difficulties in explaining the transformation from a centrally planned to a market economy. What the theory is able to achieve, at best, is to define the necessary elements of the desired new order. But even in this case, neo-classical economics is inclined to define a market economy as the negation of a planned economic order. Therefore, transformation is seen as the dismantling of institutions and procedures of central planning.

Secondly, those theories which explicitly take path-dependency and hysteresis into account seem to be more suitable in explaining the incidence of certain reform steps. Path-dependency requires the economist to take the legacy of the communist past into account, whereas non-reversibility of an economic order – the impossible task of unscrambling the eggs – demands of the economist not to define the market system in negative terms and to include institution building as a major element in the transformation. A market economy needs special institutions in order to function.

Thirdly, institution building is a matter of economic regulation. Certain theories of political economy have shown regulation to be vulnerable to pressure groups. These groups will try to shape regulations in such a way that is perceived most beneficial to their specific interest and not to the interest of the whole society. It is clear that the transformation is certainly not in the interest of the bureaucracy. But it is also a mistake to hold that enterprises would be interested in market reforms.

Fourthly, regarding the regulatory aspect of the transformation, this study has shown that the countries which were most reformist in the twilight of the communist era were most likely to face effective pressure-group behaviour and, therefore, were certainly not in the most favourable position for transformation. Since, for example in Hungary, reforms in the 1970s and 1980s implied decentralization in economic decision making, it was more difficult to monitor and control other aspects of the processes of transformation, such as further liberalization and the transfer of ownership rights. In the countries which had inherited a past of 'enlightened' communism, a system of diffuse property rights had emerged.

Fifthly, despite the observation of different pasts triggering different paths of transformation, it should also be noted that there is a convergence in economic performance of the Central European countries. This remark is not meant as any kind of 'indifference statement' concerning the strategies chosen for the transformation from a centrally planned to a fully-fledged market economy, but rather points to the fact that instead of merely focusing on the differences among the countries in transition, it is also important not to overlook common mistakes.

NOTES

1. In Chapter 5, it has already been noted that Poland is expected to be the first country. To this can be added that Slovenia will also be able to reach the 'magic marker' in 1998. Regarding the Czech Republic, Hungary and Slovakia, prognoses indicate this to be the case in 1999 (see European Bank for Reconstruction and Development, 1997; World Bank, 1996).

2. Strictly speaking, distributional effects are not due to market failures. However, they are often an incentive to government regulation.

3. In another context, this point has been made by characterizing Stalin as the owner of the Soviet Union (Olson, 1992).

4. This section is built on ideas of the author's article in *Comparative Economic Studies* (Hoen, 1996). I feel indebted to the publisher for the permission to use that publication.

References

Ábel, I. and Bonin, J. (1993), 'State Desertion and Convertibility: the Case of Hungary', in Székely, I.P. and Newbery, D.M.G. (eds), *Hungary: An Economy in Transition*, Cambridge: Cambridge University Press, pp. 329–41.

Ábel, I. and Prander, K. (1994), 'Impediments to Financial Restructuring in Hungarian Enterprises', in Jackson, M. and Bilsen V. (eds), *Company Management and Capital Market Development in the Transition*, Aldershot: Avebury, pp. 227–39.

Adam, J. (1993), 'Transformation to a Market Economy in the Former Czechoslovakia', *Europe–Asia Studies*, 45, pp. 627–45.

Aghion, P. and Blanchard, O. (1993), 'On the Speed of Transition in Central Europe', European Bank for Reconstruction and Development, Working Paper, No. 6, London.

Altmann, F.-L. (1988), 'Zu den Versuchen der "Vervolkommnung" des Außenwirtschaftssytems in der ČSSR', in Haendcke-Hoppe, M. (ed.) *Außenwirtschaftssysteme und Außenwirtschaftsreformen sozialistischer Länder; Ein intrasystemarer Vergleich*, Berlin: Duncker & Humblot, pp. 129–42.

Angresano, J. (1996), 'Poland after the Shock', *Comparative Economic Studies*, 38, pp. 87–111.

Arato, A. (1994), 'Election, Coalition and Constitution in Hungary', *The Hungarian Quarterly*, 35, pp. 3–13.

Ausch, S. (1972), *Theory and Practice of CMEA Cooperation*, Budapest: Akadémiai Kiadó.

Balcerowicz, L. (1995), *Socialism, Capitalism, Transformation*, Budapest, London and New York: Central European University Press.

Baldwin, R.E. (1994), *Towards an Integrated Europe*, Centre for Economic Policy Research, London.

Barany, Z.D. (1990), 'On the Road to Democracy: The Hungarian Elections of 1990', *Südosteuropa*, 39, pp. 318–29.

Barry, B. and Hardin, R. (eds) (1982), *Rational Man and Irrational Society? An Introduction and Source book*, Beverly Hills: Sage.

Bauer, T. (1976), 'The Contradictory Position of the Enterprise under the New Hungarian Mechanism', *Co-existence*, 13, pp. 65–80.

Bauer, T. (1978), 'Investment Cycles in Planned Economies', *Acta Oeconomica*, 21, pp. 234–60.

Bauer, T. (1983), 'The Hungarian Alternative to Soviet-Type Planning', *Journal of Comparative Economics*, 7, pp. 304–16.

Belka, M. (1994), 'Financial Restructuring of Banks and Enterprises in Poland', *Moct-Most*, 4, pp. 71–84.

Berend, I.T. (1996), *Central and Eastern Europe 1944–1993. Detour from the Periphery to the Periphery*, Cambridge: Cambridge University Press.

Berg, A. (1994), 'Does Macroeconomic Reform Cause Structural Adjustment? Lessons from Poland', *Journal of Comparative Economics*, 18, pp. 376–409.

Berg, A. and Sachs, J. (1992), 'Structural Adjustment and International Trade in Eastern Europe: The Case of Poland', *Economic Policy*, 14, pp. 117–55.

Biessen, G. (1996), *East European Foreign Trade and System Changes*, Amsterdam: Thesis Publishers.

Blaug, M. (1987), *Economic Theory in Retrospect*, 4th edition, Cambridge: Cambridge University Press.

Blejer, M., Calvo, J.B.A., Coricelli, F. and Gelb, A.H. (1993), 'Eastern Europe in Transition: From Recession to Growth?', The World Bank, Discussion Paper, No. 196, Washington D.C..

Blue Ribbon Commission (1990), 'Hungary in Transformation to Freedom and Prosperity: Economic Programme Proposals of the Joint Hungarian–International Blue Ribbon Commission', The Hudson Institute, Indianapolis.

Bolton, P. and Roländ, G. (1992), 'Privatization Policies in Central and Eastern Europe', *Economic Policy*, 15, pp. 275–310.

Bornstein, M. (1994), 'The Soviet Centrally Planned Economy', in Bornstein, M. (ed.), *Comparative Economic Systems; Models and Cases*, 7th edition, Burr Ridge, Boston and Sydney: Irwin Publishers, pp. 411–43.

Brada, J.C. (1991), 'The Political Economy of Communist Foreign Trade Institutions and Policies', *Journal of Comparative Economics*, 15, pp. 211–38.

Brada, J.C. (1993), 'Regional Integration in Eastern Europe: Prospects for Integration within the Region and the European Community', in De Melo, J. and Panagariya, A. (eds), *New Dimensions in Regional Integration*, Centre for Economic Policy Research, Cambridge: Cambridge University Press, pp. 319–47.

Brada, J.C. and King, A. (1992), 'Is There a J-curve for the Economic Transition from Socialism to Capitalism?', *Economics of Planning*, 25, pp. 37–53.

Brainard, L. (1991), 'Strategies for Economic Transformation in Central and Eastern Europe: Role of Financial Market Reform', in Blommestein, H. and Marrese, M. (eds), *Transformation of Planned Economies: Property Rights Reform and Macroeconomic Stability*, OECD, Paris, pp. 95–108.

Brakman, S. (1991), *International Trade Modelling: Decomposition Analysis*, Groningen: Wolters-Noordhoff.

Brown, J.F. (1994), *Hopes and Shadows; Eastern Europe after Communism*, Harlow: Longman.

Bruno, M. (1992), 'Stabilization and Reform in Eastern Europe: A Preliminary Evaluation', *IMF Staff Papers*, 39, pp. 319–47.

Burda, M. (1993), 'Unemployment, Labour Markets and Structural Change in Eastern Europe', *Economic Policy*, 16. pp. 101–38.

Business Central Europe (1995), 'Is Slovakia Privatising?', 3(23), pp. 15–16.

Calvo, G. and Coricelli, F. (1992), 'Stabilizing a Previously Centrally Planned Economy: Poland 1990', *Economic Policy*, 14, pp. 176–226.

Canning, A. and Hare, P (1994), 'The Privatization Process – Economic and Political Aspects of the Hungarian Approach', in Estrin, S. (ed.), *Privatization in Central & Eastern Europe*, London and New York: Longman, pp. 176–217.

Charap, J. and Zemplinerova, A. (1993), 'Restructuring in the Czech Economy', European Bank for Restructuring and Development, Working Paper, No. 2, London.

Ciechocińska, M. (1992), 'Development of the Private Sector in Poland in 1989–90', *Communist Economies and Economic Transformation*, 2, pp. 215–36.

Cline, W.R. (1984), *International Debt: Systemic Risk and Policy Responses*, Institute for International Economics, Cambridge (Massachusetts) and London: MIT Press.

Commission of the European Union (1995), 'White Paper. Preparation of the Associated Countries of Central and Eastern Europe for Integration into the Internal Market of the Union', COM(95) 163 final/2 Annexe, Brussels.

Csaba, L. (1983), *Economic Mechanism in the GDR and in Czechoslovakia*, Hungarian Scientific Council for World Economy, Budapest.

Csaba, L. (1990), *Eastern Europe in the World Economy*, Budapest: Akadémiai Kiadó.

Csaba, L. (1993), 'Economic Consequences of Soviet Disintegration for Hungary', in Székely, I.P. and Newbery, D.M.G. (eds), *Hungary: An Economy in Transition*, Cambridge: Cambridge University Press, pp. 27–43.

Csaba, L. (1994), 'Hungary and the IMF: The Experience of a Cordial Discord', Kopint-Datorg Economic Research, Marketing and Computing Co. Ltd., Discussion Paper, No. 22, Budapest.

Csaba, L. (1996), *The Capitalist Revolution in Eastern Europe*, Aldershot: Edward Elgar.

Deutsche Bank Research, 'Eastern Europe Heading for Reform; Facts, Problems, Prospects', Deutsche Bank Research Series, Fankfurt am Main, various issues.

De Weydenthal, J.B. (1991), 'The Visegrád Summit', *Report on Eastern Europe*, 2, pp. 28–32.

Dittus, P. (1994), 'Corporate Control in Central Europe: The Role of Banks', Bank for International Settlements, mimeo, Basel.

Dobszay, J. (1994), 'Back to the Future; The 1994 Elections', *The Hungarian Quarterly*, 35, pp. 9–14.

Edwards, S. (1992), 'Stabilization and Liberalization Policies for Economies in Transition: Latin American Lessons for Eastern Europe', in Clague, C. and Rausser, G. (eds), *The Emergence of Market Economies in Eastern Europe*, Cambridge (Massachusetts) and Oxford: Basil Blackwell, pp. 129–59.

Eggertsson, T. (1990), *Economic Behavior and Institutions*, Cambridge: Cambridge University Press.

Ellman, M. (1993), 'General Aspects of Transition', in Admiraal. P. (ed.), *Economic Transition in Eastern Europe*, Oxford: Basil Blackwell, pp. 1–32.

Estrin, S. (1994), 'Economic Transition and Privatization: The Issues', in Estrin, S. (ed.), *Privatization in Central & Eastern Europe*, London and New York: Longman, pp. 3–30.

Estrin, S., Hare, P. and Suranyi, M. (1992), 'Banking in Transition: Development and Current Problems in Hungary', *Soviet Studies*, 44, pp. 785–808.

Eucken, W. (1990), *Grundsätze der Wirtschaftspolitik*, 6th edition, Tübingen: Mohr.

European Bank for Reconstruction and Development (1996(a)), 'Transition Report 1995; Investment and Enterprise Development', London.

European Bank for Reconstruction and Development (1996(b)), 'Transition Report Update; April 1996', London.

European Bank for Reconstruction and Development (1997), 'Transition Report 1996; Infrastructure and Savings', London.

Falk, M. and Funke, N. (1993), 'Zur Sequenz von Reformschritten: Erste Erfahrungen aus dem Transformationprozeß in Mittel- und Osteuropa', *Die Weltwirtschaft*, 2, pp. 196–206.

Fidrmuc, J., Foltín, J., Huber, P., Jarošová, M., Kohútová, J., Kosír, I., Kováč, R., Ochotnický, P., Szerdahelyiová, S. and Wörgötter, A. (1994), *The Slovak Republic After One Year of Independence*, Bank Austria, Wien.

Fink, G. (1996), 'Enlargement of the European Union', *Studien des Institutes für den Donauraum und Mitteleuropa*, Background Material, Wien.

Fisher, S. (1993), 'Economic Development in the Newly Independent Slovakia', *Radio Free Europe/Radio Liberty Research Report*, 2, pp. 42–8.

Fornalczyk, A. (1993), 'Competition Policy in the Polish Economy in Transition', in Estrin, S. and Cave. M. (eds), *Competition and Competition Policy: A Comparative Analysis of Central and Eastern Europe*, London: Pinter Publishers, pp. 28–43.

Fries, S.M. and Lane, T.D. (1994), 'Financial and Enterprise Restructuring in Emerging Market Economies', International Monetary Fund, Working Papers, No. 94/34, Washington D.C.

Friss, I. (1978), 'Ten Years of Economic Reform in Hungary', *Acta Oeconomica*, 20, pp. 1–19.

Frydman, R., Rapaczyński, A. and Earle, J.S. (1993), *The Privatization Process in Central Europe*, Budapest, London and New York: Central European University Press.

Gács, J. (1994), 'Trade Liberalization in the CSFR, Hungary, and Poland: Rush and Reconsideration', in Gács, J. and Winckler, G. (eds), *International Trade and Restructuring in Eastern Europe*, Heidelberg: Physica-Verlag, pp. 123–53.

Gardner, S. (1983), *Soviet Foreign Trade: The Decision Process*, Boston; Kluwer-Nijhoff.

Garretsen, H. (1992), *Keynes, Coordination and Beyond. The Development of Macroeconomic and Monetary Theory since 1945*, Aldershot: Edward Elgar.

GATT (1972), 'GATT-activities in 1970/71', Geneva.

Gerrits, A.W.M. (1990), *The Failure of Authoritarian Change. Reform, Opposition and Geo-Politics in Poland in the 1980s*, Aldershot: Dartmouth.

Gomułka, S. and Jasiński, P. (1994), 'Privatization in Poland 1989–1993: Policies, Methods, and Results', in Estrin, S. (ed.), *Privatization in Central & Eastern Europe*, London and New York: Longman, pp. 218–51.

Grosfeld, I. (1990), 'Reform Economics and Western Economic Theory: Unexploited Opportunities', *Economics of Planning* 23, pp. 1–19.

Guzek, M. (1993), 'Die CEFTA aus polnischer Sicht', in Hölscher, J., Jacobsen, A., Tomann, H. and Weisfeld, H. (eds), *Bedingungen ökonomischer Entwicklung in Zentralosteuropa, Band 1: Aspekte des wirtschaftlichen Umbruchs*, Marburg: Metropolis-Verlag, pp. 185–95.

Handbook of Statistics; Countries in Transition 1995 (1995), Wiener Institut für Internationale Wirtschaftsvergleiche, Wien.

Hanel, P. (1992), 'Trade Liberalization in Czechoslovakia, Hungary, and Poland Through 1991: A Survey', *Comparative Economic Studies*, 34, pp. 34–53.

Hanson, P. (1982), 'The End of Import-Led Growth? Some Observations on Soviet, Polish, and Hungarian Experience in the 1970s', *Journal of Comparative Economics*, 6, pp. 130–47.

Hare, P. and Révész, T. (1992), 'Hungary's Transition to the Market: The Case against a Big Bang', *Economic Policy*, 14, pp. 227–64.

Hartmann, M. (1995), 'Notwendigkeit und Chancen einer Reform der GAP vor dem Hintergrund einer EU-Osterweiterung', Kopint-Datorg Economic Research, Marketing and Computing Co. Ltd, Discussion Paper, No. 35, Budapest.

Hayek, F.A. (1945), 'The Use of Knowledge in Society', *American Economic Review*, 35, pp. 519–30.

Hedri, G.I. (1993), 'Die EG und die Staten des "Visegráder Dreiecks"', *Osteuropa*, 43, pp. 154–66.

Hoen, H.W. (1994), 'Regional Economic Integration in Central Europe', *Moct-Most*, 4, pp. 115–31.

Hoen, H.W. (1995), 'Theoretically Underpinning the Transition in Eastern Europe: An Austrian View', *Economic Systems*, 19, pp. 59–77.

Hoen, H.W. (1996), 'Shock versus Gradualism in Central Europe Reconsidered, *Comparative Economic Studies*, 38, pp. 1–20.

Hoen, H.W. (1997), 'Is Economic Theory Able to Underpin the Transition in Eastern Europe', *Journal of International and Comparative Economics*, 6, pp. 153–75.

Hoen, H.W. and Van Leeuwen, E.H. (1991), 'Upgrading and Relative Competitiveness in Manufacturing Trade: Eastern Europe versus the Newly Industrializing Economies', *Weltwirtschaftliches Archiv*, 127, pp. 369–79.

Hoen, H.W. and Van Leeuwen, E.H. (1996), 'Hungary's Restructuring of Foreign Trade during the First Years of Transformation', *Current Politics and Economics of Europe*, 5, pp. 203–25.

Holzman, F.D. (1966), 'Foreign Trade Behavior of Centrally Planned Economies', in Rosovsky, H. (ed.), *Industrialization in Two Systems: Essays in Honor of Alexander Gerschenkron*, New York: John Wiley & Sons, pp. 237–65.

Horsefield, J.M. (1969), *The International Monetary Fund 1945-1965: Twenty Years of International Monetary Cooperation, Volume I, Chronicle*, Washington D.C.

Hrnčíř, M. (1991), 'Transition to a Market Type Economy: The Case of Czechoslovakia', *Moct-Most*, 1, pp. 21-32.

Járai, Zs. (1993), '10 per cent already Sold: Privatisation in Hungary', in Székely, I.P. and Newbery, D.M.G. (eds), *Hungary: An Economy in Transition*, Cambridge: Cambridge University Press, pp. 77-83.

Jasiński, P. (1990), 'Two Models of Privatization in Poland. A critical Assessment', *Communist Economies*, 3, pp. 373-401.

Jasiński, P. (1992), 'The Transfer and Redefinition of Property Rights: Theoretical Analysis of Transferring Property Rights and Transformational Privatization in the Post-STEs', *Communist Economies and Economic Transformation*, 2, pp. 163-90.

Jeffries, I. (1993), *Socialist Economies and the Transition to the Market: a Guide*, London and New York: Routledge.

Jepma, C.J. (1986), *Extensions and Application Possibilities of the Constant Market Shares Analysis; The Case of the Developing Countries' Exports*, PhD thesis, Groningen.

Jermakowicz, W. (1992), *Privatization in Poland: Aims and Methods*, Centrum Prywatyzacji, Warsaw.

Juchler, J. (1994), *Osteuropa im Umbruch, politische und gesellschaftliche Entwicklungen 1989-1993*, Gesamtüberblick und Fallstudien, Zürich: Seismo Verlag.

Kilényi G. and Lamm, V. (1990), *New Tendencies in the Hungarian Economy. Studies on Hungarian State and Law*, Budapest: Akadémiai Kiadó.

Kirzner, I.M. (1979), *Perception, Opportunity, and Profit: Studies in the Theory of Entrepreneurship*, Chicago and London: The University of Chicago Press.

Klaus, V. (1992), 'Transition – An Insider's View', *Problems of Communism*, 41, pp. 73-5.

Kornai, J. (1980), *Economics of Shortage*, Amsterdam: North Holland Publishing.

Kornai, J. (1983), 'Comments on the Present State and Prospects of the Hungarian Economic Reform', *Journal of Comparative Economics*, 7, pp. 225-52.

Kornai, J. (1986), 'The Hungarian Reform Process: Vision, Hopes, and Reality', *Journal of Economic Literature*, 24, pp. 1687-737.

Kornai, J. (1990), *The Road to a Free Economy. Shifting from a Socialist System: The Example of Hungary*, New York and London: Norton.

Košta, J. (1978), *Abriß der sozialökonomischen Entwicklung der Tschechoslowakei 1945-1977*, Frankfurt am Mein: Suhrkamp Verlag.

Kouba, K. (1994), 'Systemic Changes in the Czech Economy after Four Years (1990-1993)', *Acta Oeconomica*, 46, pp. 381-8.

Kregel, J. (1983), 'Post-Keynesian Theory: An Overview', *The Journal of Economic Education*, 14, pp. 32-43.

Kregel, J., Matzner, E. and Grabler, G. (eds) (1992), *The Market Shock: An Agenda for the Economic and Social Reconstruction of Central and Eastern Europe*, Austrian Academy of Sciences, Wien.

Křovák, J., Levcik, F., Lukas, Z., Pick, M. and Turek, O. (1993), 'The Czech and Slovak Economies After the Split', Wiener Institut für Internationale Wirtschaftsvergleiche, Forschungsberichte, No. 199, Wien.

Krueger, A.O. (1974), 'The Political Economy of the Rent-Seeking Society', *American Economic Review*, 64, pp. 291–303.

Krug, B. (1991), 'Die Transformation der sozialistischen Volkswirtschaften in Zentraleuropa: Ein Beitrag der Vergleichende Ökonomische Theorie von Institutionen', in Wagener, H.-J. (ed.), *Anpassung durch Wandel: Evolution und Transformation von Wirtschaftssytemen*, Berlin: Duncker & Humblot, pp. 39–60.

Krzak, M., (1995), 'The Experience of East European Countries with Different Exchange-Rate Regimes', Wiener Institut für Internationale Wirtschafts-vergleiche, Forschungsberichte, No. 217, Wien.

Kushnirsky, F.I. (1982), *Soviet Economic Planning, 1965–1980*, Boulder (Colorado): Westview Press.

Laski, B., Avramovic, D., Fath, J., Landesmann, M.A. and Rosati, D.K. (1993), 'Transition from the Command to the Market System: What Went Wrong and What to Do Now?', Wiener Institut für Internationale Wirtshaftsvergleiche (mimeo), Wien.

Lavigne, M. (1995), *The Economics of Transition: From Socialist Economy to Market Economy*, Houndmills, Basingstoke, Hampshire and London: Macmillan.

Leamer, E.E. and Stern R.M. (1970), *Quantitative International Economics*, Chicago: Aldine Publishing Company.

Leijonhufvud, A. (1968), *On Keynesian Economics and the Economics of Keynes. A Study in Monetary Theory*, New York and London: Oxford University Press.

Levcik, F., Pick, M., Turek, O. and Pöschl, J. (1994), 'The Czech Economy: Internal and External Developments Since 1989 and Future Options', Wiener Institut für Internationale Wirtschaftsvergleiche, Forschungsberichte, No. 203, Wien.

Lipton, D. and Sachs, J. (1990), 'Creating a Market Economy in Eastern Europe: The Case of Poland, *Brookings Papers on Economic Activity I*, 1, pp. 75–147.

Mackintosh, M., Brown, V, Costello, N., Dawson, G., Thompson, G. and Trigg, A. (1996), *Economics and Changing Economies*, London: Thomson Business Press.

Mason, E.S. and Asher, R.E. (1973), *The World Bank since Bretton Woods*, Washington D.C.

Matejka, H. (1986), 'The Foreign Trade System', in Kaser, M.C. (ed.), *The Economic History of Eastern Europe, 1919–1975, Institutional Change within a Planned Economy*, Volume III, Oxford: Clarendon Press, pp. 250–88.

Matejka, H. (1990), 'Central Planning, Trade Policy Instruments and Centrally Planned Economies within the Framework of the General Agreement on Tariffs and Trade', *Journal of Development Planning*, 20, pp. 142–62.

McKinnon, R.I. (1991), *The Order of Economic Liberalization; Financial Control in The Transition to a Market Economy*, Baltimore and London: The Johns Hopkins University Press.

Merkies, A.H.Q.M. and Van Der Meer, T. (1988), 'A Theoretical Foundation for the Constant Market Shares Analysis', *Empirical Economics*, 13(2), pp. 65–80.

Messerlin, P. (1992), 'The Association Agreements between the EC and Central Europe: Trade Liberalization versus Constitutional Failure?', in Flemming, J. and Rollo, J.M.C. (eds), *Trade and Payments Adjustment in Central and Eastern Europe*, Royal Institute of International Affairs and European Bank for Reconstruction and Development, London, pp. 111–43.

Mihályi, P. (1993), 'Hungary: A Unique Approach to Privatisation – Past, Present and Future', in Székely, I.P. and Newbery, D.M.G. (eds), *Hungary: An Economy in Transition*, Cambridge: Cambridge University Press, pp. 84–117.

Mizsei, K. (1993), 'Regional Cooperation in East-Central Europe', in Székely, I.P. and Newbery, D.M.G. (eds), *Hungary: An Economy in Transition*, Cambridge: Cambridge University Press, pp. 44–50.

Mueller, D.C. (ed.) (1983), *The Political Economy of Growth*, New Haven: Yale University Press.

Murrell, P. (1982), 'Comparative Growth and Comparative Advantage: Tests of the Effects of Interest Group Behaviour on Foreign Trade', *Public Choice*, 38, pp. 352–66.

Murrell, P. (1991), 'Can Neoclassical Economics Underpin the Economic Reform of the Centrally Planned Economies?', *Journal of Economic Perspectives*, 5, pp. 59–76.

Murrell, P. (1992), 'Evolutionary and Radical Approaches to Economic Reform', *Economics of Planning*, 25, pp. 79–95.

Murrell, P. and Olson, M. (1991), 'The Devolution of Centrally Planned Economies', *Journal of Comparative Economics*, 15, pp. 239–65.

Musil, J. (ed.) (1995), *The End of Czechoslovakia*, Budapest, London and New York: Central European University Press.

Myant, M. (1989), *The Czechoslovak Economy 1948-1988: The Battle for Economic Reform*, Cambridge: Cambridge University Press.

Náray, P. (1987), 'A Külkereskedelmi Szervezeti és Intésményi Reformja' (Organizational and Institutional Reforms of Foreign Trade), *Külgazdaság*, 20, pp. 643–59.

Nelson, R.R. and Winter, S. (1982), *An Evolutionary Theory of Economic Change*, Cambridge (Massachusetts): Harvard University Press.

North, D.C. (1990), *Institutions, Institutional Change and Economic Performance*, Cambridge: Cambridge University Press.

Nunnenkamp, P. (1997), 'Governing the Economic Transition of Hungary, Poland and Former Czechoslovakia', *Journal of International and Comparative Economics*, 5, pp. 137–52.

Nuti, D.M. (1992), 'Privatization in Hungary', in Keren, M. and Ofer, G. (eds), *Trials of Transition. Economic Reform in the Former Communist Bloc*, Boulder (Colorado): Westview Press, pp. 193–202.

Oblath, G. (1994), 'Exchange Rate Policy and Real Exchange Rate Changes in Economic Transition', in Gács, J. and Winckler, G. (eds), *International Trade and Restructuring in Eastern Europe*, Heidelberg: Physica-Verlag, pp. 15–46.

O'Driscoll, G.P. and Rizzo, M.J. (1985), *The Economics of Time and Ignorance*, Oxford: Basil Blackwell.

OECD (1991(a)), *Hungary, OECD Economic Surveys*, Paris.

OECD (1991(b)), *Czech and Slovak Federal Republic, OECD Economic Surveys*, Paris.

OECD (1994(a)), *The Czech and Slovak Republics, OECD Economic Surveys*, Paris.

OECD (1994(b)), *Industry in the Czech and Slovak Republics*, Paris.

OECD (1994(c)), *Barriers to Trade with the Economies in Transition*, Paris.

OECD (1994(d)), *Poland, OECD Economic Surveys*, Paris.

OECD (1995), *Review of Industry and Industrial Policy in Hungary*, Paris.

OECD, *Trade by Commodities*, Paris, various issues.

OECD Transition Brief, Newsletter of the Centre for Co-operation with the Economies in Transition, Paris, various issues.

Okolichanyi, K. (1993), 'The Visegrád Triangle's Free Trade Zone', *Radio Free Europe/Radio Liberty Report*, 2, pp.19–22.

Olson, M. (1965), *The Logic of Collective Action: Public Goods and the Theory of Groups*, Cambridge (Massachusetts): Harvard University Press.

Olson, M. (1982), *The Rise and Decline of Nations. Economic Growth, Stag-flation, and Social Rigidities*, New Haven: Yale University Press.

Olson, M. (1992), 'The Hidden Path to a Successful Economy', in Clague, C. and Rausser, G.C. (eds), *The Emergence of Market Economies in Eastern Europe*, Cambridge (Massachusetts) and Oxford: Basil Blackwell, pp. 55–75.

Orenstein, M. (1994), 'The Political Success of Neo-Liberalism in the Czech Republic', Center for Economic Research and Graduate Education – Economics Institute of the Academy of Sciences of the Czech Republic, Working Paper, No. 68, Prague.

Pheby, J. (ed.) (1989), *New Directions in Post-Keynesian Economics*, Aldershot: Edward Elgar.

Pissula, P. (1990), 'Experiences of the Centrally Planned Economies in the General Agreement on Tariffs and Trade', *Journal of Development Planning*, 20, 191–200.

PlanEcon Report, Washington, various issues.

Posner, R.A. (1974), 'Theories of Economic Regulation', *Bell Journal of Economics and Management Sciences*, 5, pp. 335–58.

Pryor, F.L. (1963), *The Communist Foreign Trade System*, London: George Allen & Unwin.

Raiser, M. (1994), 'Ein Tschechisches Wunder? Zur Rolle politikinduzierter Anreizstrukturen im Transformationprozeß', Institut für Weltwirtschaft, Kieler Diskussionsbeiträge, No. 233, Kiel.

Raiser, M. and Nunnenkamp, P. (1993), 'Output Decline and Recovery in Central Europe: The Role of Incentives before, during and after Privatisation', Institut für Weltwirtschaft, kieler Arbeitspapiere, No. 601, Kiel.

Reich, A.A. (1993), 'The Central European Initiative: To Be or Not to Be?', *Radio Free Europe/Radio Liberty Report*, 2, pp. 30–37.

Report on the Czech and Slovak Republics, International Institute for the Study of Politics of the School of Law of the Masaryk University, Brno, various issues.

Richter, S. (1992), 'Is there a Future for Regional Cooperation in Eastern Europe?', in Keren, M. and Ofer, G. (eds), *Trials of Transition. Economic Reform in the Former Communist Bloc*, Boulder (Colorado): Westview Press, pp. 255–69.

Richardson, J.D. (1970), *Constant-Market-Shares Analysis of Export Growth*, Ann Arbor: Michigan University Press.

Richardson, J.D. (1971(a)), 'Constant-Market-Shares Analysis of Export Growth', *Journal of International Economics*, 1(1), pp. 227–39.

Richardson, J.D. (1971(b)), 'Some Sensitivity Tests for a "Constant-Maket-Shares" Analysis of Export Growth', *The Review of Economics and Statistics*, 53(3), pp. 300–304.

Richter, S. and Tóth, L.G. (1993), 'After the Agreement on Free Trade Among the Visegrád Group Countries: Perspectives for Intra-Regional Trade in East-Central Europe', Wiener Institut für Internationale Wirtschaftsvergleiche, Forschungsberichte, No. 195, Wien.

Roländ, G. (1994), 'The Role of Political Constraints in Transition Strategies', Centre for Economic Policy Research, Discussion Paper, No. 943, London.

Rosati, D.K. (1991), 'Institutional and Policy Framework for Foreign Economic Relations in Poland', in Economic Commision for Europe, *Reforms in Foreign Economic Relations of Eastern Europe and the Soviet Union*, Economic Studies No. 2, United Nations, New York, pp. 21–31.

Rosati, D.K. (1992), 'Problems of Post-CMEA Trade and Payments', in Flemming, J. and Rollo, J.M.C. (eds), *Trade and Payments Adjustment in Central and Eastern Europe*, Royal Institute of International Affairs and European Bank for Reconstruction and Development, London, pp. 75–101.

Sachdeva, G. (1994), 'Privatization: An Interpretative Endeavor', Kopint-Datorg Economic Research, Marketing and Computing Co. Ltd, Discussion Paper, No. 21, Budapest.

Sachs, J. (1993), *Poland's Jump to the Market Economy*, Cambridge (Massachusetts): MIT Press.

Salgó, I. (1986), 'Economic Mechanism and Foreign Trade Organization in Hungary', *Acta Oeconomica*, 36, pp. 271–87.

Salgó, I. (1989), *Külkereskedelmi Vállalat, Külkereskedelmi Szervezet* (Foreign Trade Companies, Foreign Trade Organization), Budapest: Közgazdasági és Jogi Könyvkiadó.

Schmieding, H. (1993), 'From Plan to Market: On the Nature of the Transition Crisis', *Weltwirtschaftliches Archiv*, 129, pp. 31–42.

Schöpflin, G. (1987), 'Domestic Politics' in Grothusen, K.D. (ed.) *Ungarn*, Göttingen: Ruprecht, pp. 67–106.

Schumpeter, J.A. (1934), *Theory of Economic Development*, Cambridge (Massachusetts): Harvard University Press.

Senior Nello, S. (1991), *The New Europe: Changing Economic Relations between East and West*, New York and London: Harvester Wheatsheaf.

Sereghyová, J. (1995), 'Trade Policy in Central Eastern Europe', in Hölscher, J., Jacobsen, A., Tomann, H. and Weisfeld, H. (eds), *Bedingungen ökonomischer Entwicklung in Zentralosteuropa, Band 3: Field Studies on Transition*, Marburg: Metropolis-Verlag, pp. 253–77.

Slay, B. (1994(a)), 'Rapid versus Gradual Economic Transition', *Radio Free Europe/Radio Liberty Report*, 3, pp. 31–42.

Slay, B. (1994(b)), *The Polish Economy; Crisis, Reform, and Transformation*, Princeton: Princeton University Press.

'Stabilization and Convertibility: Economic Policy Action Programme' (1991), *The Hungarian Economy: A Quarterly Economic and Business Review*, 19, pp. 1–7.

Spulber, N. (1957), *The Economics of Communist Eastern Europe*, London: Chapman & Hall.

Stadler, J. (1993), 'Competition Policy in Transition', in Székely, I.P. and Newbery, D.M.G. (eds), *Hungary: An Economy in Transition*, Cambridge: Cambridge University Press, pp. 118–25.

Stigler, G.J. (1971), 'The Theory of Economic Regulation', *Bell Journal of Economics and Management Sciences*, 2, pp. 3–21.

Stiglitz, J.E. (1992), 'The Design of Financial Systems for the Newly Emerging Democracies of Eastern Europe', in Clague, C. and Rausser, G.C. (eds), *The Emergence of Market Economies in Eastern Europe*, Cambridge (Massachusetts) and Oxford: Basil Blackwell, pp. 161–84.

Stolze, F. (1996), 'The Central and East European Currency Phenomenon Reconsidered', Wiener Institut für Internationale Wirtschaftsvergleiche, Forschungsberichte, No. 232, Wien.

Švejnar, J., Terell, K., Munich, D. and Strapec, M. (1994), 'Explaining Unemployment Dynamics in the Czech and Slovak Republics', Center for Economic Research and Graduate Education – Economics Institute of the Academy of Sciences of the Czech Republic, Working Paper, No. 60, Prague.

Szamuely, L. (1984), 'The Second Wave of the Economic Mechanism Debate and the 1968 Reform in Hungary', *Acta Oeconomica*, 33, pp. 43–67.

Székely, I.P. and Newbery, D.M.G. (eds) (1993), *Hungary: An Economy in Transition*, Cambridge: Cambridge University Press.

Takla, L. (1994), 'The Relationship between Privatization and the Reform of the Banking Sector: The Case of the Czech Republic and Slovakia, in Estrin, S. (ed.), *Privatization in Central & Eastern Europe*, London and New York: Longman, pp. 154–75.

Tinbergen, J. (1959), 'The Theory of the Optimum Regime', in Klaassens, L.M., Koyck, L.M. and Witteveen, H.J. (eds), *Jan Tinbergen: Selected Papers*, Amsterdam: North Holland Publishing, pp. 264–304.

Tőkés, R.L. (1990), 'Hungary's New Political Elites: Adaptation and Change, 1989–90', *Problems of Communism*, 39, pp. 44–65.

Tőkés, R.L. (1991), 'From Visegrád to Krakow: Cooperation, Competition, and Coexistence in Central Europe', *Problems of Communism*, 40, pp. 100–114.

United Nations, *Commodity Trade Statistics*, New York, various issues

Vachudova, M.A. (1993), 'The Visegrád Four: No Alternative to Cooperation?', *Radio Free Europe/Radio Liberty Report*, 2, pp. 38–47.

Van Brabant, J.M. (1973), *Bilateralism and Structural Bilateralism in Intra-CMEA Trade*, Rotterdam: Rotterdam University Press.

Van Brabant, J.M. (1991), 'Property Rights Reform, Macroeconomic Performance, and Welfare', in Blommestein, H. and Marrese, M. (eds), *Transformation of Planned Economies: Property Rights Reform and Macroeconomic Stability*, OECD, Paris, pp. 29–49.

Van Brabant, J.M. (1993), 'Lessons from the Wholesale Transformation in the East', *Comparative Economic Studies*, 35, pp. 73–102.

Van Brabant, J.M. (1995), *The Transformation of Eastern Europe; Joining the European Integration Movement*, New York: Nova Science Publishers.

Van Ees, H. and Garretsen, H. (1993), 'How to Derive Keynesian Results from First Principles: A Survey of New-Keynesian Economics', *De Economist*, 141, pp. 323–52.

Van Ees, H. and Garretsen, H. (1994), 'The Theoretical Foundations of the Reforms in Eastern Europe: Big Bang versus Gradualism and the Limitations of Neo-classical theory', *Economic Systems*, 18, pp. 1–13.

Várhegyi, É. (1993), 'The Modernization of the Hungarian Banking Sector', in Székely, I.P. and Newbery, D.M.G. (eds), *Hungary: An Economy in Transition*, Cambridge: Cambridge University Press, pp. 149–62.

Wagener, H.-J. (1979), *Zur Analyse von Wirtschaftssystemen. Eine Einführung*, Berlin and Heidelberg: Springer-Verlag.

Wagener, H.-J. (1992), 'Debate on the Transition of Post-Communist Economies to a Market Economy: The Legacy of the Past and the Uncertainty of the Future', *Acta Oeconomica*, 44, pp. 363–70.

Wagener, H.-J. (1993), 'Some Theory of Systemic Change and Transformation', in Wagener, H.-J. (ed.), *On the Theory and Policy of Systemic Change*, Heidelberg: Physica-Verlag, pp. 1–20.

Wass von Czege, A. (1987), 'Special-Interest Groups and their Impact on Balance of Payments-Oriented Investment Strategies', in Rabá, A. and Schenk, K.-E. (eds), *Investment System and Foreign Trade Implications in Hungary*, Stuttgart and New York: Gustav Fisher Verlag, pp. 229–53.

Winiecki, J. (1988), 'East European Economies: Forced Adjustment Forever?', Institute for International Economic Studies, Seminar Paper, No. 413, Stockholm.

Winiecki, J. (1993), 'Heterodox Stabilisation in Eastern Europe', European Bank for Reconstruction and Development, Working Paper, No. 8, London.

Wolf, C. (1979), 'A Theory of Nonmarket Failure: Framework for Implementation Analysis', *Journal of Law and Economics*, 22, pp 107–39.

Wolf, T.A. (1985), 'Exchange Rate Systems and Adjustment in Planned Economies', *IMF Staff Papers*, 32, pp. 211–47.

World Bank (1994(a)), 'Poland; Policies for Growth with Equity', World Bank Country Study, World Bank, Washington, D.C.

World Bank (1994(b)), 'Slovakia; Restructuring for Recovery', World Bank Country Study, World Bank, Washington, D.C.

World Bank (1995), 'Hungary; Structural Reforms for Sustainable Growth', World Bank Country Study, World Bank, Washington, D.C.

World Bank (1996), 'World Development Report 1996; From Plan to Market', New York: Oxford University Press.

World Economic Research Institute (1995), 'Poland; International Economic Report 1994/95', Warsaw School of Economics, Warsaw.

Zloch-Christy, I. (1987), *Debt Problems of Eastern Europe*, Cambridge: Cambridge University Press.

Zloch-Christy, I. (1994), *Eastern Europe in a Time of Change: Economic and Political Dimension*, Westport (Connecticut) and London: Praeger.

Index